D1591419

Who's Next?

Who's Next?

HOMELESSNESS, ARCHITECTURE, AND CITIES

Edited by
Daniel Talesnik and Andres Lepik

DAKLOZEN

BEZDOMOVCI

HJEMLØSE

BEZPAJUMTNIEKI

DAOINE GAN

OBDACHLOSE

BENAMIAI ŽMONĖS

ROUGH

SEM-ABRIGO

BREZDOMCI

HAJLÉKTALAN

KODUTUD INIMESED

БЕЗДОМНЫЕ

SENZATETTO

BEZDOMNY

BESKUĆNICI

DÍDEÁN

PERSOANE FĂRĂ ADĂPOST

ΑΣΤΕΓΟΣ

SLEEPERS

NIES BLA DAR

INDIGENTE

EMBEREK

SANS-ABRI

KODITTOMAT

BOSTADSLÖSA

Who's Next?

HOMELESSNESS, ARCHITECTURE, AND CITIES

190 The Importance of Design, or What Can Architecture Do?

Artwork in a car park in Cheltenham, United Kingdom

The Crisis on Our Doorstep?

Andres Lepik

In many big cities around the world, a humanitarian plight has become even more acute in recent years: the number of people camping at underpasses, under bridges, and in parks, or in sleeping bags on subway exhaust shafts, has grown rapidly. The personal misery of the individuals affected is the visible result of a systemic social breakdown. In fact, architecture and homelessness have long been opposing yet inseparable concepts in industrialized societies. This means that even though the number of new residential buildings has steadily increased in many regions of the world, the rate of homelessness and people with no permanent housing has risen dramatically at the same time. In New York, for example, the number of homeless individuals sleeping in shelters grew by 143 percent (to 18,700) between 2009 and the end of 2019.[1] In London, the figure of homeless people increased by 18 percent (to 8,855) in just a single year, that is, between 2018 and 2019, something that the mayor, Sadiq Khan, has branded a "national disgrace."[2] But the estimated figure of 41,000 homeless individuals in Germany (in 2018) is also a national disgrace, because there is still no nationwide strategy for reducing or even eliminating the situation in one of the richest countries in the world.[3]

During the past year, the already precarious situation of the homeless has been further exacerbated around the globe by the coronavirus pandemic, since it was only possible for the majority of emergency shelters to be used in a limited way or not at all due to the newly introduced hygiene measures and social distancing guidelines. Last winter, many homeless individuals thus froze on the streets or died of a Covid-19 infection because no vaccines had reached them. And a further intensification is to be expected in the coming months of this year (2021), after the pandemic-related ban on the eviction of tenants in the United States comes to an end during the summer.[4]

According to estimates by the United Nations, roughly 1.6 billion people around the world currently live in inadequate housing or have no permanent accommodations. And approximately 15 million individuals are forcibly evicted from their homes each year. Young people are thus more and more at risk of becoming homeless, and this risk is increasing in a measurable way for families as well. For these reasons, the United Nations passed the first resolution to combat homelessness in February 2020, so as to prompt governments to adopt swift and decisive countermeasures.[5] A variety of action plans for redressing homelessness have meanwhile been enacted and the necessary funding approved. Great Britain, for instance, has made £236 million available for the objective of eliminating homelessness entirely by 2024.[6] Finland has been leading by good example since 2016 and is hitherto the only country in the European Union to have succeeded in reducing the number of homeless individuals so radically that no one sleeps on the streets there anymore.[7] The European Parliament passed a resolution in November 2020 that obligates member states to take measures to eliminate homelessness by 2030.[8]

It is increasingly important to remember that the absolute majority of homeless individuals did not voluntarily opt for life on the streets. Homelessness is an individual fate related to a range of structural and societal factors. One central cause lies in growing income inequality, which has meanwhile increased to an extreme in many countries throughout the world. People with a low income have the greatest risk of sliding into homelessness.[9] Another reason is the decreasing amount of social housing that has been constructed in recent years. The liberalization of the housing market and the withdrawal of governments from housing development have resulted in a declining number of residential units available for people with a low income. While citizens with a mid-range or high income are competing more and more intensively for the allocation of rental and owner-occupied housing, those with the lowest incomes are increasingly falling by the wayside. Individual factors such as personal misfortune, excessive debt, and illness are often additional factors that lead to people becoming homeless.

The progression from lack of housing to homelessness is generally a one-way street: once someone has arrived at the bottom of the spiral into poverty, they rarely find their way back into social welfare systems or attain economic self-sufficiency. This is because, without a fixed address and a registration card, one is unable to get a regular job, and without a steady income they cannot, in turn, afford housing. The system of emergency accommodations is thus set up (not only in Germany) in such a way that, apart from a place to sleep, homeless individuals are given no private sphere, no registered address, no access to the Internet, nor are they able to store personal items there. The logic behind this is brutally simple: homeless people should be given no incentives to settle down permanently in emergency accommodations. That is why many people who have become homeless prefer other solutions, for instance finding a place to stay on the street. Yet they put themselves in an extreme situation of vulnerability and danger nonetheless. The social exclusion of homeless individuals can be seen in many areas. In addition to their existential crisis, affected individuals are also punished with disregard by and spatial segregation from the rest of society, which in many cases is even heightened by aggressive, violent behavior toward them. Addiction issues, depression, and other physical and psychological problems are often the consequence, but not the cause, of homelessness.

Confronted with this social and humanitarian drama, what can be done? There is a wide range of organizations offering assistance to homeless individuals. Whether religious or nondenominational organizations, whether semigovernmental or private initiatives: they all try with great commitment to alleviate the individual distress of those affected and deserve the greatest respect for these humanitarian efforts. But it is clear that even though individual suffering is mitigated by soup kitchens, clothing donations, and emergency medical care, such services cannot combat the reasons for the growing misery.

Tokyo, 2002

What inescapably follows from the insight that society is responsible for the increasing number of homeless individuals is the political duty to develop and implement systemic approaches to solutions. The sociological foundations and planning concepts for doing so have been available for a long time. Housing First, for instance, is one successful strategy that has already resulted in the achievement of a decisive turnaround in countries like Finland and cities like Berlin.

But what role can architecture play in this problem area? It is clear that only a few architects (and schools of architecture) have examined the topic of homelessness in recent years, even though it represents a fundamental spatial and design-related task. The treatment of the homeless by society, that is, the exclusion and pushing aside of affected individuals and their distress in general, is reflected in the limited attention, not to say flagrant neglect by the discipline. This is why it seems urgently necessary to bring the few positive exceptions to the attention of the public. In the 2010 exhibition *Small Scale, Big Change: New Architectures of Social Engagement* at the Museum of Modern Art in New York, Michael Maltzan's Inner City Arts Center in Los Angeles was among the projects presented, and his New Carver Apartments for the Skid Row Housing Trust were highlighted in the catalogue introduction.[10] New Carver is a building in which homeless individuals are given accommodations in permanent apartments thanks to the support of a private initiative. This example clearly shows how the design of this housing for the formerly homeless requires highly sophisticated spatial concepts in order to be successful. "Success" here is measured first and foremost in the fact that the formerly homeless have a long retention rate in this building. But, in this context, the Carver Apartments have not only been a gain for the affected individuals personally; indeed, due to the apartments' great appreciation in the public sphere, they have inspired further planning based on the experience obtained.

Therein lies the central aspiration of our exhibition project *Who's Next? Homelessness, Architecture, and Cities*. As the architecture museum of the Technische Universität München (TUM), we have dedicated ourselves since 2013, in exhibitions and publications, to the question of the social mandate of the discipline. Our aim is to determine the backgrounds of relevant topics, to shed light on theoretical, historical, and methodological approaches, and to thus identify best practices through joint research in seminars and exercises with architecture students. The scientific insights are transposed into curatorial concepts and brought to the awareness of the public by means of presentations. And, since 2010, numerous other buildings that provide permanent accommodations for the formerly homeless—and thus give those affected opportunities to find their way back into society—have been realized not only in Los Angeles, but also in other places around the world. These projects build in part on approaches and experiences from

Michael Maltzan's practice; and it has also been possible to develop and implement new perspectives, for instance the trailblazing projects of Alexander Hagner from Austria or Peter Barber from London. What is hence important is that they are buildings that give affected individuals back their dignity and make them feel that they are included, not excluded, by the rest of society.

With this exhibition and the accompanying publication, we thus wish to provide the basis for broader public awareness, but also to inspire the next generation of designers to take up this complex task. Indeed, well-planned, attractively designed, and cleverly conceived buildings make it possible not only for those affected to obtain new perspectives, but also for architecture to attain new social relevance.

1   Coalition for the Homeless, "State of the Homeless 2020," March 2020, https://www.coalitionforthehomeless.org/wp-content/uploads/2020/03/StateofTheHomeless2020.pdf (all URLs accessed in August 2021).

2   Patrick Butler, "London rough sleeping hits record high with 18% rise in 2018–19," *The Guardian,* June 19, 2019, https://www.theguardian.com/society/2019/jun/19/london-rough-sleeping-hits-record-high-with-18-rise-in-2018-19.

3   "Wohnungslosigkeit: Kein Ende in Sicht," press release by the Bundesarbeitsgemein-schaft Wohnungslosenhilfe e.V., a federal working group providing assistance to the homeless; see https://www.bagw.de/fileadmin/bagw/media/Doc/PRM/PRM_2019_11_11_Schaetzung_Zahl_der_Wohnungslosen.pdf. Nationwide statistics will not be collected until 2022: German Federal Government, "Bundesweite Erhebungen: Statistik zur Wohnungslosigkeit," https://www.bundesregierung.de/breg-de/suche/wohnungslose-in-deutschland-1672730.

4   Sema K. Sgaier and Aaron Dibner-Dunlap, "How Many People Are at Risk of Losing Their Homes in Your Neighborhood?," *The New York Times,* July 28, 2021, https://www.nytimes.com/2021/07/28/opinion/covid-eviction-moratorium.html?action=click&module=Opinion&pgtype=Homepage.

5   United Nations, Department of Economic and Social Affairs, "First-ever United Nations Resolution on Homelessness," https://www.un.org/development/desa/dspd/2020/03/resolution-homelessness/.

6   Peter Walker, "Government pledges £236m to tackle rough sleeping," *The Guardian,* February 26, 2021, https://www.theguardian.com/society/2020/feb/26/government-pledges-236m-to-tackle-rough-sleeping.

7   Jon Henley, "'It's a miracle': Helsinki's radical solution to homelessness," *The Guardian,* June 3, 2021, https://www.theguardian.com/cities/2019/jun/03/its-a-miracle-helsinkis-radical-solution-to-homelessness.

8   European Parliament, "How Parliament wants to end homelessness in the EU," November 24, 2020, https://www.europarl.europa.eu/news/en/headlines/society/20201119STO92006/how-parliament-wants-to-end-homelessness-in-the-eu.

9   Press release of August 4, 2021, by the Hans Böckler Foundation on the situation in Germany: https://www.boeckler.de/de/pressemitteilungen-2675-13-prozent-haushalte-stadten-miete-existenzminimum-34612.htm.

10 See Andres Lepik, ed., *Small Scale, Big Change: New Architectures of Social Engagement,* exh. cat. The Museum of Modern Art, New York (Basel: Birkhäuser, 2010), pp. 63–72.

First temporary sanctioned tent encampment for the homeless, San Francisco, 2020

Unfolding Homelessness

Daniel Talesnik

Aware of the rising numbers around the world, in the fall of 2019 we started thinking about an exhibition on homelessness. Quickly questions began to stack up: Where should research efforts be directed? What should be displayed in order to address such an urgent topic? How to do it in a respectful yet critical way? Which of the many crises that houselessness reveals should be highlighted? While developing a strategy on how to break down the topic, it became clear that it would not be a "traditional" architecture exhibition celebrating this or that aspect of an architect, architectural topic, or architectural period. Although the connection to architecture is evident, what is at issue here is the lack of buildings. Developing this exhibition required not only a critical gaze, but also that we go beyond architecture as a technical field and/or academic discipline.

During the coronavirus pandemic it became evident that homelessness is a collective issue. The urgency of this crisis became even more visible, starting with the impossibility of people experiencing homelessness to respect physical distance without a dwelling. As cities attempted to "protect" their houseless by relocating them from public space, the inherent shortcomings of the situation, and at times the limited capacity for reaction, became evident. As 2020 advanced, images like that of the homeless tent encampment on gridded rectangles drawn on Fulton Street around Pioneer Monument—which is situated in front of the Civic Center Plaza and has San Francisco City Hall as a backdrop—started to appear, and headlines on how cities around the world were moving rough sleepers into hotels began to fill the newspapers.[1] Practically every week, if not every day, news outlets report on homelessness and the housing crisis, as well as on related topics. In London, the number of people experiencing homelessness over the last ten years has doubled; and according to the statistics of the Coalition for the Homeless, in 2020 over 120,000 different homeless men, women, and children slept in the New York City municipal shelter system.[2] Meanwhile, Germany is dealing with acute housing shortages, which includes homelessness, and Chancellor Angela Merkel promised to dedicate a budget of €6.85 billion to housing solutions in 2018.[3] Although we are aware that numbers can be misleading, it is clear that the situation is escalating worldwide.

Street homelessness can be considered an extreme version of poverty—though not all homeless individuals sleep on the streets—and, as such, it mirrors the standards and flaws of the communal or state order where it occurs. In many ways, homelessness at large is a compendium of all the failures of a society. It is a symptom of economic crisis, and it also illustrates the extreme polarity of the distribution of wealth. Moreover, it not only involves housing, but also areas like education, health care, and justice. The reasons that someone might end up without a home are manifold: unemployment, family crises, mental health issues, and addiction are listed as some of the common causes. But when researching the topic in detail, a more nuanced picture arises, one that identifies the problem's roots within the challenges of society at large: people living on the streets might also be war veterans with PTSD, refugees, legal and illegal migrants who have become stranded and chronically unemployed, victims of domestic violence, or teenagers expelled from their homes after coming out. As such, homelessness is often the most extreme locus for issues of gender, race, class, and even climate change.[4] More than that, it is increasingly touching larger parts of our societies, including individuals and families who cannot find affordable housing in spite of being employed, and by extension involving an alarming number of both children and senior citizens without a home.

In order to address the expansive topics related to homelessness, the exhibition *Who's Next? Homelessness, Architecture, and Cities,* along with the accompanying publication, includes original research on multiple themes and cities, a survey of architectural case studies, and interviews with experts. On the one hand, the aim is to attract the attention of specialists—architects, urban designers, and planers in particular—and to share the knowledge coming from different places and fields. On the other, we want to unfold a topic that is literally in plain sight in urban and rural environments around the world, in order to understand why and how it occurs, and to hopefully also change the outlook on it.

Topics About and Around Homelessness: A Polyphonic Approach

As we started doing research, we began to engage with specialists around the world. The eight essays stemming from this collaborative project are organized within four categories. The rubric of "Housing Systems" is closely connected to the housing market and related to such long-debated texts as Friedrich Engels's 1872 "Zur Wohnungsfrage" (The Housing Question). In the 1980s, the lawyer Peter Marcuse was already arguing that in countries like the United States "homelessness exists not because the system is failing to work as it should, but because the system *is* working as it must."[5] The sociologist David Madden, a student and collaborator of Marcuse's, picks up the baton and writes about "Homelessness and the Housing System," not only questioning the suitability of the terms based on a thorough understanding of the American and British systems, but also delving deep into the subjects they attempt to define. Also, the geographers Stephen Przybylinski and Don Mitchell, in their essay "Tent City: Living (Rather Than Dying) at the Limits to Capital," focus on a case study in Portland, Oregon, and the right to live outside the hegemony of capitalism, understanding, just like Madden, that through logic such as that of the housing market, homelessness is produced in parallel to housing.

The second rubric focuses on "Terminology" and discusses the language about and around the expanded topic of homelessness, within the understanding that words create realities and vice versa, and that there is huge stigmatization coming from our vocabulary of choice. In the United States, the term *homeless* implies the absence of a home, which includes the absence of a building; in German, *obdachlos* can be interpreted as pointing toward the absence of a building element (the roof), which is similar to the Italian *senza-tetto,* and not far from French's absence of shelter in the term *sans abri.* In England, however, the concept of choice is *rough sleeper,* which points directly to a bodily act and triggers an understanding of an experience. The Spanish term *indigente,* in turn, comes from the Latin *indigēns,* which means "needing" or "requiring." The difficulty of definition, which presents itself when comparing the related terminology in multiple languages, is exemplified by the choice between homelessness and houselessness, since the latter simply denotes the absence of a place to live, while the former is more evocative and can go beyond the idea of a physical space. For the English title, we settled on "homelessness" because we deal with multiple aspects of the expanded topic in the exhibition, while within the research context a distinction is made by the specialists themselves, some of whom prefer the term "houselessness." The anthropologist Luisa Schneider's "Loving and Living at the Limit" reveals the everyday experience of some of the terms we question. What does it mean to raise a family in public space? How can life unfold when privacy is just a concept? Or, said differently, what are personal spaces and opportunities for intimacy with oneself and others when there is no place to retreat to at the end of the day? Also, the curator Juliane Bischoff's "Overlooked Remembrance and the Language of Social Exclusion: The Example of the Term 'Asocial'" takes us deep into Germany's darkest period and unfolds how the homeless during National Socialism were catalogued under the devious rubric of *Asoziale* and how many unhoused ended up in concentration camps. Strangely, today the term *asozial* is still used to point at people on the fringes of society who are "unwanted."

The third relevant rubric is "The Legality of Homelessness," where we explore societal duties and rights, and how not having a home leaves people on the fringes of the law, but also without a right to participate in civil society and represent themselves. The architect Jocelyn Froimovich's "The Right to Sleep in the City" questions, citing several cities, why sleeping is not catered to in the same way as other basic activities like eating and defecating, arguing that sleeping in public should also be a human right and have its own public infrastructures. In her essay "Forbidding Homelessness: The Lockdown Law as a Pharmakon," the architectural historian Samia Henni directly connects homelessness with the coronavirus crisis and breaks down the housing system in France using the official terminology of the state machinery.

Finally, the rubric "Land Value" is related to who owns land and property in a city and thus who controls open space and the housing market. The architects Alejandra Celedón and Nicolás Stutzin, in "Life in Tents: From Land Occupation to Urban Reclamation," analyze the emergence of individual tents as opposed to informal encampments in Santiago de Chile during the coronavirus pandemic and detect a variation of the Lefebvrian "Right to the City." Finally, the sociologist Fraya Frehse's "On the Spatialities of the Homeless' Street in Covid-19 São Paulo" connects the long-term problem of homelessness to its extreme pandemic version by examining the production of domestic space on the sidewalks of South America's largest city.

As we have seen, this essay section marks different entry points toward the understanding of homelessness and some of the multiple problems associated with it. The complexity of the expanded themes related to this topic is evident in these original essays due to their specificity and at times detailed approach. Although all essays discuss the same social crisis, the issues they reflect upon cover only some of the many related topics around homelessness, a fact that perhaps best illustrates the challenges that our societies face when trying to solve such a multifold set of problems.

Homelessness in Cities: A Comparative Global Outlook

While the causes of homelessness vary, the consequences of finding oneself without shelter are similar for everyone who experiences it; collectively, the homeless are unequivocally among the least protected members of our societies. Homelessness is not only a personal tragedy, but also a systemic problem that requires systemic solutions. As our exhibition plans advanced, it became evident that one way to approach the topic is by looking into cities. Accepting the challenge, and also the limits of how to compare cities, we established conditions for our considerations, focusing on large, powerful economic centers in countries with a level of urban prosperity that in all cases collides with extreme poverty. Also, none of the city case studies are in Europe, based on the premise that Europe still has a welfare system in place—albeit a faulty and shrinking one—that should be preserved and made more robust.

Amid the coronavirus crisis, it was clear that we could not do this research alone. We invited researchers to participate and write city biographies addressing the state of homelessness, as well as to analyze a specific topic of their choice that is particular to each city. Aya Maceda and James Carse in New York write about "Alternative Equity Models in the Development and Preservation of Long-Term, Deeply Affordable Housing," Valentina Rozas-Krause and Trude Renwick in San Francisco about "Tech and the Conundrum of Homelessness," María Esnaola Cano in Los Angeles about "Climate Change and Equity for the Los Angeles Homeless," Clara Chahin Werneck and Joao Bittar Fiammenghi in São Paulo about "Toward a New Agency: Notes on Architecture and Homelessness in São Paulo," Tatiana Efrussi in Moscow about "Experiencing and Dealing with Homelessness in Moscow:

Work as Reason, Exploitation, Salvation, and Solution," Aditya Sawant in Mumbai about "Homelessness and the Image of the City," Zairong Xiang and Elena Vogman in Shanghai about "Shanghai: China's Financial Capital without Homelessness," and Helena Čapkova and Erez Golani Solomon in Tokyo about, respectively, "Hidden Homelessness" and "Too Few Too Many: The Imbalance of People and Housing." Also, Leilani Farha, a former United Nations Special Rapporteur on adequate housing and the founder of The Shift, an international movement working to secure the right to housing, writes about her experience dealing with the challenges of homelessness in cities around the world.

How Do We Talk About Homelessness? What Should We Talk About?

In addition to the essays and city research, we commissioned three original documentary films that in some cases allow individuals experiencing homelessness to come to the fore, in others institutions that work for or support them, while fostering an appreciation of certain public buildings' role in their daily lives, an outlook on hostile urban environments, or a combination of these and other scenarios. The films present both the shortcomings and the positive efforts seen in the cities of Munich (directed by Nicole Huminski, Nikolai Huber, and their team), Hong Kong (directed by Matthew Ho and his team), and São Paulo (directed by Fraya Frehse and her team). In this publication, there are also three interviews: one by Lluís Alexandre Casanovas Blanco, an architect, scholar, and curator, with the lawyer Robert M. Hayes, cofounder of the Coalition for the Homeless in the United States and current president and CEO of the Community Healthcare Network; another by Binyamin Appelbaum, the lead writer on business and economics for the editorial board of *The New York Times*, with Veronica Lewis, a community leader and director of HOPICS in Los Angeles; and also one by Giovanna Borasi, the director of the Canadian Centre for Architecture in Montreal, with the architects Michael Maltzan in Los Angeles and Alexander Hagner in Vienna, which echoes and goes deeper into some of the topics of the documentary film *What It Takes to Make a Home* (Daniel Schwartz, 2019), also shown in the exhibition.

What Can Architecture Do?

Although architecture alone cannot solve homelessness, the question remains as to how architects can collaborate on short-, medium-, and long-term solutions for people experiencing homelessness. There is a long history of buildings for those in need of a bed, and a quick overview on the topic could include buildings like God's House in Ewelme, England (1437), Ferdinando Fuga's Albergo dei Poveri, in Naples, Italy (ca. 1750), and Le Corbusier's iconic Cité de Refuge de l'Armée du Salut in Paris, France (1929–33). However, a historical and genealogical approach like this one apparently did not unveil the responsibilities of the architectural field today. Another avenue that arose was to concentrate on established strategies such as Housing First, a radical idea which started in the United States in the late 1980s that prioritizes providing permanent housing to people experiencing homelessness and that considers the urgency of a place to live before attending to all other associated needs like a job or rehabilitation for substance abuse. Although this concept has found success in some cities, we know enough by now to also consider how its implementation can be a challenge. For example, often there are either too few units or they are too centralized, creating a ghetto-like situation for the formerly homeless that can favor the very conditions that led people to live in the street, such as sensitive environments for addiction. Reintegration to the housing system not only requires a dwelling, but also a support system ensuring that people stay housed in the long term.[6]

In the end, our main focus is on housing projects oriented toward people who have previously experienced houselessness. In some cases, programmatic and/or formal aspects of the architecture of the buildings stand out, in others the integration of health and social services, while in some cases an idea of "best practice" comes to the fore, meaning that they are buildings that set interesting standards worth highlighting and are seen in comparison to other examples. We present nineteen housing projects that include two by Michael Maltzan Architecture in Los Angeles, one by Alexander Gorlin Architects in New York City, two by gaupenraub+/- in Vienna, one by Michel Müller, Heiner Blum, Jan Lotter, and HKS Architekten in Frankfurt, one by Peter Barber Architects in London, and several other projects by different firms in cities like Essen, Landsberg am Lech, Salzburg, Zurich, and Washington, DC.

Besides the recently built examples, we found several non-housing projects, like a mausoleum in Santiago de Chile; a refurbished factory in Hartford, Connecticut; an integrated housing, farming, and restaurant compound in Paris; and the Seattle Public Library. All of these projects in one way or another expand the question of "What can architecture do?" Additionally, in the exhibition we have also included some projects coming from university students, a design project for Mumbai, an analysis of the shelter system in New York, a manifesto-like set of urban interventions in Munich, and a documentary film set in London, thus expanding the imaginary around the topic by representing approaches to design and research.

Homelessness is a global problem that requires local discussions and solutions. The question is: What and which roles can architecture play? Or, to be more precise, how can architecture collaborate with other disciplines in developing ways to house those who do not have a home? The exhibition *Who's Next? Homelessness, Architecture, and Cities* and this publication attempt to explore and understand a problem that involves national, regional, and city agencies, nongovernmental organizations, religious insitutions, academic disciplines, and scientific fields. In brief, this book is a choral attempt to break down a topic into as many parts as needed so that the specificities and complexities of one of the most urgent crises of our days come to the fore.

By embracing the possibilities of bringing visibility to this complicated reality, we hope to contribute to getting one step closer to finding solutions, much in the same way that the architectural and urban disciplines—and particularly architects and urban specialists around the world—are able to use their practical and critical tools to engage in this conversation.

1   Vivan Ho, "'It's barely a Band-Aid': Life inside San Francisco's first sanctioned tent camp," *The Guardian,* May 22, 2020, https://www.theguardian.com/us-news/2020/may/22/san-francisco-sanctioned-tent-camp-homeless-covid-19 (all URLs accessed in August 2021); Mark Townsend, "UK hotels to become homeless shelters under coronavirus plan," *The Guardian,* March 21, 2020, https://www.theguardian.com/world/2020/mar/21/uk-hotels-homeless-shelters-coronavirus.

2   See https://www.trustforlondon.org.uk/data/rough-sleeping-borough/ and https://www.coalitionforthehomeless.org.

3   Sophia Wanyonyi, "Homelessness in Germany on the Rise," The Borgen Project, January 5, 2020, https://borgenproject.org/homelessness-in-germany-on-the-rise/.

4   In the United States, for example, most minority groups experience homelessness at higher rates than Whites, and therefore make up a disproportionate share of the homeless population. African Americans make up 13 percent of the general population, but more than 40 percent of the homeless population. See National Alliance to End Homelessness, "Racial Inequalities in Homelessness, by the Numbers," June 1, 2020, https://endhomelessness.org/resource/racial-inequalities-homelessness-numbers/.

5   Peter Marcuse, "Neutralizing Homelessness," *Socialist Review* 88, no. 1 (1988), pp. 69–97, esp. p. 93.

6   I am indebted to Luisa Schneider, a contributor to this book, for her help with this critical assessment of Housing First.

Tokyo, 2002

Hanging by a Thread: Confronting Urban Homelessness with Human Rights

Leilani Farha

All human beings are born free and equal in dignity and rights.
—Universal Declaration of Human Rights (Article 1, 1948)

In cities across the globe, I have met with people living in homelessness. On sidewalks in San Francisco and Delhi, under bridges in Paris and Lagos, in parks in Valparaíso and Belgrade, in tents in Los Angeles and Vancouver, in shelters in Barcelona and London, in abandoned buildings in Mexico City, in cars in San Diego. Each encounter as powerful as the one before.

I was appointed United Nations Special Rapporteur on adequate housing in 2014, a post I held until 2020. For six years I was the world's top watchdog, charged with investigating housing conditions across the globe and holding governments accountable to their human rights commitments under the Universal Declaration of Human Rights and the many international human rights treaties they have signed which protect housing as a human right. These commitments are well defined: as members of the human family, we each have the right to life, security of person, and an adequate standard of living, including adequate housing, food, water, and sanitation. All of which are required for human dignity—the essence of human rights.

It quickly became clear to me that where housing is concerned, the world is in a mess— all the signs of a global housing crisis, as serious and as pressing as the climate crisis is, were graffitied on the wall. They still are. Unaffordability, evictions, lack of social housing, discrimination, and, worst of all, growing homelessness, especially in the most affluent countries. All of which suggests that governments are failing to abide by their international human rights law obligations and are doing so with impunity.

To solve a problem, you need to understand that problem. Where human rights practice is concerned, you go to the source—those whose rights are most at risk. I needed to talk with people in their homes, wherever those homes happen to be. I made it my opportunity to meet those living in homelessness in all my travels. These were my most cherished conversations—ones I carry with me. Regardless of the city and its relative affluence, the geographic location, the weather—there are patterns and shared experiences.

It always begins with warm greetings. I am offered to stay and talk for a bit, to have a sip of juice, a biscuit, something procured out of nothing. One man washes his hands with bottled water before shaking mine; a woman plucks her eyebrows and puts her lipstick on outside the tent where she lives; another shows me her spotless space, adorned with a battered family photo. Each seemingly acutely aware that what holds them together, what defines them, is their dignity, under constant threat, hanging by a thread. No toilets. No showers. No beds. No roof.

I am told stories of despair, of lack, of wanting, of violence, of cruelty, of loss and abandonment—etched in their eyes, their teeth, their hands, their skin. They say to me: I just want to be treated like a human being.

When I look up from the destitution and deprivation of lives lived on sidewalks, bridges, and parks, I see billboards advertising new luxury lifestyle apartments, cranes hovering over glass and steel skyscrapers, tall buildings with no occupants, and tourists rolling suitcases to their short-term rentals.

I tell the people I meet that I can't remedy their individual living conditions; it's not my job. I talk to governments to influence them to think differently and from there to do more, to do better. Often, I hear from those living in homelessness that I am the first one with power or privilege who has taken the time to listen to their experiences. They want to be seen. They want to be heard. I am a witness to their existence. And in the absence of spaces and places for them to speak to authorities, they want me to retell their needs (not their stories) to those who have abandoned them, to help make them visible to those who prefer not to see.

They are not victims. They are human rights defenders. Every tent erected, sleeping bag rolled out, toilet constructed, is a claim: a distilled human rights claim for survival and dignity. Cognizant that their living conditions are not acceptable, understanding they are part of a global trend, wanting their governments held accountable.

Each conversation provides me with a clearer, more complete picture of our world.

In my many meetings with government officials, they do not express pride regarding the rising homelessness they see in their cities. Sometimes, they even show a flicker of embarrassment, which is quickly subsumed by a rash of numbers: dollars spent, units built, support provided. And yet, there is growing homelessness.

I am struck by the numbers they don't talk about. The number of billionaires and the degree of corporate wealth within their borders. The amount of money that flows across these borders, never to return. The dollars they give away through tax breaks to those who can buy the know-how to navigate the system.

Governments won't admit to the political and legislative energy they pour into wealth creation and maximization, forsaking those who are not useful to their economic equations. They don't concede that the race for accumulation that they facilitate and foster, and the extraction of profit from every square meter of land and property, pushes people out of their homes. They obfuscate the connection between unregulated corporate activities extracting profits from real estate and the growing number of people living in homelessness.

It's double jeopardy: governments create homelessness and then punish people for their homelessness. It's not uncommon for an individual experiencing homelessness and trying to survive to be criminalized, stereotyped, silenced, and shuttered in institutions like shelters or prisons.

Upon completing my term as UN Special Rapporteur at the beginning of the coronavirus pandemic, I knew that this work was by no means complete. The years I have spent acquainting myself with those living the gross inequalities of our times have fundamentally changed me—there is no walking away. But what steps do we need to take to create a world where people experiencing homelessness are valued members of the human family? How do we make visible the invisible?

I have come to understand that homelessness is a global phenomenon that undermines human rights, as an affront to human dignity, health, and life itself. As such, local and national governments have an obligation to address and solve the crisis. This will only be done effectively through the establishment of creative and new solutions carried out in collaboration with those experiencing homelessness, service providers, housing and human rights advocates, and public officials. Connections between global finance, national economies, real estate, corruption, and housing precarity and homelessness must also be recognized and addressed. At the end of the day, governments and private protagonists must be held accountable for upholding human rights.

It is to these ends that I founded The Shift—a new human rights project and global movement. Born through a unique partnership with the UN Office of the High Commissioner for Human Rights and with United Cities and Local Governments (UCLG), we are working collaboratively to shift the narrative, to shift how people think about homelessness, and to shift local and global responses.

One thing is clear: it will take all of us, and all of our strategies, such as protests in the street, to achieve legislative reform, research, documentary film, photography, art, and the written word.

Housing Systems

Housing systems are made up not only of buildings and properties, but also of the political and economic speculation that controls their development. Through commercial interests and an ever-increasing privatization of property, more and more city districts around the world are in the process of becoming gentrified. Neighborhoods are beautified, building blocks renovated and sold to high-bidding private investors, all of which leads to climbing rent for tenants, speculation, and vacancy. Some cities, like Vienna, still own a majority of the buildings, which gives them the opportunity to configure their use and helps to keep rent at a controlled price. However, most cities around the world are structurally oriented to private owners, which makes them increasingly expensive to live in. Housing systems are thus one of the main reasons for the growing number of homeless people in cities. Although other factors, such as an unstable private life, mental illness, or substance abuse, also play a role in destabilizing living situations, the intrinsic hierarchy of the housing market prevails as the cause of someone not obtaining or losing a home. Instead of looking at the problem as the individual responsibility of the unhoused, societies need to develop a structural approach to fighting homelessness due to the increasingly difficult housing market.

Park in Munich, 2020

Homelessness and the Housing System

David Madden

Social problems are inseparable from how they are defined, understood, and measured. Defining a problem is a political act itself. The ways that a problem is imagined and delineated shape the extent to which an issue can be acted upon. Our definitions determine if something is seen as a problem in the first place, as opposed to being seen as natural, normal, or unchangeable.

Homelessness is a paradigmatic example of a social problem that is ill-served by dominant forms of understanding. It is often portrayed as a straightforward moral problem, as a condition that primarily afflicts those who cannot or will not live up to the behavioral standards of contemporary capitalist society. This is blatant victim blaming, but it helps to perpetuate the fiction that the housing system works well and if some people are unhoused, then that is their problem. This view is institutionalized in legal mechanisms such as the British concept of "intentional homeless," a device through which legal authorities can establish that they have no obligation to provide housing for individuals or families if they are determined to have deliberately caused themselves to become homeless.[1] The assumption here is that people choose homelessness, and thus demands for housing assistance need to be viewed with suspicion.

Others eschew such an obviously judgmental position and instead cast homelessness as a medical problem, especially as one that reflects untreated substance abuse or mental health issues. This perspective might seem to be superficially more enlightened, but it still essentially casts homelessness as the result of what is implied to be an individual deficiency. It also fails as an explanation. The majority of people who experience mental health or substance abuse challenges are not also therefore rendered homeless. And the reality of homelessness does not match the common stereotype of isolated individuals battling mental health issues in peripheral urban sites. Since the advent of what scholars call "modern homelessness"[2]—the form of homelessness that emerges in the era of neoliberalization—there has been a sustained rise in family homelessness, and especially in the number of homeless children. Some countries, including the UK and the US, have also seen a rise in the number of people considered to be "in-work homeless,"[3] defined as those who are both employed and unhoused. To be sure, housing precarity can take its own toll on mental health. Some people without housing do face mental health challenges. But so do plenty of people with stable housing, and it does not follow that homelessness is caused by mental health struggles.

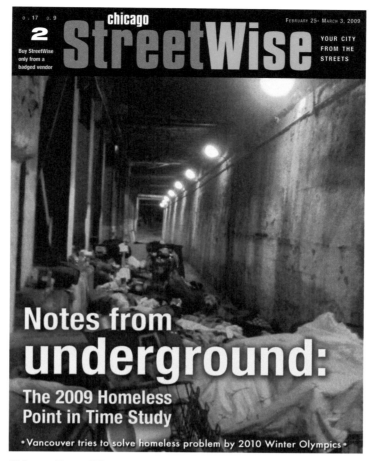

chicago

StreetWise

Notes from
underground:

The 2009 Homeless Point in Time Study

• Vancouver tries to solve homeless problem by 2010 Winter Olympics •

Chicago *StreetWise* magazine cover, Feburary 25 – March 3, 2009

Yet other voices eschew treating homelessness as either a moral or a medical problem but instead see it as an architectural one just waiting to be solved through clever design innovations. There is no shortage of novel plans for tiny houses, redesigned tents, reinforced tree houses, or coffin-sized shelters for people experiencing homelessness. An award-winning UK proposal would have attached plywood pods to the exterior walls of buildings, and these barnacles would be made available to people without homes to sleep in.[4] The fact that such ideas are taken seriously in design competitions is a testament to mainstream architectural culture's lack of engagement with the housing question. A more realistic recent idea would provide "virtual addresses" at which people with no fixed abode can receive mail.[5] Projects of this sort can potentially be helpful for the people who participate in them. But they are usually rolled out as experiments, and almost never actually implemented at scale. And they are still focused on ameliorating the effects of homelessness, rather than changing the conditions that make it possible in the first place.

So what sort of problem *is* homelessness? I want to offer what I think is a more sociologically informed perspective: homelessness is neither a personal condition nor an

architectural challenge, but rather a political problem that reflects particular relationships between people, property, and the state. Focusing on "the homeless" as a variety of persons obscures what is in fact a systemic issue. The phenomenon of homelessness has its origins not in individual choices but in systemic factors. And its impact is felt well beyond those who are compelled to experience it directly.

In order to make sense of homelessness, we need to understand the functions that it serves within the housing system. The term "housing system" invokes a bird's-eye view, referencing not any specific tenure or housing form in isolation, but the totality of housing types and tenures in any given territory and the ways in which they relate to social structures more broadly. The housing system includes the residential built environment, the political-economic structures that produce it, and the ideas and ideologies that animate it. Housing systems vary across places and can change in response to political contestation, policy shifts, new building technologies, and other factors.[6]

Homelessness is often imagined as a kind of purgatorial position outside of the housing system, but I would argue

Chicago *StreetWise* magazine cover,
July 1 – July 7, 2009

that it should instead be seen as an integral part of the housing system. This means, first of all, that homelessness is fundamentally the result of systemic causes. The recent increase in rough sleeping in the UK, for example, was not precipitated by a rapid rise in behavioral issues amongst individuals, but by the shifting role of housing within British political and economic life over the past three decades, which has resulted in the underfunding of local councils, the diminishment of public housing, and the sustained decoupling of the cost of housing from wages and local housing need. As an essential part of the housing system, homelessness is as much a creature of political and economic policy and decision-making as is any other type of housing tenure or residential form.

If we are to consider homelessness to be not a condition outside of the housing system but instead a fundamental part of it, it follows that within any given social formation, homelessness serves a number of specific purposes. Homelessness clearly interfaces with other housing forms and tenures, impacting the overall shape of the housing system, as well as the way people move between structural locations within it. The key is figuring out what homelessness does, as a residential, social, and political phenomenon. Significant social-scientific attention and philanthropic resources are devoted to tracing the impact

of homelessness on those who experience it. Although this is vitally important work, it is equally important to understand how homelessness impacts the housing system as a whole.

One of the functions of homelessness within the housing system is to serve as a threat. In largely privatized, unequal societies like the UK and the US, homelessness acts as the ultimate social warning to keep up with rent or mortgage payments. In no other economic sector does non-payment carry such devastating consequences for entire households. The very existence of rent as an institution relies on the threat of eviction and homelessness. If there were no possibility of eviction leading to homelessness, then rent and landlordism would not be able to exist in their current forms. Similarly, the debt relations surrounding homeownership are intimately tied to the threat of foreclosure. Precisely because they carry the risk of the loss of one's home, foreclosure and eviction are powerful instruments for maintaining the primacy of landlords, banks, and other financial actors.

Homelessness is also drafted into the service of the housing system to provide ideological support. The moralized, individualistic assumptions that surround homelessness serve to obscure its origins and functions within contemporary urban political economy. The belief

Chicago *StreetWise* magazine cover,
July 29 – August 4, 2009

that homelessness is caused by personal shortcomings— rather than by political-economic arrangements—is both supported by and supportive of the privileged role that private property enjoys in what the housing scholar Richard Ronald calls "homeowner societies."[7] In these societies, owner-occupation is valorized, naturalized, and privileged; the very notion of "home" is equated with property ownership. And while homeownership is viewed as a symbol and source of autonomy and respect, home- lessness is stigmatized as "an incarnation of a failed selfhood."[8] The inescapable stigma of homelessness and the inherent dignity of homeownership are mutually supportive ideological inventions that serve to justify existing housing hierarchies.

The fact of the matter is that for people who occupy the dominant positions in the housing system, it is comforting to believe that those in subordinated positions somehow deserve their fate. If they don't—if homeless- ness is not an individual failing but a contingent relation- ship generated by alterable political-economic arrange- ments—what does that say about the housing system as a whole and their privileged position in it? Maintaining the stigma that is attached to the experience of home- lessness becomes an ideological necessity if the housing system is to secure the privileged role of private property.

So how should we respond to the problem of homeless- ness? To truly address the homelessness crisis facing many cities, there needs to be a change in the way that issue is framed as a public problem. Changing this frame- work requires creating a new way of talking about housing and homelessness, one that avoids the stigmatizing, individualizing logic that currently dominates public debates. To start with, the word "homeless" should not be used to describe a category of person. Homelessness is not an essence. Someone who is homeless in one residential-political-economic context could be housed in a different context. There is, in fact, no homogenous group that we can label "homeless people." Homeless- ness is actually a relationship between people, the state, the market, and a racialized, gendered housing system. It is a relationship that occurs in conditions of inequality, hyper-competitiveness, and social austerity. Homeless- ness is also something that is *done* to particular groups. It is important to highlight this active dimension to the issue; rather than referring to "homeless people," it is more sociologically accurate to speak about specific groups who are forced into homelessness or relegated to housing precarity.

But beyond merely changing how we speak about homelessness, addressing the crisis requires a different politics of homelessness to be brought to the fore. Rather

Chicago *StreetWise* magazine cover,
March 31 – April 6, 2010

than exclusively focusing on the development of emergency policies to aid people who are currently experiencing homelessness, what is required is a deeper transformation of the housing system that prevents homelessness from being produced in the first place. Solving homelessness requires a widespread strengthening of tenancy rights, of legal aid for renters, and of support for struggling homeowners. It demands a reinvigorated and expanded public and social housing sector. It must entail a broader push to definancialize and decommodify housing as part of an effort to reorient the housing system as a whole.

Even the Housing First model, which seeks to provide housing to those in need regardless of their situation, does not address broader questions of who and what the housing system is for. Although Housing First certainly represents an improvement over less supportive policy models, it still represents a response to the problem of homelessness that is focused on those who are considered "chronically homeless," which is itself a problematic term.[9] Like all such reforms, Housing First should be part of a broader strategy that addresses homelessness at its root.

While truly engaging the housing crisis requires systematic change, this does not mean that there is no role for short-term policy changes or urban design interventions.

There is definitely a need for emergency support and the provision of special services to people who have been rendered homeless, as well as for immediate reforms that make urban spaces less hostile to them. It would still be a sign of progress, for example, to remove hostile architecture elements from public spaces or to develop approaches to urban planning that are not predicated upon removing people that urban gurus like William H. Whyte referred to as "undesirables."[10] However, simply adding a right to emergency housing to a fundamentally unchanged housing system would allow residential precarity and insecurity to persist unchallenged.

Homelessness in its current form ultimately reflects the shallowness of contemporary citizenship. The only truly effective response to the problem of homelessness is a politics that seeks to create substantive equality and social citizenship and that reshapes cities and housing systems accordingly. To solve homelessness, states must be pushed to create a deeper and broader right to home.

1   On the concept of intentional homelessness,
     see Simon Mullings, "Enacting 'Intentional
     Homelessness,'" *Socialist Lawyer* 84 (2020),
     pp. 40–43.

2   Peter H. Rossi, *Down and Out in America: The
     Origins of Homelessness* (Chicago: University
     of Chicago Press, 1991).

3   Katy Jones, Anya Ahmed, Iolo Madoc-Jones,
     Andrea Gibbons, Michaela Rogers, and Mark
     Wilding, "Working and Homeless: Exploring the
     Interaction of Housing and Labour Market
     Insecurity," *Social Policy and Society* 19, no. 1
     (2020), pp. 121–32.

4   Liz Connor, "A London architect is building
     spacious pods for London's homeless to bed
     down in," *Evening Standard,* July 23, 2015.

5   Katie Prescott, "'Having an address got me
     a job when I was homeless,'" *BBC News,*
     April 2, 2021.

6   See David Madden and Peter Marcuse, *In
     Defense of Housing: The Politics of Crisis*
     (London: Verso, 2016).

7   Richard Ronald, *The Ideology of Home Owner-
     ship: Homeowner Societies and the Role of
     Housing* (New York: Palgrave Macmillan, 2008).

8   Craig Willse, *The Value of Homelessness:
     Managing Surplus Life in the United States*
     (Minneapolis: University of Minnesota Press,
     2015), p. 150.

9   Ibid., pp. 139–68.

10   William Hollingsworth Whyte, *The Social
     Life of Small Urban Spaces* (New York:
     Conservation Foundation, 1980).

Tent City: Living (Rather Than Dying) at the Limits of Capital

Stephen Przybylinski and Don Mitchell

Tent cities have been a feature of the American landscape, sometimes tolerated, sometimes abhorred, since the earliest days of the country's industrialization. Though they mushroom during times of severe economic crisis— New York's Central Park, for example, hosted a large shantytown during the Great Depression and there was something of a media frenzy over the explosion of tent cities in the wake of the Great Recession after Oprah Winfrey visited Sacramento's sprawling tent city—they never go away. Indeed, tent cities have positively flourished during the various economic booms of the late twentieth and early twenty-first centuries, as the forces of real-estate capital have increasingly turned America's cities into playgrounds (and bedrooms) for the rich.

The predominant policy response to the rise of tent cities in the United States has been, and remains, to bulldoze them, wiping them off the face of the cityscape in hopes that their denizens will likewise disappear. Indeed, making houseless people disappear is a primary leitmotif of the increasingly mean streets of the American city.[1] Sometimes this means rendering them invisible by ensuring that any services and shelters are located far away (sometimes tens of kilometers away) from prestige districts. Oftentimes it means forcing them out through laws and policing—so-called sit-lie laws that make it impossible for people experiencing houselessness to

hang out on the streets, anti-camping ordinances, anti-begging laws, and aggressive "zero-tolerance" police strategies—that make the pursuance of everyday life close to impossible for people without shelter. Increasingly it may also mean buying them a one-way bus ticket out of town.

Under such conditions, America's mean streets are also deadly streets. While no full statistics exist, various studies show that people who are unstably housed die at elevated rates—from exposure to otherwise manageable diseases like hypertension and tuberculosis, at the hands of police violence and other assaults, due to automobile accidents, and more (to say nothing of the iniquitous ravages of Covid-19). Bulldozing tent cities is merely part of the regular violence visited against the shelterless in the world's most successful capitalist democracy.

Alongside the meanness and the deadliness of America's streets there also exist, of course, spaces of respite: voluntary and government-run shelters, for example, have always been a central, if also inadequate, part of the American response to houselessness, creating an archipelago of intervention that is at once ameliorative and disciplinary. Over the past two decades, an increasing number of cities have added sanctioned tent cities to this archipelago. Such encampments are often located in

The commons and tiny houses at Dignity Village

out-of-the-way places, typically operated by government agencies and local charities, and are governed by a hierarchical, top-down management with stringent rules regulating residents' behavior. The geographer Jessie Speer calls these sorts of houseless compounds "tent wards," and they do indeed share much in common with old ward-based "total institutions" like prisons and mental asylums, as well as newer ones like refugee camps.[2]

A small number of American cities, however, have been home to experiments to sanction and support self-governing encampments. Portland, Oregon offers a primary example of this model. Although the city continues to bulldoze houseless people's encampments, it has also, for nearly twenty years now, approved and even provided services to several self-governing tent cities. The first of these encampments, dating to the early 2000s, is called Dignity Village (DV). It began as a space of protest, decrying the lack of housing and shelter options for low-income and houseless people in the city. In 2003, Portland's city government agreed to host the encampment on an industrial site on the northeast part of the city, where it still operates to this day.

The significance of DV cannot be overstated; it not only provided a model for Portland's other encampments, but it has come to be seen throughout the United States as a

primary example of how houseless communities can effectively self-govern. DV's operations are managed by its residents, and governance is regulated through the village's collectively decided bylaws. An elected governing council holds weekly meetings, during which residents decide how to divide necessary communal labor and spend community finances. The council holds votes on a range of issues, organizes relations with outside organizations and the surrounding community, and arbitrates disputes among residents when they arise.

For most of the first decade of the twenty-first century, DV was Portland's only sanctioned encampment. As the Great Recession deepened, however, more tent cities sprouted up across the city. After an intense period of struggle, in 2011 the city sanctioned a second encampment, called Right 2 Dream Too.[3] Later, in 2015, Portland declared a "State of Emergency on Housing and Homelessness," allowing the city to suspend certain zoning laws and approve a small number of additional encampments, despite sometimes-virulent neighborhood opposition. These more recent tent cities typically house one- or two-dozen residents and are also governed on the DV model. The primary benefit of these encampments to the city is that they provide low-cost shelter which provides residents with a certain degree of stability, thereby helping to ameliorate the perceived disorder that

The security desk of Right 2 Dream Too in front of the men's and women's sleeping tents

houseless people bring to city streets. Meanwhile, to the residents, the encampments provide an opportunity to shape and control the environment in which they live, providing them with a sense of empowerment, dignity, agency, accountability, and even urban citizenship, to say nothing of the health benefits that having a more secure sleeping space entails.

The jewel in the crown of Portland's new "emergency" solution to houselessness is its recent pilot project, the Kenton Women's Village (KWV). Opened in the summer of 2017, KWV is the result of years of planning by city government, neighborhood associations, local architects, and advocacy groups. Located on Portland's industrial north side, KWV hosts twenty neatly ordered tiny houses, designed by architects at a nearby university and built with volunteer labor, a commons with a kitchen, and shared toilets. In roughly three years, KWV has helped more than forty women move into permanent supportive housing and aided even more in receiving necessary services and more stable incomes.[4] Backed by the resources of Portland's government and powered by the organizing and building skills of the city's activist and advocacy communities, KWV illustrated how the model of self-organized houseless communities can provide stability to precariously housed people while simultaneously calling attention to the plight of houselessness

as a broader condition of society, not just a trait inherent to vulnerable individuals.

Beyond the social benefits of the encampments, the quality of infrastructure is also of importance, especially given Portland's rainy climate. While most of the city's encampments began with makeshift tents and tarps, over time, they have slowly upgraded to a (sometimes somewhat haphazard) collection of tiny houses. In contrast, for KWV, architects worked closely from the start with potential residents to design their spaces, and later with volunteer contractors and general laborers to construct the site, paying attention both to matters of urban planning (like street layout) and domestic architecture. Similarly, at Agape Village located on the city's far east side, tiny houses were built by a nonprofit that hired only houseless individuals who resided in other tent cities. Others still, like Right 2 Dream Too and the thus-far unsanctioned Hazelnut Grove, have relied on donated resources from a local building center to develop infrastructure and replace tents with tiny houses. Typically, construction is accomplished by organizing "work parties," where housed and unhoused supporters of the encampments work with residents to construct the spaces together. Each of Portland's tiny-house encampments now hosts between twenty and sixty structures, nearly all of which were built or rebuilt in the last few

Tiny houses at the original location of Kenton Women's Village

years, providing residents with protection from the elements and the privacy and safety that having personal space affords.

Given the social and physical benefits of the self-organized shelter model, the city of Portland is amending its land use ordinances to allow tiny-house encampments to become permanent after the sunset of the State of Emergency on Housing and Homelessness. These changes in zoning regulations will make Portland the first city in the United States to legally allow self-organized encampments to operate on municipally owned properties. While such a move is no doubt beneficial to houseless residents—and likely to their surrounding communities—its implications should nonetheless give us pause. On one hand, the encampments provide a sense of dignity and agency for many of their residents, qualities that are regularly denied to houseless people who live even more precariously on the streets or in crowded shelters. Nevertheless, these encampments cannot match the scale of need in Portland (much less the country), nor do they satisfy the desires of people living in them, who ultimately wish to find more permanent, stable housing. Even if the encampments themselves are made permanent, it is nonetheless understood that they will continue to serve only as temporary, emergency forms of shelter.

In other words, self-organized encampments are not a solution to the crisis of houselessness in capitalist America. So why, then, have they become so embedded into the urban landscape? In part it is because they indicate, if only tacitly, a significant shift in dominant thinking about houselessness, its causes, and what can—and cannot—be done about the issue. They demonstrate a dawning understanding that, under current political and economic conditions, there *is no solution to houselessness in American capitalism*. The growth of Portland's constellation of government-sanctioned encampments may have been made possible by the "State of Emergency" declaration, which responded to a growing belief that houselessness was a *crisis* that had to be urgently addressed. But the making permanent of these encampments indicates that houselessness is not a crisis at all, but rather a condition *endemic* to capitalism. Tent cities are a permanent part of the landscape because houselessness is a permanent part of capitalism. Portland is merely recognizing and sanctioning a condition that has always existed and a reality that cities in the Global South have always known about: the global reserve army of labor has to live somewhere and, if no space is provided for them, then they will create space for themselves, however "informally."

But why now? What is it about this historical moment that has led Portland to recognizing this reality? Over the last

Building foundations for tiny houses at Right 2 Dream Too

couple of generations, capitalism has changed its stripes. Typically, we understand this political-economic shift through the twin lenses of globalization and neoliberalism, but there is also another factor at work. Back in 1970s, the spatial theorist Henri Lefebvre declared that we were in the midst of an urban revolution.[5] By this he was not simply referring to the fact that a larger (now majority) share of the global population was living in cities. Rather, Lefebvre was noting that the center of capitalism's gravity was shifting from the industrial production of commodities to the production of urban space. As urban space became increasingly commodified, the urban landscape itself was transformed into a primary site for capital circulation and accumulation. And he was right. As we all know by now, the success or failure of whole economies rests on the fortunes of the real-estate market, and this recent trans-formation produces houselessness more ruthlessly than ever before. The whole point of accumulation through the built environment is to make urban space, especially housing, *unaffordable*. Houselessness is produced not only through the normal workings of capitalism (the constant production of a reserve labor army), but also even more directly by throwing people onto the streets to make room for higher paying residents and businesses.

Under these conditions, houseless people illustrate the limits to capital and to capitalism.[6] Capitalism cannot provide decent housing, decent sanitation, or a modicum of decency for houseless people because to do so would threaten the very model of accumulation. At the same time, however, houseless people are themselves a limit to capital: they are a threat to that accumulation and a significant problem of management. If, for three decades now, the primary mode of management has been to police and to kill or let die, that mode has done nothing to eliminate houselessness or the threat to the system that houseless people embody. The meanness of America's streets has nothing to show for itself but spite. Perhaps Portland's tent cities stand as a frank admission of this fact, as well as a dawning recognition that it is just as possible to let houseless people live, and not merely die, at the limits to capital.

1   Throughout this essay we use the term "houseless" or "houselessness" rather than homeless or homelessness. In doing so, we follow the language used by encampment residents in Portland to describe their situations. Using the term houseless prioritizes what houseless individuals need most: housing.

2   Jessie Speer, "The Rise of the Tent Ward: Homeless Camps in the Era of Mass Incarceration," *Political Geography* 62 (2018), pp. 160–69.

3   Stephen Przybylinski, "Securing Legal Rights to Place: Mobilizing around Moral Claims for a Houseless Rest Space in Portland, Oregon," *Urban Geography* 42, no. 4 (2021), pp. 417–38.

4   Catholic Charities, "Kenton Women's Village," https://www.catholiccharitiesoregon.org/ services/housing-services/kenton-womens-village/ (accessed in September 2021).

5   Henri Lefebvre, *The Urban Revolution* (1970; repr., Minneapolis: University of Minnesota Press, 2003).

6   Don Mitchell, *Mean Streets: Homelessness, Public Space, and the Limits of Capital* (Athens, GA: University of Georgia Press, 2020).

Terminology

Language. Does it describe or create reality? Words define, and, as the previous question implies, they also determine realities. Moreover, words frequently involve issues of rights and duties; language can be inclusive or exclusive; and it can qualify matters in neutral, positive, or negative ways. Using appropriate words can be the starting point toward a shift of awareness within a society. This starts with the decision of whether to say "houseless," which is limited to the idea of a place, or "homeless," which can evoke an idea of community and is also a way of labeling individuals, implying that they are limited to, or even represent, their situation of being without an abode. Moreover, words can modify (or add to) meaning over time, and this dynamic dimension of language is critical when speaking about such sensitive topics as homelessness, evictions, and marginalization. By way of a glossary, and the effort of concisely defining each selected term, we are addressing the relevance of understanding different meanings. We also suggest that there are certain words which one should know during the process of comprehending the multiple dimensions of homelessness and its relation to architecture and cities. Language empowers; it enables us to think and reflect on problems. Every active member of society needs to first reflect on these problems before deciding how to act upon them, what to demand from politicians, what to expect from municipalities, and/or simply how to engage in dialogue about it.

Avenida Paulista, São Paulo, 2016

Loving and Living at the Limit

Luisa Schneider

Imagine a day in the life of a couple or a family. What do you imagine them doing? Where do you see them returning to in the evening to sleep? And where do they enjoy quality time together, free from unwanted interruptions? While the ways of living you imagine may be vastly diverse, they are almost always likely to involve a home.

This is not surprising. Many of our basic rights, and the protections in place to prevent interference with them, are dependent on the separation of the private sphere from the public sphere. This boundary, between the public and private realms, is usually delineated by the walls of tenancy-protected housing. As such, our rights, and much of German domestic law as well,[1] are based on the underlying assumption that those subject to the law have access to some form of housing. Housing has thus become intimately linked to our sense of safety and well-being, providing us with a safe space to address our most fundamental needs without fear of intrusion or surveillance.

The rights to privacy and intimacy are two such internationally recognized basic human rights that are closely linked to our conception of housing.[2] As a result of this sociolegal constellation, of how our rights and private and public spheres are delineated by housing, our relationships have become entwined with the domestic realm.

For unhoused people,[3] the separation between the house and the street collapses, making it extremely challenging to attain the rights to privacy and intimacy. For starters, ordinances often forbid sleeping or engaging in intimate acts in public places. And even if authorities choose to look away, living on the streets provides little in terms of security or stability. In addition, child protection laws prevent unhoused parents from maintaining custody of their children, while domestic violence laws and restraining orders are impossible to enforce for those who dwell on the streets. Ultimately, those without housing cannot find protection from violations of the rights to privacy and intimacy.

The realities of houselessness often fall outside our normative assumptions and the laws and protections we consider basic or universal. However, houselessness is a reality in all societies, and the rights of the people who experience it also deserve to be protected.

Based on long-term ethnographic fieldwork with unhoused people in Leipzig, Germany, this essay examines how people who live on the streets or in shelters experience intimate relationships, including parenthood and family life. What practical, legal, political, and emotional challenges do unhoused people face in finding privacy and intimacy? And what does this tell us about how we take for granted the connections between love, family, and domesticity?

The Happyland, 2020. Section of an abandoned building in the arsenal behind Leipzig's main station which has been designated as a space for intimacy where couples can enjoy the privacy they seldomly find on the streets. This building has been torn down.

The Kissing Booth, 2020. Space devoted to exchanging intimacy in an abandonded building in Leipzig which has been labeled with the word *Knutschen* (smooching)

Creating Spaces for Love

Isa, Mike, Bernt, Sebastian, Vera, Lina, and Chantal, all in their late twenties or early thirties,[4] are lying on the cement floor of one of the abandoned buildings that used to form Leipzig's customs area. Isa lies in Mike's arms as they gaze at the open sky through the last remainders of a roof that had long ago collapsed. Mike kisses her and, after exchanging a look, they stand up and disappear into the dark, behind bare brickwork that designates a separate room over which someone has written *Knutschen,* or "smooching." We can hear their movements in the kissing booth, but we can no longer see them.

During my research, I met several couples who, like Mike and Isa, fell in love while experiencing houselessness. While older men and women, the latter of whom often live almost invisibly on the streets, tend to navigate homelessness alone, younger people almost always form communities, which they often refer to as their "chosen families." Living on the streets comes with many dangers, which are particularly pronounced for young women. The murder of one of my research collaborators, a woman in her twenties, is only one example of the severe challenges that are faced by people who are unstably housed.[5] After my research collaborator's relationship ended and coronavirus restrictions forced unhoused people apart, she had no choice but to sleep alone, putting her at greater risk of danger.

Chosen families may occupy abandoned buildings or stairways. They may erect tents under bridges or deep inside city parks. They protect each other and, together, try to meet their basic survival needs. However, these makeshift homes usually share a common trait: their residents are rarely able to experience privacy.

This lack of privacy makes it difficult for couples to find ways to be intimate. Walking off into the dark is not always a safe or viable alternative due to policing, the presence of passersby and, in some cases, people who rely on acquisitive crime. Unhoused groups, recognizing the simultaneous needs for privacy and protection, often attempt to create spaces where they can safely carry out their intimate needs without unwanted interruptions. Some encampments offer a tent or oversized sleeping bag for lovers to use; others have created signage systems—red may mean "do not disturb" and green may mean "unoccupied." Those living in abandoned buildings develop similar mechanisms, such as the kissing booth used by Mike and Isa and the Happyland, both of which are rooms, albeit without most of their walls or windows. However, while these solutions may protect those engaging in acts of intimacy from unwanted onlookers, noise still travels. These places are a far cry from the privacy afforded by a personal bedroom or house.

The red disc signals that this tent in Leipzig is occupied and may not be entered. Since the photograph was taken in 2020, the members of this camp have been evicted.

The Long and Arduous Road to Housing

Many of the unstably housed couples I conducted research with hope to find an apartment where they can live together but are unable to do so. Even for those who do receive benefits, the size of an apartment for two cannot exceed 60 square meters or cost more than €387.69. Competition is fierce, and landlords ultimately decide whom to rent to. The best way to qualify for an apartment is to navigate the houseless aid system, which usually requires people to advance through steps to prove that they are "housing ready." Unhoused people first sleep in emergency shelters while they receive immediate assistance to address the issues that allegedly prevent them from securing and maintaining housing. They then move into supervised accommodations, a shared apartment, or temporary housing before transitioning to an independent apartment.

One core issue, however, is that, while a few cities across Germany do offer accommodations for unhoused couples, for the most part, the country's homeless aid system is based on individualized care. Emergency shelters, which serve as the entry point to the aid system, tend to be separated by gender and require couples to split up to be placed. Couples are not eligible to receive an apartment without first meeting the preliminary requirements, which require them to proceed individually.

Lena, fifty-four, and Tim, fifty-five, who were evicted from their home after living there for twenty-nine years, are one such example of a couple that was forced to choose between staying together and finding shelter.[6] After spending one night in separate emergency shelters, they decided they would rather sleep on the streets together than in a bed apart. Throughout my research, I only met one couple out of forty that agreed to split up in order to enter the shelter system. Most others gave shelters a chance for a few weeks or months but, like Lena and Tim, ultimately stopped using them regularly. This placed them back on the streets and therefore out of the aid system, making it extremely difficult for them to reach their goal of obtaining housing.

Family and Children

Whenever children are involved, Germany does its best to offer unhoused families accommodations, an approach that is also meant to encourage parents to exit violent or abusive relationships. However, before receiving housing, child services must assess whether parents are able to take care of their children. The fear and stigma of losing custody and being separated from one's children ultimately prevents many parents from seeking shelter or leaving violent relationships.

The green disc indicates that the tent is unoccupied and may be used to enjoy privacy or exchange intimacy.

Furthermore, if unhoused people become pregnant, maintaining custody of their newborn children can be extremely difficult. Even if they are able to find housing and show that they can provide for their children, maintaining custody is not a certainty. One example of this is Janine, a woman in her twenties who was able to independently secure housing and other necessities for her baby during her pregnancy. However, she was still not allowed to take her child home after giving birth, as child services was concerned that she would be unfit to be a mother due to her unhoused past. Janine's infant daughter was taken into state custody and she was only able to see her during supervised visits. And although the state's plan was for Janine to take parenting lessons and then reunite her with her daughter, Janine's struggle with the separation eventually led her to experience depression. This situation was aggravated by the pandemic, which impeded her from seeing her daughter for long periods of time. Janine eventually lost custody of her daughter altogether.

My research is full of parents who have lost custody of their children because they cannot secure housing. Many get a dog with whom they form deep bonds and from whom they are unwilling to separate. As a result, a few cities across Germany have created shelters where people can stay with animals, but Leipzig is not one of them. Like other unhoused individuals who refuse to give up their relationships for shelter, many of them ultimately have no choice but to live on the streets.

Existential Relationships

If couples have no housing and thus neither the space nor legal protections to enjoy privacy and intimacy, if covering basic needs like food and safety requires intense efforts, if teamwork and coordination are a necessity for survival, then the dynamics of a relationship and its emotional interactions are likely to be severely affected. Where other couples can enjoy getting to know one another while dating, the relationships of individuals who are unstably housed are strained by numerous and ongoing challenges. These challenges begin with everyday questions: Where will we find food today? Where can we sleep? How can we find the space to be alone? They end with more complex questions: How can we create a stable foundation for our relationship, given our circumstances? While relationships between unhoused individuals may face many obstacles, couples that endure such a trying experience together may become very close very quickly. They not only form an emotional unit, but also a practical team that works together to complete the tasks that are necessary for survival.

Love as the Road to and from the Streets

Many people are driven to houselessness after experiencing drastic relationship changes, such as a breakup, the death of a loved one, or a separation. Furthermore, life crises like unemployment, debt, and mental health breakdowns can become unsurmountable if people do not have healthy social support networks to lean on.

While strained relationships can be one factor that can lead to houselessness, unhoused people also go to great lengths to protect their relationships and to create spaces where they can experience love and intimacy. For many, love and parenthood serve as drivers that provide them with the necessary strength to travel the long and arduous road to obtaining housing. In order to best support people who are unstably housed, public services must acknowledge the endurance and importance of these relationships and allow the people in them to navigate hurdles together.

Germany treats houselessness as an individual problem, caused by the personal failings of those who are unstably housed. As such, the solutions to the problem are also individualized. Unhoused people are frequently forced to make a choice between shelter and their most intimate relationships. These choices are made even more difficult by the fact that our notions of home are often intrinsically tied to our loved ones.

In order to improve our response to the ongoing housing crisis affecting cities across the world, we must better understand how our relationships are tied to domesticity and better protect the rights to privacy and intimacy for those who are unhoused. This is particularly important now, considering that the number of people without housing in Germany has tripled in the last decade, a situation that may be further aggravated by the coronavirus crisis.

1   The "allgemeine Persönlichkeitsrecht (APR)," or personality rights, developed by Germany's Federal Court of Justice in 1954, recognizes the spheres of privacy and intimacy, which are protected from intrusion and surveillance. The APR is drawn from Art. 2 para. 1 *Grundgesetz* (Free Development of Personality), in conjunction with Art. 1 para. 1 *Grundgesetz* (Protection of Human Dignity).

2   Privacy refers to the activities that happen outside of the public sphere—in the domestic arena—whereas intimacy pertains to, among other things, a person's inner, emotional, and sexual life.

3   I use the term "unhoused" because, to my research collaborators, "home" and "house" are not synonyms. While they are "unhoused" (without housing) they refuse to be labeled "homeless" (without a home). See Luisa T. Schneider, "'My home is my people': Home-making among Rough Sleepers in Leipzig, Germany," *Housing Studies* (2020), pp. 1–18.

4   The names and identifying details of the research collaborators who wish to remain anonymous have been changed.

5   Saxony Police, "Leblose Person," *Sachsen.de,* March 16, 2020, https://www.polizei.sachsen. de/de/MI_2020_71356.htm (all URLs accessed in September 2021). Alexander Bischoff, "Die Tote von den Bahngleisen: Frau (25) wurde in Leipzig im Streit erschlagen," *Tag 24,* March 18, 2020, https://www.tag24.de/ leipzig/leipzig-die-tote-von-den-bahngleisen-frau-wurde-im-streit-erschlagen-1462512.

6   Schneider, "'My home is my people,'" pp. 1–18.

Overlooked Remembrance and the Language of Social Exclusion: The Example of the Term "Asocial"

Juliane Bischoff

It's difficult to play a role if there are no grounds for that role any more, difficult to stay in your place when you've lost that place or to exist in another person's dwelling when you yourself have no fixed abode, are without hearth or home, are almost nameless.

—Marc Augé, *No Fixed Abode*

Introduction

Social fragmentation and disintegration are particularly prevalent in times of crisis. Rapid societal changes give rise to insecurities, which are often expressed as fear of losing one's social status. Right-wing extremist and populist movements use this to their advantage, manipulating perceived truth to mobilize against minorities. The marginalization and devaluation of vulnerable populations are also reflected in public discourses that play off facts against perceptions through the use of language. As early as the 1930s, the playwright and poet Bertolt Brecht had already called for critical reflection on exclusionary language when he stated that, "[i]n times when deception is demanded and errors are encouraged, the thinker strives to correct whatever he reads and hears."[1]

What does the exclusion of vulnerable groups say about a society? The persecution of individuals who were stigmatized as "asocial" during the National Socialist period in Germany, and their long-overlooked stories of suffering in the postwar era, tell of the long-lasting effects of ideologically charged language and how it can impact perceptions of reality. To this day, ways in which allegedly socially deviant behavior is dealt with reflects an ideology of inequality that can serve as an indicator for the state of our social coexistence.

Social Conditions in the Early 1930s

The social developments of 1920s-era Germany, a time characterized by a liberal zeitgeist, social emancipation, and the acquisition of new rights and freedoms, among others, came to an abrupt end with the global economic crisis that began in 1929. Rapidly increasing unemployment and privation, poverty, and mass impoverishment now shaped day-to-day life. The crisis impacted not only the economic, but also the social foundations of the Weimar Republic, to the benefit of right-wing extremist and populist forces who took advantage of the moment to breed a politics of hate. Originally, the National Socialist German Workers' Party (Nationalsozialistische Deutsche Arbeiterpartei, NSDAP) staged itself as a protest movement directed against the liberal values of the Weimar Republic and thus succeeded in attracting voters from all sectors of society, particularly from the middle and lower-middle classes. The National Socialists grew rapidly throughout the early 1930s, a result of their aggressive rabble-rousing and propaganda, but also facilitated by the population's willingness to subordinate themselves to an extremist

Table showing how various categories of prisoners were designated at the Dachau concentration camp, ca. 1940

leader in exchange for the promise of stability.[2] On the eve of the National Socialist seizure of power, the sociologist Theodor Geiger described "a society ruled by fears of displacement, loss of prestige, and defensiveness"[3] in all strata of society. In this, he saw "the vanguard importance of a younger generation that was removing itself from history, stylizing itself as an agent of national activism and, in doing so, turning the rumble of fear into the engine of a new age. Today we know that these ranks produced the ideological avant-garde of the totalitarian era . . ."[4]

The NSDAP's electoral success led to the appointment of Adolf Hitler as Reichskanzler on January 30, 1933. What followed was a step-by-step dissolution of democratic structures and the establishment of a dictatorship. Under the catchword of a "people's community" (Volksgemein-schaft), the National Socialists promised to satisfy the needs and desires of one segment of the population, regarded as "racially pure," at the expense of others. Political adversaries and individuals ostracized as "foreign to the community" (Gemeinschaftsfremde) and "harmful to the people" (Volksschädlinge) were radically excluded and persecuted.[5]

Social policy became one of the first areas to be trans-formed by National Socialist ideology, as the party aimed to break with the social welfare principles of the Weimar Republic based on the values of solidarity and support. One of the NSDAP's early campaign pledges was to eliminate "asociality," a term that encompassed a wide range of behaviors that were considered to deviate from norms, including the aversion to work and homelessness.[6] At the same time, the National Socialists developed health policies based on the principles of heredity and race, which measured the value of a person on the basis of "racial biology" (rassenbiologisch). Policies supposedly identified individuals who were "biologically inferior" and were therefore deemed a burden on the "collective genetic pool," making them ineligible to receive financial aid and social support. Wilhelm Frick, the Reich's Minister of the Interior, had already formulated these guidelines by 1933, as is evidenced in a speech he delivered before the so-called Advisory Council for Population and Racial Policy (Sachverständigenrat für Bevölkerungs- und Rassenpolitik), during which he vilified all those members of society who were no longer considered productive due to illness or their social situation. Frick announced a program of "selection and eradication," which by 1945 had resulted in a 70 percent reduction of outpatient services, mass internment, a structural undersupply of public welfare services, and even targeted murders.

The notion of the inherited inferiority of certain groups and individuals was promulgated countless times by the National Socialists, and terms like "antisocial," "foreign to society," "dangerous to society" (gemeinschaftswidrig), and "hereditarily incapable" (erbuntüchtig) were brought into welfare discourses in order to advance National Socialist ideology. The National Socialists thus created the prerequisites for a radical shift away from a notion of welfare oriented to democratic principles and toward a society guided by principles of utility.

The Persecution of "Asocials" under National Socialism

The ideology of the Volksgemeinschaft ensured that only the segment of the population that was legitimated as Volks-genossen (the "people's comrades") would be guaranteed protection and social support. As a result of this policy, the number of welfare recipients decreased considerably after the National Socialists came to power. By contrast, political opponents, as well as individuals singled out due to anti-Semitic and racist motivations, were increasingly excluded and persecuted. Instead of receiving welfare, individuals who were seen to partake in socially deviant lifestyles were categorized as groups that needed to be combated and excluded from society.[7] This soon turned into a battle cry: several disparate groups were branded as "asocials." Targeted groups included the homeless, beggars, sex workers, migrant workers, Yenish people, Sinti and Roma who were pejoratively referred to as "Gypsies," and other people derogatively described as "traveling people living in a Gypsy manner." They were subjected to a practice of repressive persecution that frequently resulted in arrests, forced sterilization, and internment in psychiatric clinics, workhouses, and concentration camps.[8]

The National Socialists' first racial hygiene law, the Law for the Prevention of Hereditarily Diseased Offspring, came into effect in July 1933 and argued for the existence of a relationship between criminality and heredity. Completely ignoring how social conditions and structural issues impact civil society, the National Socialist dictatorship instead opted for the criminalization of socially vulnerable sectors of society. With the so-called beggar raids (Bettlerrazzia) of September 1933, persecution reached its first climax: tens of thousands of people experiencing homelessness under the Reich were arrested within just one week.[9]

The term "asocial" rapidly gained currency in the mid-1930s as it morphed into a collective, all-encompassing term for deviant behavior. The term was never clearly defined and did not represent any specific group of people, allowing it to be imposed from the outside in connection with various undesirable behaviors. Under National Socialism, the question of who exactly was ultimately counted among the "asocials" and "individuals foreign to society" remained largely unexplained.[10]

Language of Exclusion

By examining and recording semantic shifts in the language of the National Socialist dictatorship, the literary scholar Victor Klemperer analyzed the ways in which words serve as a projection surface for social reality. According to Klemperer, the National Socialists asserted their worldview not so much through the employment of newly created terminology but by charging existing terms with the ideas of racial hygiene.[11] In his journal entries, Klemperer documented how language can be used to establish who is included and excluded from a community. He describes an oppressive reality characterized by increasing radicalization, the humiliation of socially excluded individuals, anti-Semitic and racial persecution, and even expulsion and eradication.

Klemperer traced the mechanisms and strategies of the "language of the Third Reich," revealing that, for the most part, the National Socialists did not invent propagandistic terms, but instead changed the value and frequency of use of already-established terms:

The Third Reich coined only a very small number of the words in its language, perhaps—indeed probably— none at all. In many cases, Nazi language points to foreign influences and appropriates much of the rest from the German language before Hitler. But it changes the value and the frequency of their occurrence, it makes common property out of what was previously the preserve of an individual or a tiny group, . . . and in the process steeps words and groups of words and sentence structures in its poison. Making language the servant of its dreadful system, it procures it as its most powerful, most public, and most surreptitious means of advertising.[12]

As such, it was not individual speeches by the National Socialists that had an impactful influence, but rather the figures of speech and terms that found their way into people's everyday language—that "were taken on board mechanically and unconsciously."[13]

Such is the case with the term "asocial," which was already included in the Duden German-language dictionary in 1929. This and other terms used in National Socialist propaganda significantly impacted how social reality was interpreted: the National Socialists presented the individuals that were affected by societal hardship as the problem, rather than the threat of poverty as its structural condition.[14]

Over the years, as new groups came into the crosshairs of the National Socialists, the radical persecution of "asocials" expanded to include more and more individuals. In 1937, Wilhelm Frick's Ordinance for the Prevention of Crime (Grunderlass zur vorbeugenden Verbrechensbekämpfung) made the police, rather than welfare agencies, responsible for individuals in need. As a result, the summer of 1938 was witness to two waves of detention by the Gestapo and the criminal police (Kriminalpolizei). Referred to today as the Action Against the Work-Shy (Aktion Arbeitsscheu Reich), more than ten thousand individuals were arrested.[15] According to the historian Wolfgang Ayaß:

The number of detainees in German concentration camps thus doubled in size as a result of the arrival in the camps of a hitherto unknown group of detainees. They were for the most part beggars, vagrants, and indigent alcoholics . . . , as well as many Roma and Sinti . . . , [while] homeless individuals represented the largest group. Beggars and vagrants were, in part, arrested directly in facilities providing assistance to the homeless. For a time, 'asocials,' who were designated by a black triangle, made up the by far largest group of detainees in the existing camps.[16]

In the context of this ordinance, several Jewish individuals were also forcibly deported to concentration camps.

Though no other comparable crackdowns occurred after 1938, over the years, more and more individuals continued to be detained as "asocials." Even people engaged in comparatively smaller acts of deviant behavior were increasingly categorized as "asocial": during the Second World War, unsatisfactory job performance and frequent absenteeism also came to be encompassed by the term. While the word "asocialism" (Asozialität) was not new, and neither public authorities nor the majority of the population had condoned deviant behavior prior to 1933, what was new, according to Ayaß, "was the radical, strict, terroristic conduct and the increasingly widespread view that deviant behavior was ultimately explained by a person's genetic pool."[17]

Overlooked Remembrance

During the National Socialist period, between 63,000 and 82,000 individuals branded as "asocial" were interned in concentration camps.[18] Meanwhile, it was not until February 2020 that the Bundestag, Germany's Federal Parliament, officially recognized as victims of the National Socialist regime those persecuted as "asocial" or as "professional criminals" (Berufsverbrecher).[19] Persistent precarious living conditions and increasing and sustained discrimination against many of these groups had hitherto led to their stories being excluded from discourses on remembrance. Moreover, because the term "asocial" had encompassed a very heterogeneous group of individuals, their collectivization was largely impossible.[20] Unlike other groups of detainees, there was no single organization that could step in to advocate for their right to remembrance. According to Lothar Evers, "Among the groups of marginalized and persecuted individuals, the 'asocials' had particular difficulties formulating their claim for compensation.... Their experience of a first damaged, then brutally persecuted life could barely be articulated in the hermeneutics of the 1950s."[21]

Continuities of Devaluation

When Klemperer published his notebooks on the language of the National Socialists in 1947, he shrewdly noted that some of the terms that had become charged with racist ideology in the preceding years continued to be in use: "But it appears that the language of the Third Reich is to survive in the form of certain characteristic expressions; they have lodged themselves so deep below the surface that they appear to be becoming a permanent feature of the German language."[22] In fact, the term "asocial" continued to show up in public discourses in the postwar period—both in the German Democratic Republic (GDR) and the Federal Republic of Germany (FRG). In the GDR, "asociality" was included in the penal code, where it was also used to encompass a wide array of undesirable behaviors that were assumed to lead to criminal conduct, until the unification of Germany in 1990.[23] Until 1967, homelessness was also criminalized in the Federal Republic; people could be arrested simply for being unsheltered under the rationale of "self-protection." Throughout Germany's "economic miracle" during the 1950s, when almost full employment prevailed, there was particularly little sympathy for the impoverished, the unemployed, and the homeless, as their situation was generally perceived as being self-inflicted.[24] Even today, the term "asocial" continues to be found in our language, employed to discredit people or to describe behaviors that are perceived as negative.

The resulting individualization of the question of responsibility for poverty and precariousness shifts attention away from the systemic causes of hardship. In a long-term study conducted between 2002 and 2011, the sociologist Wilhelm Heitmeyer examined the link between attitudes toward social minorities and economic relationships.[25] The study revealed that forms of disparagement based on economic status steadily increased during the time of his study. His results applied to perceptions of the homeless and the unemployed, as well as to migrant workers, who oftentimes represent competition for jobs. According to the sociologist Heinz Bude, what is expressed in this rise in contempt is representative of a change in the mode of social integration—from a promise of advancement for all to a threat of exclusion.[26] This is accompanied by the increasing economization of society, underpinned by a flexible capitalism and neoliberal policies. Social inequality is no longer addressed by means of social services, but instead through calls for self-discipline. The structural conditions and determinants are thus obscured, eroding social solidarity. People in need, such as those experiencing homelessness or the unemployed, are frequently subjected to animosity and are shamed as "asocials," losers (Abgehängte), expendable, bums, or freeloaders.[27] They are often accused of refusing to work and are regarded as useless or even detrimental to a society that prizes efficiency. This stigmatization arises from their assigned belonging to a social group and is expressed as group-focused enmity. Individuals perceived as "useless" are not seen as a legitimate part of society and are therefore met with hostility.[28] This devaluation can be described as a form of Social Darwinism, which, in addition to racism, anti-Semitism, nationalism, and anti-pluralism, represents a significant ideological element of the radical right. However, it is also present in wider public discourses.

In July 2000, four young right-wing extremists in Ahlbeck beat to death Norbert Plath, a fifty-four-year-old homeless man. According to police reports, the perpetrators stated that "asocials and vagrants do not belong in society."[29] Under this worldview, the social condition of poor individuals is intrinsic to their characters and determined by origin.[30] The Specialist Office for Gender, Group-Focused Enmity, and Right-Wing Extremism (Fachstelle Gender, Gruppenbezogene Menschenfeindlichkeit und Rechtsextremismus) has reported that, among the 193 fatalities of right-wing extremist violence between 1990 and 2019, twenty-six were individuals experiencing homelessness. Of these victims, eight were regarded as "asocials" by their perpetrators.[31]

Insecurity and Threats to Democratic Values

The exclusion of individuals experiencing homelessness or poverty is expressed by disparagement, by their displacement from central areas of cities, by physical violence and assaults. In his research, Heitmeyer detected the greatest level of enmity against social minorities around the 2009 global financial crisis: more than one-third of the individuals surveyed agreed with statements implying that society cannot or should no longer afford human mistakes or people of little value, that too much consideration is given to "losers," and that moral laxness is a luxury we can no longer afford.[32] According to Heitmeyer, the exclusion and displacement of individuals based on the ideology of inequality serves as a "projection screen for interpreting social reality and as a basis for legitimizing discrimination against, exclusion of, and violence toward individuals and groups."[33] Rising social inequality and instability reinforce this view and make people more susceptible to populist promises and conspiracy theories, as is currently shown by the high levels of participation in demonstrations by self-proclaimed "lateral thinkers" (Querdenker) throughout Germany or the increase of visitors to the online platform for QAnon.

Times of crisis, such as today's coronavirus pandemic, make us more likely to experience economic, political, social, or personal instability. Recognizing the conditions and structural causes of social problems is critical for strengthening the values of solidarity, fairness, and equality and for preventing the ongoing erosion of democracy. Marginalization and exclusion make people invisible and exclude them from participating in social opportunities. As part of our social world, language can play an important role in fostering social inclusion. We must thus understand language as part of our broader public discourse because, as the journalist Ronen Steinke states in his book *Antisemitismus in der Sprache,* "words have a tone, words have a history, a range of associations."[34]

1   Bertolt Brecht, "On Restoring the Truth," in *Brecht on Art and Politics,* ed. Tom Kuhn and Steve Giles, trans. Laura Bradley, Steve Giles, and Tom Kuhn (London: Bloomsbury Methuen Drama), pp. 133–40, esp. p. 133.

2   Winfried Nerdinger, ed., *Munich and National Socialism: Catalogue of the Munich Documentation Centre for the History of National Socialism* (Munich: C. H. Beck, 2015), p. 91.

3   Heinz Bude, *Society of Fear,* trans. Jessica Spengler (Cambridge: Polity, 2018), p. 2.

4   Ibid., p. 4.

5   See Nerdinger, *Munich and National Socialism,* p. 133.

6   See Britta-Marie Schenk, "Eine Geschichte der Obdachlosigkeit im 19. und 20. Jahrhundert," in *Aus Politik und Zeitgeschichte: Wohnungslosigkeit* 68, nos. 25–26, ed. Bundeszentrale für politische Bildung (2018), pp. 23–39, esp. p. 26.

7   A few homeless individuals and families that were considered "Aryan" were placed in makeshift housing or in hostels for the homeless; see Schenk, "Eine Geschichte der Obdachlosigkeit," p. 27. This legitimized form of homelessness was not supposed to be visible in public spaces, and affected individuals were instead relegated to isolated spaces; see Nadine Recktenwald, "Räume der Obdachlosen: Städtische Asyle im Nationalsozialismus," in *Städte im Nationalsozialismus: Urbane Räume und soziale Ordnungen,* ed. Winfried Süß and Malte Thießen, vol. 33 of *Beiträge zur Geschichte des Nationalsozialismus* (Göttingen: Wallstein, 2017), pp. 67–88, esp. p. 67.

8   Wolfgang Ayaß, "'Demnach ist z.B. asozial...': Zur Sprache sozialer Ausgrenzung im Nationalsozialismus," in *Ungleichheiten im Dritten Reich: Semantiken, Praktiken, Erfahrungen,* ed. Nicole Kramer and Armin Nolzen, vol. 28 of *Beiträge zur Geschichte des Nationalsozialismus* (Göttingen: Wallstein, 2012), pp. 69–89, esp. 73–74.

9   Wolfgang Ayaß, "'Asoziale': Die verachteten Verfolgten," in *Dachauer Hefte: Studien und Dokumente zur Geschichte der nationalsozialistischen Konzentrationslager,* vol. 14, no. 14, ed. Wolfgang Benz and Barbara Distel (Munich: Dtv, 1998), pp. 50–66, esp. p. 54.

10 Ayaß, "'Asoziale': Die verachteten Verfolgten," p. 51.

11 See Ayaß, "'Demnach ist z.B. asozial...': Zur Sprache sozialer Ausgrenzung im Nationalsozialismus," p. 88.

12 Victor Klemperer, *The Language of the Third Reich: LTI – Lingua Tertii Imperii; A Philologist's Notebook,* trans. Martin Brady (London and New York: Bloomsbury Academic, 2013), p. 16.

13 Ibid., p. 15.

14 This was also consistent with the logic of "protective or preventive custody" (*Schutzhaft*) and the Decree for the Protection of the German People (*Verordnung zum Schutz des deutschen Volkes*), which was directed toward members of the political and Jewish opposition, who could be arrested and imprisoned solely on the basis of police orders and without judicial control.

15 See Wolfgang Ayaß, "'Wohnungslose im Nationalsozialismus': Eine Wanderausstellung der BAG Wohnungslosenhilfe," in *Integration statt Ausgrenzung: Gerechtigkeit statt Almosen,* ed. Werena Rosenke (Bielefeld: Bundesarbeitsgemeinschaft Wohnungslosenhilfe, 2006), pp. 170–87, esp. p. 180.

16 Ibid.

17 Ayaß, "'Asoziale': Die verachteten Verfolgten," p. 53.

18 See Julia Hörath, *"Asoziale" und "Berufsverbrecher" in den Konzentrationslagern 1933 bis 1938,* vol. 222 of *Kritische Studien zur Geschichtswissenschaft* (Göttingen: Vandenhoeck & Ruprecht, 2017), p. 323.

19 The appeal, initiated on April 18, 2018, was recognized by the German Bundestag on February 14, 2020; see https://www.change.org/p/deutscher-bundestag-anerkennung-von-asozialen-und-berufsverbrechern-als-opfer-des-nationalsozialismus (all URLs accessed in June 2021).

20 Awareness of this omission has been repeatedly called for by historians and sociologists, including Julia Hörath, Andreas Kranebitter, Frank Nonnenmacher, and Wolfgang Ayaß, among others, as well as by artists like Tucké Royal, who initiated the Zentralrat der Asozialen in Deutschland as an artistic project in 2012, or Willem de Rooji with his conceptual work *Vorhaben zum Gedenken an "Asoziale" und "Berufsverbrecher"* (2019–ongoing), to name just a couple of artists.

21 Lothar Evers, "'Asoziale': NS-Verfolgte in der deutschen Wiedergutmachung," in "minderwertig" und "asozial": *Stationen der Verfolgung gesellschaftlicher Aussenseiter,* ed. Dietmar Sedlaczek et al. (Zurich: Chronos Verlag, 2005), pp. 179–83, esp. p. 182.

22 Klemperer, *The Language of the Third Reich,* p. 14.

23 See Susanne Gerull, "'Unangenehm', 'arbeitsscheu', 'asozial': Zur Ausgrenzung von wohnungslosen Menschen," in *Aus Politik und Zeitgeschichte: Wohnungslosigkeit* 68, nos. 25–26, ed. Bundeszentrale für politische Bildung (2018), pp. 30–36, esp. p. 39.

24 Schenk, "Eine Geschichte der Obdachlosigkeit im 19. und 20. Jahrhundert," p. 28.

25 Wilhelm Heitmeyer, ed., *Deutsche Zustände,* 10 vols. (Frankfurt am Main: Suhrkamp, 2002–11).

26 Bude, *Society of Fear,* p. 8.

27 Lucius Teidelbaum, "Zwischen 'Geh' arbeiten, Du Penner' und 'Penner klatschen': Wohnungs- und Obdachlose als Opfer von Ausgrenzung und rechter Gewalt," in *All Inclusive? Inklusion als Herausforderung in der politischen Bildung,* ed. Bundesarbeitskreis Arbeit und Leben (Wuppertal: Bundesarbeitskreis, 2013), p. 20.

28 Wilhelm Heitmeyer, Manuela Freiheit, and Peter Sitzer, *Rechte Bedrohungsallianzen: Signaturen der Bedrohung II* (Berlin: Suhrkamp et al., 2008), pp. 18–19.

29 Amadeu Antonio Stiftung, "Norbert Plath," https://www.amadeu-antonio-stiftung.de/todesopfer-rechter-gewalt/norbert-plath-staatlich-anerkannt/.

30 Teidelbaum, "Zwischen 'Geh' arbeiten, Du Penner' und 'Penner klatschen,'" p. 20.

31 "Was ist das? Feindschaft gegen Obdachlose," *Bell Tower,* February 6, 2019, https://www.belltower.news/was-ist-das-feindschaft-gegen-obdachlose-80951/.

32 Heitmeyer et al., *Rechte Bedrohungsallianzen: Signaturen der Bedrohung II,* p. 32; Teidelbaum, "Zwischen 'Geh' arbeiten, Du Penner' und 'Penner klatschen,'" p. 21.

33 Heitmeyer, *Rechte Bedrohungsallianzen,* p. 20.

34 Ronen Steinke, *Antisemitismus in der Sprache: Warum es auf die Wortwahl ankommt* (Berlin: Dudenverlag, 2020), p. 9.

Being without a house comes with a range of difficulties spanning from physical strain to mental exhaustion—states of being that are not particular to an individual's constitution, but first and foremost framed and supported by a contextual and legal scaffold. Although the United Nations asserts that everyone should have the right "to an adequate standard of living for himself and his family, including adequate food, clothing and housing," reality is far from this social pact. Homelessness is on the rise, and our housing systems, which can't attend to the housing necessities of all, are supported by our legal systems that provide the related backdrop. Climbing rent and skyrocketing land value tend to be paired with landlord-oriented rights that are mirrored by weak tenancy rights, easily exposing dwellers to eviction. The right to a permanent home is therefore not only a question of social improvement; it also reveals how the housing market works. Once without a home, the legal framework of daily life and the prospect of returning to stable housing are multilayered and can be counterproductive. Those experiencing homelessness are marginalized and lose civic rights, such as the right to sleep undisturbed, voting rights as one lacks an address for registration, and the right to intimacy. This is also vividly evident in the legality surrounding the use and appropriation of public space, including the banning of homeless people through hostile architecture in urban areas, such as parks or the commercial centers of cities.

"You Can't Stay Home If There Is No Home. Racism Kills." Banner out of a window in Berlin, March 2020

The Right to Sleep in the City

Jocelyn Froimovich

The need for humans to address their bodily functions has spurred the creation of architectural forms in the public realm. Eating and drinking have found a proliferation of public expressions, from leisurely picnics to water fountains and food carts. And although urinating and defecating have been historically relegated to the private sphere, public toilets nonetheless dot our streets and parks. However, of the three primary bodily functions—eating, defecating, and sleeping—sleeping has been the least integrated into the urban public realm. Rarely do we find public places designed for the civic display of sleeping; if anything, street furniture is more often designed to prevent it.

We have lost the right to sleep in public spaces. Those driven by indigence, desperation, or exhaustion to sleep on the street strike us as vulnerable and out of place. Sleeping in public is looked at as a symptom of economic or personal weakness.

In modern Western tradition, sleep is normally an activity that takes place on a bed within a dwelling. Nonetheless, across our cities we still find people sleeping on street and park benches, on subways and buses, on lawns and sidewalks. However, our cities lack public places specifically designed for addressing the need for sleep.

Regardless of social class, income, or age, we all experience exhaustion and require adequate amounts of rest. From transient workers and slaves of hyperproductivity to overachieving schoolchildren and jet-lagged tourists, many of us sleep less than we biologically should.

The capitalist obsession with productivity has killed the dream of a good sleep, driving some to even feel as though time slept is time wasted. Sleep thwarts our fantasies of endless economic growth and carries economic, social, and political implications that go beyond the frontiers of pragmatism.

As a civic concern, sleeping has not been thoroughly analyzed from an urban perspective. Freed from the bed and the dwelling, how can public sleeping transform the ways in which we understand our cities?

The Japanese culture of napping (*inemuri*) allows for sleep to expand into the public domain.

Do Not Sleep

— Boise, Idaho, USA

The Eighth Amendment of the Constitution of the United States, adopted in 1791, bars the government from imposing excessive fines or cruel and unusual punishment upon its citizens.

In 2009, Janet Bell, Robert Martin, and nine other homeless people sued the city of Boise over ordinances that banned people from sleeping in public spaces. Bell had been cited twice, once for sitting on a riverbank with her backpack and another time for lying on a sleeping mat in the woods, for which she received a thirty-day suspended sentence. Meanwhile, Martin, a man with physical disabilities, was fined $150 for resting near a shelter. During the trial, known as Martin v. Boise, the plaintiffs argued that the enforcement of the ordinances violated their Eighth Amendment rights, noting that criminalizing them for carrying out the basic bodily function of sleep constituted cruel and unusual punishment.

While the United States Court of Appeals for the Ninth Circuit did rule in favor of the plaintiffs in 2018, United States Circuit Judge Marsha Berzon noted that "only ... municipal ordinances that criminalize sleeping, sitting, or lying in all public spaces, *when no alternative sleeping space is available*, violate the Eighth Amendment," minimizing the extent to which the ruling can protect people experiencing homelessness or otherwise driven to sleep on the street. As long as cities can claim that there is space available in shelters, they can continue to clear homeless encampments and arrest or fine those who refuse to leave. Cities are left with ample power to police and punish homeless people, as well as to regulate and restrict their access to public space.[1]

Rather than lamenting more international examples of inhumane regulations against sleeping in public and the legal battles against them, this essay will quickly move on to more hopeful examples of public sleeping, describing present-day case studies where public sleeping in the city is framed as a basic human right. In order to do so, I will focus on episodes that make sleep a communal

Sleeping pod companies in international airports provide resting niches for those willing and able to pay.

matter. By doing so, I hope to inspire the empathy required to truly comprehend what it means to have no place to sleep.

Let's Sleep, But . . .

— Japan

Inemuri is a millenary Japanese practice of napping while in public, often translated as "sleeping on duty" or "sleeping while present."[2] Although most common in workplaces, people may also nap in department stores, cafés, restaurants, or even in a cozy spot on a busy sidewalk.[3] *Inemuri* is especially prevalent on commuter trains. Regardless of how crowded they may be, trains in Japan often turn into communal bedrooms.

One reason public sleeping may be so common in Japan is that people get little sleep at home. A 2015 government study found that more than a third of Japanese adults slept less than six hours per night.[4]

And while public sleeping may be a socially acceptable practice in Japan, one unwritten rule of *inemuri* is that those practicing it must sleep in a compact and discrete manner, without invading the personal space of others.

Taking up several seats on a train or splaying out on a park bench, for example, could draw reproach as socially disruptive acts.[5]

— International Airports

Airport layovers have become more bearable for those willing and able to pay for access to a place to sleep. Sleeping pod companies provide weary travelers with such safe havens, whether in the form of a reclining cocoon chair or a queen-sized luxury bed.[6]

In 2010, Jussi Piispanen, CEO and founder of GoSleep, was motorcycling across Europe when his bike broke down and he was forced to take a taxi to Paris Charles de Gaulle Airport and book a flight back to Finland.[7] With the next available flight back home scheduled for the following morning and the airport hotel fully booked, Piispanen's only option was to spend the night at the airport. "A night of misery was ahead," the sleeping pod company founder states on GoSleep's website. At midnight, he woke up to find himself being pushed with a broomstick by a member of the airport cleaning crew, who was displeased with the fact that Piispanen had removed the armrests from a bench to fashion himself a makeshift bed. After the employee threatened

In Mumbai, a city with a history of temporary sleeping, a room of the Rotary Club serves as an impromptu resting facility.

to call security, Piispanen quickly reassembled the armrests and thought, "There has to be a solution for this."

According to Piispanen, this experience prompted him to found his company: "Misery was our motivation to create the GoSleep pay-per-use concept."[8] Some price references: Tokyo Narita's 9H pods cost €10.50 per hour, Napcabs in Munich go for €30 per hour, and a nap at Amsterdam Schiphol's YotelAir costs €42 per hour, with a minimum four-hour stay.

— Los Angeles, California, USA

In 2016, the city of Los Angeles decriminalized living in vehicles with Section 85.02 of the Los Angeles Municipal Code. The change to the code allowed people to dwell in their cars while outlining strict regulations around the activity: "From 6 a.m. to 9 p.m., persons are allowed to use a vehicle for dwelling, subject to posted parking restrictions, in most areas of the City that are more than 500 feet from licensed schools, pre-schools, day care facilities or parks."[9] The city of Los Angeles also developed a series of maps to assist the public in identifying where exactly vehicular dwelling was allowed.[10]

But unhoused Los Angeles residents who own or have access to a car still do not have many options. According to the "Greater Los Angeles Homeless Count" conducted in 2020 by the Los Angeles Homeless Services Authority (LAHSA), vehicular homelessness represents approximately a third of the 58,936 individuals experiencing homelessness in Los Angeles County.[11] While the city offers Safe Parking sites, which are usually run by nonprofits and are equipped with security officers and services, an LAHSA Safe Parking program flyer from April 2020 counted only 640 of these parking spots in the entire county.

Let's Enjoy our Sleep!

— Mumbai, India

When I visited Mumbai in 2010, I came across a place that made me reconsider how we sleep. The place was a corner shop located at a busy intersection in the upscale coastal area of Bandra.

It was the middle of the day and the sliding door entrance was slightly open. I peeked in and saw a room with a surface of approximately 40 square meters. In it, there were eight middle-aged men wearing shorts and T-shirts lying on the floor, sleeping. Other clothing items (I presume theirs) hung from the walls. The room's sparse stainless-steel furnishings had been pushed to the edges, leaving most of the space empty. Outside, a sign read, "Sir Mangalds Nathubhai Kapol Charitable Dispensary Physio-therapy Clinic – Sponsored and Managed by Rotary Club of Bombay Seaface Charities Trust." At the time of writing this article, I was unable to locate this place and verify if it still exists, nor have I been able to reach the Rotary Club to gather additional information.

The city of Mumbai has a history of temporary sleeping rooms, and the room I described above is exemplary of many of them. As workers migrated en masse to the city during the 1940s, Mumbai experienced a housing short-age that led to a rise in homelessness and the growth of slums, particularly near factories, mills, and workshops. To this day, Mumbai's high density leads its inhabitants to devise unique scenarios for living and resting that blur the line between public and private.[12]

Providing significantly more protection than precarious street dwellings, which leave their users quite vulnerable, the Physiotherapy Clinic's functional potential brings up a vast array of urban possibilities. With varying schedules and often working multiple jobs, Mumbai workers with access to these spaces can distribute their sleep more flexibly around their work hours. Furthermore, assuming that these locations are scattered across the city, workers can find places to sleep while on the go, optimizing their resting time between commutes, rather than having to return home to their beds.

— Zurich, Switzerland

The Akademischer Sportverband Zürich (Academic Sports Association of Zurich, ASVZ) was commissioned by the three main local universities[13] to provide athletic facilities in different city locations for all of its members (including students and staff). In three of ASVZ's loca-tions there are relaxation rooms. A more upscale model of Mumbai's sleeping rooms for migrant workers, ASVZ's relaxation rooms are equipped with reclining chairs and daybeds, each with headphones for noise-canceling or relaxing auditory experiences. According to ASVZ, "With short relaxation and recovery phases, also called power naps, you can reduce stress and regain valuable energy and vitality. In our relaxation rooms, relaxation / audio / sound beds . . . invite you to regenerate . . ."[14]

All enrolled university students (approximately 60,000) are members of ASVZ, which also counts among its ranks 5,000 university employees and 5,000 alumni and their

domestic partners. All pay between 180 and 500 Swiss francs (an equivalent to €163 to €452) per year.[15] Even those members who are not actively seeking to relax subsidize these rooms.

Although relaxation rooms are common in the corporate world and have been adopted by other universities, ASVZ's rooms serve as an interesting model. At a rela-tively low cost, a sizable community of members can effectively enjoy access to well-equipped and well-maintained sleeping rooms (along with multipurpose athletic facilities) at different locations around the city.

— Ulm, Germany

Ulmer Nest is a solar-powered architectural prototype designed for Ulm, Germany, which is meant to serve as a last-resort shelter for people experiencing homeless-ness, protecting them from extreme weather conditions and hypothermia.[16] The shelter, which began with a commission from Ulm's Social Affairs Department to create a structure to protect against frostbite, was developed by a team of product, interface, hardware, and software designers.[17] While carrying out research to develop their prototype, they found that, while the city of Ulm provides plenty of shelter options, there are several reasons why people may choose not to stay in more traditional homeless shelters, ranging from mental health issues to fear of crime and violence in larger facilities.

Important material and safety considerations included structural stability and fire protection, as well as the provision of a secure locking system. Sensor technology and a user-friendly communication platform monitored fresh air, safety, waste, and pollution. The legal liabilities of providing safe shelter under harsh climate conditions led the team to build a field prototype.[18] Data collected during the prototype's trial phase has been crucial in evaluating the emergency shelter's overall performance. It is still to be determined if and how Ulmer Nest will be affected by vandalism, but the success of the prototype means that Ulmer Nest shelters may be deployed throughout the city in the near future.

— Santiago, Chile

Costanera Center is a real-estate project by Cencosud, the largest retail company in Chile and the third largest in Latin America.[19] The multi-programmatic complex was controversial from the start.[20] The project's urban impact is immense, as it is located in a heavily trafficked and commercialized part of the city, adjacent to the

The riverside park across from Costanera Center in Santiago de Chile has been claimed by locals and passersby as a place to rest.

Mapocho River that runs through the city. The program originally consisted of a set of four buildings totaling 710,000 square meters.[21] Gran Torre Santiago, the tallest of the four and the tallest skyscraper in South America until 2020, was the only building that was completed.[22] The base of the office tower includes a six-story shopping center and two five-story hotels.

As a result of the 2008 global economic crisis, all construction work at the Costanera Center site was stopped for the majority of 2009, leaving nearly 2,000 people unemployed. The structures, in one of the most economically thriving sectors of Santiago, remained half-finished for over a year.[23]

Throughout construction and during the work stoppage, workers would meet along the Mapocho River, just across the street. The 20-meter-wide riverbank park provided an ideal space for workers to rest, and napping along the

river during breaks became a routine practice.[24] Still today, this riverside park serves as a convenient resting spot for workers in the area. In contrast to the poor street condition and landscape design of Santiago's financial icon, this modest, rather narrow, inclined grass plane, acoustically sheltered by the river, and bathed in sunlight throughout the day, welcomes construction and white-collar workers, visitors, and passersby alike to enjoy a pleasant nap.

The Right to Sleep in the City

In his book *24/7: Late Capitalism and the Ends of Sleep*, the art critic and essayist Jonathan Crary explores how human sleep cycles have been disturbed around the world by a culture that dismisses sleep as a waste of time. The term "24/7" is itself representative of "a time of indifference, against which the fragility of human life is increasingly inadequate."[25] The term "renders plausible, even normal, the idea of working without pause, without limits."[26] 24/7 is a time without sleep.

The notion of the eight-hour sleep cycle, established during the Industrial Revolution, is still deeply engrained in Western societies. Even so, many of us still struggle to get our suggested eight hours: urban congestion and long commutes, as well as working across different time zones or during night shifts, force us into disrupted or shortened sleep schedules. While polyphasic sleep patterns, where individuals sleep in intervals throughout the day, could prove to be a suitable alternative to the eight-hour sleep cycle, as long as our conception of sleep is constrained to a bed in a home, such alternatives remain an impossibility. Even so, can we imagine alternative urban scenarios where polyphasic sleeping is, in fact, a possibility and not an exception? What would such cities look like?

The decriminalization of homelessness is an important—but certainly not the only—reason to fight for the public provision of rest and for the reinstatement of sleep as a basic human right.[27] As the case studies of construction and white-collar workers napping in Santiago and Japan show, a group of people sleeping together in the public realm may well be the last remaining example of the daily experience of collective vulnerability. Yes, we could all use some sleep.

1   "Eighth Amendment—Criminalization of Homelessness—Ninth Circuit Refuses to Reconsider Invalidation of Ordinances Completely Banning Sleeping and Camping in Public.—Martin v. City of Boise, 920 F.3d 584 (9th Cir. 2019)," *Harvard Law Review* 133 (December 10, 2019), p. 699, quoting Bell v. City of Boise.

2   Bryant Rousseau, "Napping in Public? In Japan, That's a Sign of Diligence," *The New York Times,* December 16, 2016, https://www.nytimes.com/2016/12/16/world/what-in-the-world/japan-inemuri-public-sleeping.html (all URLs accessed in September 2021).

3   "Inemuri is most prevalent among more senior employees in white-collar professions. Both sexes indulge in inemuri, but women are more likely to be criticized for it, especially if they sleep in a position that is considered unbecoming." Ibid.

4   It also helps that Japan has a very low crime rate, which makes it safer for people to fall asleep in public spaces.

5   Rousseau, "Napping in Public?"

6   The following is a list of airports with sleeping pods: Abu Dhabi, Dubai, Helsinki, Tallinn, Amsterdam, Tokyo Haneda, Belo Horizonte (GoSleep), Atlanta, Philadelphia, Dallas (Minute Suites), Munich, Berlin Tegel (Nap Cabs), Hanoi (SleepPod), New Delhi (Sams Snooze at My Space), Dubai (SnoozeCube), London Heathrow, London Gatwick, Amsterdam Schiphol, Singapore Changi, Istanbul, Paris Charles de Gaule (YotelAir), Bergamo Orio al Serio (Zzzleepandgo), Tokyo Narita (9H). At the time of this article, most sleeping pod services had been suspended due to the coronavirus pandemic. See "Airport Sleeping Pods," *Sleeping in Airports,* December 15, 2015, https://www.sleepinginairports.net/blog/airport-sleeping-pods.htm.

7   Today, the GoSleep pods have found their way to dozens of industries, including airports, hospitals, offices, sports clubs, and universities. Jussi Piispanen, "Our Story," *GoSleep,* https://gosleep.fi/about-us/.

8   Ibid.

9   "REVISED LAMC-SECTION 85.02 Los Angeles City Municipal Coderegarding Vehicle Dwelling," *Empower LA,* https://empowerla.org/wp-content/uploads/2017/01/REVISED-LAMC-SECTION-85.02-Los-Angeles-City-Municipal-Code-regarding-Vehicle-Dwelling-2.pdf.

10   The maps and pamphlets on Section 85.02 of the Los Angeles Municipal Code were publicly available on the city's website and through the city's Zone Information and Map Access System (ZIMAS), as well as at local city halls, libraries, and community police stations. See ibid.

11   Los Angeles Homeless Services Authority, "Homelessness Statistics by City," https://www.lahsa.org/documents?id=5201-homelessness-statistics-by-city.pdf.

12   Tithi Sanyal, "The Chawls and Slums of Mumbai: Story of Urban Sprawl," *Agora Journal of Urban Planning and Design* 12 (2018), pp. 22–34.

13   ETH Zürich, Universität Zürich, and Zürcher Fachhochschule.

14   "Entspannen: Mit Erholung Energie tanken," *ASVZ,* https://asvz.ch/sport/245229-entspannen.

15   Universities subsidize the ASVZ with around 3 million francs per year. In addition to the subsidies, ASVZ is funded through contributions from sponsors such as General Electric, Credit Suisse, or EWZ. These contributions only make up 5 percent of the total budget of 12 million francs. See Peer Teuwsen, "Zwanghaft sportlich," *Neue Zürcher Zeitung,* December 14, 2016, https://www.nzz.ch/karriere/studentenleben/akademischer-sportverband-zuerich-zwanghaft-sportlich-ld.134346.

16   "Ulmer Nest is not an alternative to spending the night in a controlled and secure environment like a homeless shelter. The closed and isolated construction reduces and minimizes wind, moisture, coldness and other negative influences. Nevertheless it can become dangerously cold inside." See "Goals," *Ulmer Nest,* https://ulmernest.de/ziele.

17   Ulmer Nest was created as part of the Wilhelmsbüro project, which took place in the fall of 2018 as a part of Ulm's "Stürmt die Burg" (Storm the Castle) initiative, which was meant to revitalize Ulm's century-old Wilhelmsburg (Wilhelm's Castle). See "How it all started …," *Ulmer Nest,* https://ulmernest.de/ursprung.

18   The prototype was presented to the public, workers who provide homeless services, fire department representatives, the police, citizen services, medical staff, cleaning staff, the waste management department, and future manufacturing partners. See ibid.

19   Cencosud is owned by Horst Paulmann, a German-Chilean billionaire entrepreneur. See Wikipedia, s.v. "Horst Paulmann," last modified April 23, 2021, https://en.wikipedia.org/wiki/Horst_Paulmann.

20   Costanera Center was designed by Cesar Pelli & Associates Architects and Alemparte Barreda and Associates. The project was developed and construction started without receiving municipal approval. Many of the issues had to do with its visual impact, and with the impact mitigation work that Cencosud refused to pay for over an extended period. See Juan Pablo Figueroa, "El Costo humano que deja la paralización del Costanera Center," *CIPER Chile,* January 30, 2009, https://www.ciperchile.cl/2009/01/30/el-costo-humano-que-deja-la-paralizacion-de-costanera-center/.

21   In terms of square meters, the complex was to be (and still is) the biggest one in the city.

22   Gran Torre Santiago lost the title when the 305-meter Torre Obispado, located in Monterrey, Mexico, was completed. Gran Torre Santaigo has a total area of 128,000 square meters, and a height of 297 meters. See Wikipedia, s.v. "Costanera Center," last modified April 23, 2021, https://es.wikipedia.org/wiki/Costanera_Center.

23   "Crisis paraliza emblemático proyecto Costanera Center," *Mercurio de Valparaíso,* January 29, 2009, https://www.mercurioval-po.cl/prontus4_noticias/site/artic/20090129/pags/20090129145954.html.

24   Because of the poor transportation conditions of the city, and the fact that many workers lived far from the site of the Costanera Center, it is likely that, like many other workers in Santiago, the Costanera Center's construction crew was sleep deprived. As safety measures at the construction site were very strict, workers were frequently asked to take breaks. See Figueroa, "El Costo humano que deja la paralización del Costanera Center."

25   Jonathan Crary, *24/7: Late Capitalism and the Ends of Sleep* (New York: Verso, 2014), Chapter 1, p. 9.

26   Ibid., p. 10.

27   Because of this article's brevity, I have purposefully left aside issues of race and gender inherent in the cited examples. I hope that the inclusive ambitions of embracing the idea of sleep as part of the public realm are self-explanatory.

Forbidding Homelessness: The Lockdown Law as a Pharmakon

Samia Henni

According to the research project "HOME_EU: Homelessness as Unfairness," there are approximately 3 million unhoused people in Europe, and 410,000 individuals sleep on the streets of European cities every night.[1] In the spring of 2020, in response to the coronavirus pandemic, several European countries began implementing strict mandatory national lockdowns to slow down the spread of the virus. While certain workers were labeled "essential," meaning that their labor was considered indispensable to the functioning of the country, most were designated "non-essential," meaning that they were forced to stay home and, when possible, work remotely. While meant to protect the health of residents, these restrictions neglected the existence of the millions of unhoused people across the continent. To enforce the lockdown measures, also known as confinement or stay-at-home orders, police officers were required to impose fines on people who were unable to provide official authorization for being outdoors. As a result of such policies, people experiencing homelessness were penalized for their housing conditions—for resorting to living and sleeping on the streets.

This essay explores the impact of coronavirus lockdown measures on the unhoused population of Marseille, France, based on interviews with "essential" workers interacting with the unhoused population, which were conducted following the lifting of the country's first mandatory lockdown, which spanned from March 17 to May 11, 2020. The interviews were begun during the development of the exhibition *Housing Pharmacology*,[2] which was displayed at the Museum of the History of Marseille on the occasion of the exhibition *Traits d'union.s* at the thirteenth edition of Manifesta, the European Nomadic Biennial, which took place in Marseille in 2020.[3] *Housing Pharmacology* sought to expose and juxtapose the poisons and cures that the presence or absence of dwellings engender, while reflecting on how the act of writing history or curating an exhibition can lead to the inclusion or exclusion of specific groups. Rather than continuing to plan the exhibition as if nothing was happening, following the coronavirus pandemic its content took on a conversational format that was able to respond to the ways in which state measures disregarded the very existence of homelessness. The show ultimately presented a series of fragments, competing visions, and lived experiences through audiovisual records and published sources that interrogated the past and present while aspiring to a more viable future.

In an attempt to question the role of exhibitions during a multifaceted crisis, I chose to interview inhabitants who were dealing directly with the realities on the ground, giving their voices a public podium in the form of the museum institution. Since the crisis was unfolding while the exhibition was taking place, the show, set in a museum of history, was able to feature the experiences of living

Ras le bol (discontent), a sign on one of the walls in the streets of Marseille in March 2020

beings, alongside the polished objects and declassified documents of the museum collection. The exhibition also aimed to call more attention to the stories and histories around housing (*logement*), rehousing (*relogement*), bad housing (*mal-logement*), dislodgement or eviction (*délogement*),[4] and homelessness (*sans-logement*), which form a part of every city and all histories.

While this essay focuses exclusively on the impacts of the lockdown measures and the banning of homelessness, the exhibition presented witnesses from seven professions, generations, and classes: Monique Blanc and Bernard Nos, cofounders of the nonprofit organization Vendredi 13, which shelters and feeds unhoused people in Marseille; Aicha Boutayeb, a social worker at Mouvement et Action pour le Rétablissement Social et Sanitaire (Movement and Action for Social and Medical Recovery, MARSS), which is part of l'Assistance Publique-Hôpitaux de Marseille (Public Hospitals of Marseille); Vincent Girard, a psychiatrist and cofounder of MARSS; Fathi Bouaroua, a housing activist involved in the fight for the right to housing and with community movements in Marseille; Habib, an urban bus driver for the Régie des Transports Métropolitains (Metropolitan Transport Authority, RTM); a plainclothes police officer in Marseille; and Laura Spica, an anthropologist and member of two collectives of Noailles inhabitants in Marseille: Collectif du 5 Novembre and Noailles Debout.[5]

As a social worker for MARSS, Aicha Boutayeb was considered an "essential" worker and was therefore required to continue working during France's national lockdown. During an interview conducted on May 29, 2020, Aicha described the empty streets of Marseille at the start of the pandemic and noted that all the reference points for people experiencing homelessness were shut. She also stated that some of Marseille's homeless population had not even been informed about abrupt lockdown measures. When the lockdown was hastily implemented, "They [unhoused people] totally lost their bearings. People who used to interact all day long with passers-by found themselves with no one to talk to. They were suddenly even more alone than they were to begin with."[6] Aicha stressed that state measures prevented those experiencing homelessness from asking for charity or receiving food from concerned passersby. She and other social workers and associations working in homeless services became charged with informing the unhoused about the sudden measures. They were also tasked with providing them with food, helping them fill out necessary authorizations, and placing them in temporary shelters (when possible) now that being outdoors was forbidden.

According to the Marseille police officer, who was interviewed on June 2, 2020, once the lockdown laws were implemented, he and his colleagues were required to fine everyone without an official signed authorization form,

An outdoor sleeping area in Marseille during the
first national lockdown of March 2020

including the city's unhoused population. Initially, even people who lived in the streets continued to gather in their usual places, disbanding when they saw police officers approaching and returning to their groups once police departed. Although the officers initially did fine everyone without proper authorization, they soon understood that it made no sense to fine individuals who were experiencing homelessness and were therefore on the streets out of necessity.[7] Bernard Nos, cofounder of Vendredi 13,[8] denounced some of the police officers who carried out checks on both unhoused populations and the volunteer workers who distributed meals to them. In an interview conducted on June 11, 2020, Bernard noted, "When the night shelter closed early in the morning, they [unhoused people] would go back to their house—the street—and the police would ask them to provide a special permit. They would respond: my house is the street and the place where I sleep is closed during the day. I can only go back there in the evening."[9]

In response to this pandemic-induced national prohibition of homelessness, Aicha and her colleagues began searching for accommodations for the city's unhoused population. They dialed 115, the national hotline for emergency homeless assistance, and were in contact with the Service intégré d'accueil et d'orientation (Integrated Reception and Guidance Service, SIAO), an agency that helps place people in need in shelters, and Nuit Plus.[10] In

collaboration with these groups, they were able to expand the services provided until the lockdown was lifted and even beyond. MARSS, along with several other groups providing homeless services, also worked to convince hotels, now closed to the public as a result of the pandemic, to serve as shelters for Marseille's homeless population. According to Aicha, "During the first week, we also called empty hotels and negotiated with the hoteliers to get them to agree to take in people. A lot of hotels said no but some were willing to work with us. So we sent the list of people to Nuit Plus and the SIAO so that they could write up the agreements and provide shelter."[11] Some of Marseille's social workers themselves also moved their headquarters to two large hotels from which they would communicate with street teams to help address the needs of those who found themselves unhoused. Aicha and her team, however, also worried about what would happen after the lifting of the lockdown, when people facing houselessness would be forced to return to the streets. She wondered, "What are we going to do after this? It's hard to imagine: we've gotten someone who was on the street used to a minimum level of comfort, and now we're going to tell them to go back to the street. That worries me a lot."[12]

One of the founders of MARSS is the psychiatrist Vincent Girard. Informed by his experience at the Yale Program for Recovery and Community Health,[13] he created the first

Vivre autre chose (experience/live something different), a reaction to the first national lockdown of March 2020 on a wall in Marseille

Samia Henni, *Housing Pharmacology,* 2020, History Museum of Marseille, Manifesta 13

street team in 2008 in partnership with Médecins du Monde and Marseille's public hospital. Initially, the street team was composed just of an unhoused person and himself. According to Vincent, who was interviewed on July 3, 2020, "as a psychiatrist, I could not set up a recovery program with psychiatrists, psychologists, and nurses without including the people experiencing home-lessness" because he embraced the renowned saying "Nothing about us without us.'"[14] The street team worked—first on a voluntary basis, although the program was later formalized—to improve housing services for Marseille's unhoused population, with the hopes of inspiring other cities in France and Europe, which were, and are still, dealing with similar homelessness crises. Vincent's team advocated for a Housing First approach (known as *Un chez-soi d'abord* in French), which follows the logic of Maslow's hierarchy of needs. The psychologist Abraham Maslow proposed this pyramidal hierarchy in his 1943 paper "A Theory of Human Motivation,"[15] which organizes human needs, starting with the most basic at the bottom: physiological needs, safety, love and belongingness, esteem, and self-actualization. Vincent argues that access to shelter is not only a basic physiological need, but also a basic human right and serves as "a very important social determinant of health."[16]

Fathi Bouaroua is actively involved in the fight for the right to housing in France. In an interview conducted on June 16, 2020, he argued that this right "is about the fact that a dwelling is not a commodity."[17] Although the right to housing is protected in the French constitution, Fathi

claims that it "has a complex logic linked, of course, to the right to gain access to housing, but also to remain in it, and to live there with dignity in accordance to safety and hygiene standards." To Fathi, the right to housing is made more complicated because it "is enshrined in the Town Planning Code, the Building Code, the Hygiene Code, the Commercial Code, the Civil Code, the Local Government Code, and the Social Security Code via housing assis-tance."[18] However, even though the right to housing is constitutional, it often goes unimplemented or is mistaken for the right to property. Vincent believes that, during the pandemic, "We were almost acting with a *Un chez-soi d'abord* [Housing First] approach, but in an inferior way," due, in part, to the temporary nature of the accommoda-tions that were provided. The conditions of the pandem-ic—the government's stay-at-home orders, the growing number of volunteers to provide services for the home-less, and the sudden availability of hotel rooms for un-housed people—all served to reinforce the notion of the right to housing. However, Vincent observed that the "National Public Health Agency [in France] was particu-larly ineffective and inoperative. Mainly because it does not value the experience that is valued in this institution, and because the people working for the National Public Health Agency have spent their lives in offices and are, for the most part, very far removed from the realities on the ground."[19]

Countries that ordered national lockdowns and curfews ultimately criminalized people who had previously made a home for themselves in the streets of European cities.

In this case, European emergency lockdown laws functioned as a pharmakon, serving both as a remedy and a poison. While helping to slow down the spread of SARS-CoV-2, these lockdown laws also rendered unsustainable the lives of people experiencing homelessness. By exploring and unpacking these dynamics, which were recounted by people who experienced them on the ground, *Housing Pharmacology* sought to reflect on the following questions: Who is responsible and accountable for ensuring the safety of people experiencing homelessness during a health emergency? When will inclusive and fair state measures be written and implemented? Has this experience taught politicians and civil servants that homelessness itself is an emergency and that Housing First policies and homeless' rights are in urgent need? Unfortunately, it seems that although some politicians did become more aware of the inequalities that stay-at-home orders accentuated, the right to housing and the issues of homelessness have not, so far, become a priority.

1   *HOME_EU: Homelessness as Unfairness* is a European-funded project made up of twelve organizations. Its aim is "to provide a comprehensive understanding on how the Europeans stakeholders perceive, tolerate and confront the inequality." See http://www.home-eu.org/the-project/ (all URLs accessed in September 2021).

2   Pharmacology is a condition that stipulates both poison and remedy. Drawing on Jacques Derrida's essay "Plato's Pharmacy," which proposed that writing is a pharmakon, pharmacology was theorized and broadened by Bernard Stiegler, who suggested a political analysis of and intervention on exploitative capitalist systems and destructive tendencies of consumerist societies. Pharmacology informs the ethics and politics of care.

3   *Traits d'union.s* was curated by Katerina Chuchalina, Stefan Kalmár, and Alya Sebti, and it took place in various locations in Marseille between August 8 and November 29, 2020. See https://manifesta13.org.

4   This term is used in Marseille when people are dragged from their homes in an emergency, such as the possibility of the collapse of a building, with no promise of return and sometimes with no possible return. One of the last building collapses in Marseille occurred on November 5, 2018, in the neighborhood of Noailles in the city center of Marseille.

5   On the specificities of *Housing Pharmacology,* see https://manifesta13.org/participants/samia-henni/ and https://samiahenni.com/exhibits.html. For a virtual tour of the exhibition, see https://manifesta13.org/programmings/the-port-where-histories-lie/. On all transcribed conversations in French and English, see Samia Henni, "Housing Pharmacology" (2020), https://samiahenni.com/IMG/Pharmacologie_Samia_Henni.pdf.

6   Henni, "Housing Pharmacology," p. 53.

7   Ibid., pp. 92–100.

8   Vendredi 13's core activities concern people living on the street, known in French as *sans abri* (homeless people), or *sans domicile fixe* (SDF, or those with no fixed abode).

9   Henni, "Housing Pharmacology," p. 81.

10 In Marseille and other cities in France, there is a scheme called "Nuit Plus" in which the SIAO lists all the accommodations available in suitable facilities. A homeless person is entitled to ten nights of accommodation a year paid for by the state.

11 Henni, "Housing Pharmacology," p. 50.

12 Ibid., p. 53.

13 "Recovery" is an international movement inspired by Franco Basaglia's democratic psychiatry, which was born in Italy in the 1950s and 1960s after the Second World War. Since the 1970s and 1980s, it has spread to the United States and to much of the Anglo-Saxon world.

14 Henni, "Housing Pharmacology," p. 67.

15 Abraham Maslow, "A Theory of Human Motivation," *Psychological Review* 50, no. 4 (1943), pp. 370–96, http://psychclassics.yorku.ca/Maslow/motivation.htm.

16 Henni, "Housing Pharmacology," p. 72.

17 Ibid., p. 15.

18 Ibid., p. 17.

19 Ibid., p. 73.

Land Value

The fact that the price of housing and rent is rising on the housing market has to do with land value and landowner speculation. The lack of available housing units in cities allows the price of the remaining few to skyrocket. At the same time, the value of land goes up once higher profits are to be expected from the property, for example due to reutilization for commercial purposes. This means that gentrification and rising land value are interdependent urban phenomena and can thus be seen as two sides of the same coin. The interests of private investors, along with the capitalistic gain that this system supports through its inherent characteristics of speculation and commerce, are at the root of local and global housing crises. Next to letting rent for citizens grow to inconceivable heights, rising land value also affects the support system for people who find themselves without a home due to these very circumstances. Besides social housing development and budget adjustments in the social welfare sector, some cities like Berlin have been buying back housing in order to make more housing available to those in need, but also to lower the market prices. However, due to the sellout of property in and near city centers, opportunities for development are concentrated on the outskirts, often lacking an appropriate infrastructure and further marginalizing the unstably housed or those in precarious financial situations. As a reaction, tents and informal encampments have become a regular sight in city centers or in less-accessible locations within a city, for instance under bridges and at underpasses.

Small tent city under an overpass, Oakland, California, 2018

Life in Tents: From Land Occupation to Urban Reclamation

Alejandra Celedón and Nicolás Stutzin

"Encampment" refers to the construction of a field, the establishment of a territory, the act of defining and enclosing a piece of land. In Santiago, Chile, encampments (*campamentos*) have historically served as a means to conquer urban space, as a strategy through which people solved urban housing shortages on their own terms. Throughout the twentieth century, informal settlements established around the city's periphery used tents and other forms of light construction as a first step toward gradually claiming ownership of the land, ultimately creating a pathway to formalized home ownership for those involved. The tents in the photograph from the early 1970s represent a city in which housing is the first and only element.

An image depicting two tent-like structures with wooden frames in the middle of an open field evokes this desperate claim for a house in the city. The photograph was taken on August 7, 1972, at the informal settlement of Lo Hermida in Santiago's outskirts, during an official visit by President Salvador Allende and Housing Minister Luis Matte Valdés to the new encampment, two days after violent confrontations between police forces and the settlers left one dead and several wounded. The first land occupation in the area had taken place two years earlier, following a massive rural-to-urban migration that had been faced by Operación Sitio, a national program to regularize land occupation.[1] While the tents in the image may seem like simple and rudimentary forms of shelter, resembling the primitive hut in Charles Eisen's

1755 engraving printed in *Essai sur l'Architecture,* their construction was nonetheless a feat, seeing as they were built virtually overnight out of leftover materials and scraps. In the background, we see nothing but a horizon of crops, an empty landscape on the outskirts—no city in sight.

During the coronavirus pandemic, as the streets of Santiago became lifeless and uninhabited as a result of the city's lockdown laws, tents as dwelling units proliferated. This present-day expansion of tents, however, represents quite a different phenomenon from the encampment at Lo Hermida. While similar in form, the tents we find today in central Santiago are not trying to establish a concrete form of ownership at the periphery, but rather encroach upon the city in order to benefit from immediate access to urban amenities. The proliferation of tents in central Santiago is indicative of the city's endless sprawl, following the suppression of urban limits in 1979 as part of the military dictatorship's free-market initiatives. At the time, the country's housing policy entrusted real-estate developers with the task of meeting housing shortages, while requiring of them no responsibility over the provision of public services. This resulted in a vast periphery of dormitory zones devoid of the social fabric that so defines urban life, and with limited access to basic public infrastructure for health, food, education, jobs, and transportation. The locations where tents have sprung up in the center of Santiago over the past years reveal the inherent value of these sites in the reclamation of urban

Charles Eisen, allegorical engraving of the Vitruvian primitive hut, frontispiece of Marc-Antoine Laugier, *Essai sur l'Architecture,* 2nd ed. (Paris: Duchesne, 1755)

THIS IS NOT A TENT, Armindo Cardoso, Población Lo Hermida, August 7, 1972

existence. Tents have become evidence of a broken model of urban development, one that has failed to ensure access to either housing or to the city. Unlike some peripheral encampments, the precarious tents of Santiago can access water, food, temporary jobs, and safety by their mere proximity to the urban center.

Tents as Land Struggle

Tents are manifestations of struggle. As the sociologist Andreas Folkers and the geographer Nadine Marquardt state, "the tent as heterotopia, as a space of the exceptional, is not only a place of dreams and desires, it is also a place of nightmares and despair."[2] Tents past and present represent the visible tipping point of a larger and longer confrontation. They are symptomatic of a lack of state commitment and are also emblematic of the complete distrust for the institutions that are meant to ensure collective well-being. When, after decades of waiting for solutions, people are forced to find their own way, they acquire proof that official channels to housing provision have failed them.

Both the peripheral camps of the recent past and the current scattering of self-standing tents represent violent land disputes. One portrays the power of collective manifestation, while the other is an urgent and unruly symptom of failure thrust in front of our doorsteps. While the English word "camp" comes from the Latin *campus,*

meaning "open field and level plain," the term also has roots in the Old High German *champf*, which meant "battle and struggle." As the central device in the struggle for the "right to the city," the notion of land as a battlefield is at the core of the etymology of the encampment. The words "encampament" (*campamento*) and fight (*lucha*) are usually used together, both in press coverage on land usage in Santiago as in academic papers and essays, but also in the encampment dwellers' own discourse and protest banners.[3]

The encampment is everything that a city is not. It lacks even the most minimal forms of urban infrastructure, with no schools or hospitals, no food supplies, and, often, not even drinking water or basic waste management. Generally, encampments have been located on the urban fringe, if not entirely outside the city, where density fades and land is cheap. In Chilean history, encampments emerged as a result of the organized occupation of private land, sometimes with the support of political parties that assisted occupiers through the process.[4] The terms given in Chile to these peripheral agglomerations are *campamento* (encampment) or *población callampa* (mushroom town, the local term for *favela* or *bidonvilles*). "Mushroom town" refers to the speed in which these informal settlements sprung up, literally sprouting overnight at the city fringes, by canal borders, and next to roads.

Located in the periphery, an encampment is a piece of land that aims to become a city, but that by definition finds

THIS IS NOT A CAMP, self-standing tents in downtown Santiago de Chile, May 12, 2021

itself *outside* of the city. Dwellers migrating from the countryside long for the opportunities provided by urbanity: jobs, education, and the promise of a better quality of life. While living in an encampment is not the same as living in the city, it promises occupiers access, or at least proximity, to the city. For the inhabitants of Santiago's twentieth-century encampments, the struggle centered around home ownership—a piece of land on which to settle, as close to the city as possible.

The encampment (as open field) and the city (as urbanity) form a binary view of territory, with one opposing the other. As the historian Armando de Ramón has described, "When the edges of the city advanced until they touched the rural areas, these immediately came to be called encampments, whether or not they were populated."[5] The proliferation of tents in the inner city today makes visible another form of urgent land reclamation. Tents stand for an unfulfilled demand—not only for a piece of land on which to build a home and a community, but for a piece of central, urban land that provides direct access to the city. Tents today, unlike the encampments of the recent past, allow people to actually inhabit the city. While encampments occupy private land, tents in the city squat upon public space. Whereas the encampment functioned as a last resort to access housing and to satisfy both the need and longing for community, the tent of today is individualized, dotting the landscape rather than carpeting a field or cluster. An encampment represents the struggle for homeownership, even if the city is given

up in the process. Tents are a struggle for the city, even if the ideal of the home must be sacrificed. In accordance with Lefebvre's and Harvey's ideas on "the right to the city," tents represent "the right to return."

The 2011 encampments at Puerta del Sol in Madrid or Zuccotti Park in New York City, which were triggered, in part, by protests and concerns over access to housing, catalyzed the transformation of public spaces into domestic spaces as a form of protest, making visible the political potential of the encampment-city within the city.[6] But, far from the idea of encampment or occupation, the tents that have colonized central areas of Santiago during the past decade cannot be understood as a political statement or as a form of protest; they are a direct expression of an actual (and critical) lack of access to urban space and services, a form of urgent need that remains invisible in plain sight. Unlike the inhabitants of peripheral encampments, the people living in tents in central Santiago are not invisible; they can be found outside subway stations, in business districts, and by wealthy commercial avenues— in every daily commute to and from your home. Here, tents make visible the violation of a universal human right. Article 25 of the Universal Declaration of Human Rights covers a broad range of basic human rights, including the right to adequate food, water, sanitation, clothing, medical care, and housing. The everyday presence of tents (and their inhabitants) in the center of the city serves as a reminder that these universal rights are not being met by the Chilean state.

Archizoom Associati, *No-Stop City, Residential Parking,* 1971

Tents as Technology

The tent, both symbol and tool, has served as the architecture for political action as much as the architecture for times of crisis and emergency. A contested and paradoxical technology,[7] tents are a solution that exposes the most obscure fractures of a political and economic system. As a portable shelter that functions as an alternative to housing solutions, the tent brings together two narratives: that of the adventures of life in the great outdoors, in direct contact with the surrounding environment, and that of a precarious minimum existence defined only by present need. If the encampment represents the possibility of a future city, then isolated ready-to-use tents installed within the city are probably the most fragile and futureless of infrastructures. When folded, a tent can be easily transported; when unfolded, it creates a temporary dwelling. As a technology, the tent has served both nomadic peoples and important parts of sedentary societies throughout history. But, more recently, the tent has become a global phenomenon, a contested political technology that shapes the urban landscape.

Living in a tent—like living in an encampment—represents the ultimate form of struggle to access housing, usually by one's own means. Both are tools of survival but, in the case of self-standing tents, location comes first: a mattress inside the city is better than a home outside it. Unlike the tents in encampments, which are first light and temporary

only to later become fixed and solid, tents in the city have no such aspirations to permanence; rather, they embrace their temporary, portable condition. Tents benefit from their location, choosing access to city infrastructures over land occupation or the prospect of home ownership. Encampments and tents are beasts of a different nature. Tents are linked to desperation about the present— short-term need; camps are linked to aspirations and the future—long-term longing.

Echoes of global phenomena, in Santiago tents are the expression of a dependent relationship between housing and infrastructure that the city (and the encampment) fails to meet. Behind motorways, below underpasses, in parks, underneath bridges, above plinths, under arcades, up on roofs, inside abandoned properties, and under viaducts, tent inhabitants occupy nowhere land or no-one land—the spaces that the formal city and capitalism have overlooked. Close to food markets, outside public hospitals, near sources of water, jobs, or toilets, less visible or more visible, their locations are evidence of a dependency between domestic life and the urban infrastructures that cannot be found at the periphery.

Most tents in Santiago's city center are in vacant spaces where the limits of ownership, and the boundaries between public and private, are undefined: in public parks, on the sidewalks and median strips of heavily trafficked streets, and in nooks scattered across massive modernist housing projects. An ideal location is the perfect combination of centrality and proximity to potential jobs and services. Tents are sometimes only a few blocks away from centrally located and iconic public spaces like Plaza Baquedano/ Plaza Dignidad, the currently contested epicenter of the social uprising that began in October 2019. Others are just meters away from public hospitals like Posta Central, Santiago's main emergency medical center, or popular food markets like La Vega. Most take advantage of isolating physical conditions to remain hidden in plain sight in sites located close to busy pedestrian areas, subway stations, and public service offices, narrowing the gap between tents and the city to a few steps while interfering as little as possible with urban life. Tents and their dwellers reclaim the urban experience and take advantage of centrality while inhabiting the most precarious expression of housing. The historic center, once Santiago's great urban dream, no longer resembles the utopia it promised but has instead been reduced to a combination of just two elements: tents and infrastructure, like in the dystopian images of Archizoom Associati.

1   Operación Sitio, which can be translated as Operation Plot or Operation Site, was a national self-help housing program that responded to Chile's severe housing crisis by giving people access to private plots of land on the outskirts of the city. It was an attempt to confront the proliferation of illegal land occupation in central areas of the city by placing people in uninhabited sites located at the periphery. The initiative was referred to as Operación Tiza (Operation Chalk) by its critics, since the chalk tracing of a semi-urbanized 9-by-18-meter plot was what most people received.

2   Andreas Folkers and Nadine Marquardt, "Tents," in *Making Things International 2: Catalysts and Reactions* (Minneapolis: University of Minnesota Press, 2016), p. 68.

3   This was presented by Equipo de Estudios Poblacionales, CIDU, in "Reivindicación urbana y lucha política: los campamentos de pobladores en Santiago de Chile" at the seminar "Política y Urbanización," organized by EURE, Buenos Aires, October 1971.

4   Encampment dwellers in Chile were called *pobladores,* a social subject constructed in the 1950s. Faced with a steep housing deficit, the *poblador* used the emblematic occupation of land as a means to establish the right to the city. Growing in numbers throughout the 1960s, *pobladores* became a symbol of struggle and resistance.

5   Armando de Ramón, *Estudio de una periferia urbana: Santiago de Chile 1850–1900* (Santiago: Instituto de Historia de la Pontificia Universidad Católica de Chile, 1985), p. 120. Original quote in Spanish: "Cuando los bordes de la ciudad avanzaban hasta tocar los parajes rurales, poblados o no, éstos de inmediato pasaban a ser llamados poblaciones."

6   This idea was presented by Urtzi Grau and Cristina Goberna in the article "They don't represent us," *Materia Arquitectura* 10, Santiago (2014).

7   In the sense of the Greek word *techne,* meaning craftsmanship, craft, or art, a form of knowledge directed toward an end, to the art of making as an action, implying the material aspect of forming and transforming matter. Michel Foucault's use of the word *techne* is an invitation to expand its meaning to the technologies of conception, which impacts not only material, structural, and spatial concepts but ideas about form, its generation, definition, and perception. Tents allow us to explore the social role of designed spatial objects as being crucial for understanding how politics and space are affected by changes in the material world.

On the Spatialities of the Homeless' Street in Covid-19 São Paulo

Fraya Frehse

One challenge that homelessness poses to architecture lies in its sociospatial nature, once we approach the phenomenon on the scale of the pedestrian in urban public spaces. What makes homelessness visible daily in the city streets and squares throughout the world—especially in Covid-19 times—is one specific way in which pedestrians use these public places in bodily terms. Besides moving to and fro during the daytime, increasingly more people sleep therein on a more or less regular basis at night. This particular pattern of what I elsewhere termed *body behavior*[1] goes hand in hand with, on the one hand, material and symbolic goods turned into personal and/or communal belongings; and, on the other hand, rules (regularities) of verbal and nonverbal inter-action with other human beings, whether homeless or not, as well as with nonhuman living beings such as dogs, cats, and plants.[2] In brief: human beings regularly dwell in *the street*—the theoretically paramount urban public space that comprises the empirical range of places characterized by their singularly large possible legal, physical-material, or informational access:[3] public streets, alleys, slopes, squares, et cetera.

Hence, the challenge for architecture becomes evident: How might one plan dwelling alternatives for this population, considering that street dwelling has become a decisive trait of the production of urban space world-wide? My aim here is to answer this question by arguing that architects engaged in evidence-based housing projects for the homeless have a lot to learn from the ways in which these subjects symbolically conceive the street as space during their everyday time spent therein. To put it more precisely: homeless individuals' social orderings of the street—that is, their *spatialities* of the street—during the daytime on Western workdays bear programmatic challenges relevant to architectural design.

Therefore, one has to take into account the everyday "imaginary" of homeless and formerly homeless people about the street.[4] The social and symbolic centrality of this space in these subjects' everyday life therein unfolds into verbal and photographic images of the street packed with design-productive spatialities.

São Paulo as Empirical Reference

To this end, I in this essay mainly explore thirty-one individual and group responses to the question "What is the street in your view?" The conversations were

Figure 1: A set of tents in the Mooca district (photographed on Thursday, January 21, 2021)

conducted with homeless and ex-homeless people of São Paulo's downtown districts Sé, República, Luz, and Mooca during the shop opening hours (8 a.m. to 7 p.m.) on weekdays and a Saturday between November 2020 and February 2021.[5] The data originates from semi-structured interviews with twenty-one cis men, six cis women, and four trans women, which took place in the streets, squares, or institutional locations where the everyday life of homelessness in central São Paulo has played out since the onset of the coronavirus pandemic. Moreover, for illustrative purposes I refer to photographs of downtown street dwellings taken in November 2020 and January 2021.[6]

The homeless population of the biggest Latin American city has undergone an empirically visible, albeit still unmeasured, increase since the pandemic's onset in March 2020. A mere walk through São Paulo's public places during the day from then to now (June 2021) suggests that the official figure of almost 24,500 homeless (2019) is strongly outdated. Moreover, a significantly higher number of couples with or without children are sleeping rough. The display of domestic objects socially typical of bourgeois family homes around the ever-increasing tent dwellings indicates more than one

denizen. When photographed in January 2021, the tent pictured above, for example, hosted a couple with two children (fig. 1).

Especially the historical increase of family homelessness makes the São Paulo case compelling. This circumstance has coincided with the dissemination, among the city's downtown homeless, of the conception that dwelling in the street must urgently be replaced by alternative housing alternatives. However, the street is a more intricate space. Confluences between at least two interviewees regarding their verbal images of the street disclose two spatialities which inform one conceptual program assumption that, in turn, implies three programmatic challenges for architectural projects addressing homelessness.

Unfolding Spatialities

An initial image that underpins the interview data depicts the street as a site used by pedestrians according to two different patterns of body behavior: moving around, and sleeping therein. Regarding the first rule, three male and one female interviewees imagined it as a place of regular

Figure 2: The front of two dwelling tents in the República district
(photographed on Tuesday, January 19, 2021)

physical to and fro—either by cars or by human beings—
be it for passing by or for strolling purposes. One homeless man put it succinctly: "The street is tarmac" (fig. 2).

As to sleeping rough, it was addressed by three male
interviewees. Two of them deemed the regular physical
permanence in the street for sleeping purposes to be
usual when one is not able "to pay a rent." Under such
circumstances, the street becomes, according to the
first man, "normal," a natural dwelling place, whereas the
second man sees the street as "a very strong necessity."
By contrast, the third interviewee, a self-proclaimed hobo,
told me that what made him choose the street where we
met as his dwelling place was its "tranquility": the neighbors' receptivity to his sleeping there (fig. 3).

Not only did Mário proudly tour me through the place
he called his "house" in early November 2020.[7] He was
verbally dismissive of individuals he referred to as "sidewalk dwellers," whom he considered socially inferior to
"street dwellers" due to the spatial transience implicit in
a night spent on a pedestrian sidewalk. And he was not
alone in pointing out a difference between street and
sidewalk dwellers: one man and two (cis and trans)
women, interviewed in February 2021, noted that "at the
moment" they were transient "sidewalk dwellers" rather
than individuals "dwelling in the streets."

The interviewees' verbal images of the street contain
fewer clues about how they conceived this space for
dwelling purposes than photographic images do.
The spatial orderings in the photographs speak for
themselves: carefully displayed bottles, shoes, a plant,
and a feeding bowl, alongside an improvised washbasin
between a gutter and two playful dogs, but also two
cupboards framing the red "door" of a "bedroom."

All in all, the photographs and interviews converge on the
aforementioned image of the street. This space is depict-
ed as *a place of two specific patterns of bodily use by
(homeless) pedestrians: movement and dwelling*.

A second converging image concerns the street as *a
place of existential learning processes*. One interviewed
trans woman was poignant: "One has to learn how to live
in the street" (fig. 4).

Seven additional interviewees relied on similar language
when alluding to the street. During a three-member group
interview, the man stated, "For me, the street has been
a school," to which a cis woman added, "It is a life experience I have had to go through," and her trans peer
concluded, "She said it all." The dialogue shows that the
spatial image also bears a temporal dimension: the street
is a stage of life. Two homeless men were more poetic
about the issue: while one noted that "the street is a
life phase," the other assumed this space as "a painful
learning process" that "is part of my life: part of my way,
never my destiny."

Hence we arrive at a third image of the street. Five other
men and one woman imagined this space as *a place of
morally loaded social values*. Two males ambiguously
paired adjectives such as "bad" and "good," whereas

Figure 3: Mário in front of his "house" in the Luz district
(photographed on Thursday, November 5, 2020)

attributes such as "dangerous" and "sinister," nouns like "hell," and phrases such as "the street robs the street" prevailed among the other three. On her part, the woman was most affectively explicit, asserting that "the street is a place of suffering." Hence, she indirectly suggests that although domestic violence is the major motivation for female homelessness in São Paulo,[8] the street is not devoid of anguish.

Given that morality is accompanied by normative behavior patterns, it comes as no surprise that four other men converged on an alternative, fourth and last, spatial image. Two of them understood the street as *a place of overall human physical access*, that is, as "a 'joint' place," or as "everybody's place." After all, public access does not imply an absence of rules, as was made evident by the two other interviewees: whereas the first defined the street as "having its own laws," the second proclaimed that "one has to know how to enter and exit the street."

Altogether, the four confluent images signal that the bodily (re)production of this public space owes everything to the combination of two spatialities. The street is both the *physical setting* of two patterns of bodily use, and an *institution* where irreplaceable socialization processes daily take place under the aegis of tacit, albeit longstanding, insider rules regarding physical access and coercion.[9]

Precisely this combination of spatialities is crucial for the purposes of this essay. It allows for understanding the homeless' street in Covid-19 São Paulo as an "institutionalized space."[10] However, its normative nature is opposed

to that of theoretically formalized institutionalized spaces, such as "courts" of law, for example.[11] In the street, the "effectiveness" of the bodily "order/ing" that, by transcending the individual's "own action," brings about institutionalized space[12] is due to essentially *informal* patterns of bodily and materially mediated (non)verbal interaction therein. The São Paulo homeless' street teaches us that institutions may be spatially forged through the *informal regularities* implicit in the bodily use of urban public places by their most constant and long-term users.

Three Program Challenges for Architectural Projects

Despite the qualitative and localized nature of this data, the mere existence of the aforementioned four spatial images regarding today's São Paulo downtown area shows that the homeless' street is not restricted to the physical space where mainly men—and now also more and more women and children—have been sleeping rough in Covid-19 times. Hence, a crucial conceptual clue for evidence-based architectural projects comes to the forefront: adequate housing addressing homeless populations requires that architects consider the *social* nature of the homeless' street as an independent project variable; or, better stated, as a major conceptual program presupposition.

By methodologically building on this assumption, architects are challenged to technically translate particular local traits of the street as social space into architectural spaces for people coming out of homelessness. Based particularly on the aforementioned case of São Paulo, in which the street appears as an institutionalized space of movement, of dwelling, of lifelong learning, and respectively of morally loaded values and behaviors, the program challenges are threefold:

(i) to integrate into design affective belongings that range from personal items to living beings such as animals and plants, as well as means of transport such as trolleys, buggies, and carts;

(ii) to turn the temporally more or less transitory dimension of street dwelling—expressed through the difference between street and sidewalk dwellers—into architecturally diverse yet co-extant spaces;

(iii) to qualify in architectural terms for the existentially groundbreaking socialization process implicit in street dwelling, which includes morally charged yet informal institutional rules.

Though all of this may seem too specific to São Paulo, it really is not. The street as social space is closely associated with everyday regularities—rules, patterns—that are implicit in social actions, interactions, and relations worldwide. Hence we are back at the street as an institutionalized space. Its locally specific "laws" have to be taken seriously for the sake of a *sociospatially rooted* architecture of homelessness.

Acknowledgments

I thank the Global Center of Spatial Methods for Urban Sustainability (GCSMUS) for funding the graduate students Ana Carolina Gil, Anna Carolina Martins, Caio Moraes Reis, Ednan Santos, Giovanna Olinda, Giulia Patitucci, Paula Quintão, and Tales Siqueira Cunha, who under my supervision conducted the interviews underlying this essay in the framework of the GCSMUS Action 4 (https://gcsmus.org/action-speakers-for-action-4/). Besides also being grateful to each student, I extend my gratitude to Valéria Jurado, Marcus Repa, and Tiago Queiroz/Estadão for contributing, respectively, one fieldwork photo, one video photogram, and two newspaper photos.

The Global Center of Spatial Methods for Urban Sustainability is funded by the German Academic Exchange Service (DAAD) with funds from the German Federal Ministry for Economic Cooperation and Development (BMZ).

1   See Fraya Frehse, "For Difference 'in and through' São Paulo: The Regressive Progressive Method," in *Urban Revolution Now,* ed. Lukasz Stanek, Christian Schmid, and Ákos Moravánsky (Farnham, Surrey, and Burlington, VT: Ashgate Publishing, 2014), p. 250.

2   See Fraya Frehse, "The Historicity of the Re-Figuration of Spaces under the Scrutiny of the Pre-Covid São Paulo Homeless Pedestrians," in *Spatial Transformations,* ed. Angela Million, Christian Haid, Ignacio Castillo Ulloa, and Nina Baur (New York: Routledge [forthcoming in 2021]).

3   See Fraya Frehse, "On the Everyday History of Pedestrians' Bodies in São Paulo's Downtown amid Metropolization (1950–2000)," in *Urban Latin America,* ed. Bianca Freire-Medeiros and Julia O'Donnell (London: Routledge, 2018), p. 33.

4   I draw on Henri Lefebvre's conceptualization of the "imaginary" as a socially and historically specific product, which is (hence) mediated by representations whose "forms" are the (sensitive, individually invented) "images." See, respectively, Henri Lefebvre's *La présence et l'absence* (Paris: Casterman, 1980), pp. 56 and 240; *La critique de la vie quotidienne,* vol. 2 (Paris: L'Arche Éditeur, 1961), p. 288; and *La production de l'espace* (Paris: Anthropos, 2000), pp. 49–50.

5   Besides the twenty-nine interviews by students, I conducted two myself. See Fraya Frehse, "A Rua de Máscara (São Paulo, 5 de novembro de 2020)," video documentary, 2020, https://www.youtube.com/watch?v=DDhrEFczyko&feature=emb_title (accessed in August 2021).

6   See the Acknowledgments.

7   See Fraya Frehse, "A Rua de Máscara," part 2.

8   See, among others, Fraya Frehse, "A Rua de Máscara," parts 1 and 3.

9   My reference here is an analogy between institution and language in everyday life; see Peter and Brigitte Berger, *Sociology: A Biographical Approach* (New York: Basic Books, 1972). As to recent spatial developments related to this approach to institutions, see Silke Steets, *Der sinnhafte Aufbau der gebauten Welt* (Frankfurt am Main: Suhrkamp, 2015).

10 See Martina Löw, *Raumsoziologie* (Frankfurt am Main: Suhrkamp, 2001), p. 164.

11 Ibid.

12 Ibid.

Figure 4: Alternative view of the tents' front from figure 2 (photographed on Tuesday, January 19, 2021)

Cities

Although not exclusively, homelessness is an urban problem. One of the main topics when thinking about the relationship between the housed and the unhoused in cities has to do with how visible this reality is and how invisible it can become. Almost like an ophthalmic correction, the everyday scenes of loitering in train stations, parks, and the extreme reality of rough sleeping can become imperceptible for the majority of urban dwellers. In cities like New York, public administration spends millions of dollars on transitional or permanent housing solutions, yet without managing to decrease the numbers. The definition of homelessness can vary from one urban society to another, but what remains clear is that the number of variables confronting the unhoused on the streets is increasing. For example, during the past year rough sleepers in Los Angeles have been confronted not only by the coronavirus pandemic, but also by the fumes of forest fires, water shortages, rising temperatures, a huge housing crisis, and high unemployment. Comparing the realities of different cities around the world is particularly helpful in an effort to understand what is general and what is local about the crisis of homelessness and the lives of those experiencing it.

New York City

Population
1990: 7.32 million
2000: 8.01 million
2010: 8.18 million
2020: 8.34 million

Number of Homeless People in New York City Shelters Each Night
1990 (Jan): 20,995 total, including 11,806 persons in families and 6,747 children
2000 (Jan): 22,955 total, including 16,053 persons in families and 8,863 children
2010 (Jan): 39,066 total, including 31,103 persons in families and 16,346 children
2020 (Jan): 62,679 total, including 43,669 persons in families and 21,886 children

However, the US Department of Housing and Development believes this number to be closer to 80,000, which reflects the number of people staying overnight in the city's emergency shelters **every day.**

How many people in the city are considered to be living below the poverty line by local standards?
1990: 1.38 million New Yorkers, or 19.3%
2000: 1.67 million New Yorkers, or 21.2%
2010: 1.54 million New Yorkers, or 18.8%
2019: 1.48 million New Yorkers, or 17.8%

Unemployment Rates
1990: 5.4%
2000: 4.5%
2010: 8.6%
2019: 3.9%
2020: 10.1%

Over the course of the
NYC fiscal year 2020, there were

122,926

different homeless adults
and children sleeping in the
New York City municipal shelter system.
This includes more than

39,300

homeless children.

Ownership Rate in the Housing Market
2018: 33% (in the five boroughs)

Average Buying Price per Square Meter in 2020
Manhattan: $1,657 per ft^2 (€15,323 per m^2)

Average Annual Income in 2020
Per household: $63,900 (€55,200)
Per individual: $39,800 (€33,900)

Sources, see p. 270

New York City:
Invisible Homelessness

Aya Maceda and James Carse

"Our Homeless Need Housing Now": marchers at the protest outside the Republican National Convention, New York City, 2004

Under Section 42 of New York's Social Services Law, a person deemed homeless is defined as "an undomiciled person who is unable to secure permanent and stable housing without special assistance."[1]

Every night in New York City, 83,000 men, women, and children—enough to fill a building four times the size of Madison Square Garden—find themselves on the streets, in shelters or other city-funded, nonpermanent housing. But of the city's homeless population of 83,000, only 4,000, or approximately 5 percent, live on the streets, most while dealing with significant health or mental health issues.[2] While less visible, people in shelters make up the majority of New York City's homeless population. According to a report by the Coalition for the Homeless, of the 55,500 people[3] who sleep in shelters each night, 62 percent are families and more than 30 percent are children. Data from the NYC Department of Education show that as many as 130,000 school-age children experienced homelessness at some point during the 2018–19 school year,[4] representing more than one in every ten children in the city. How is it acceptable that, each day, 18,000 children wake up in a shelter in one of the wealthiest cities in the United States?

In February 2021, New York City shelters housed 40 percent more New Yorkers, including 70 percent more school-aged children, than ten years ago. The NYC Department of Homeless Services (DHS) directly attributes this steep rise in homelessness to the city's affordable housing crisis[5]—the result of increasing rents, decreasing wages, a significant loss of existing rent-stabilized apartments, and a lack of creation of new rent-stabilized apartments. While housing is considered affordable if a third or less of a household's income is applied to rent, affordable housing in New York City is developed by calculating a geographic region's Area Median Income (AMI), which is based on the area's income distribution. In 2021, the AMI for the New York City region was reported as $107,400, a number out of reach for a majority of New York City households. According to HUD, in 2016 "a family of three . . . could afford to pay approximately $613 per month in rent and utilities—a figure well under half of the city's 2015 median gross rent of $1,317."[6] Today those numbers have diverged even more as rents continue to climb, with median rents hovering around $3,249 per month in Manhattan, $2,704 per month in Brooklyn, $2,700 per month in Queens.[7]

Eviction moratoriums put into effect during the coronavirus pandemic protected many families from losing their housing during the crisis, leading to a significant decline in the percentage of families in shelters. However, the looming expiration of these moratoriums could have a catastrophic impact on the city's homeless population: 33 percent of New York metro area renters with children state that they have not paid or have deferred rent payments in recent months, and 66 percent of low-income renters with children report slight or no confidence in making their next rental payment on time. The impact of this impending situation is not just the imminent loss of housing for families; research[8] also shows that individuals who experience homelessness as children are significantly more at risk of reentering the homeless system as adults.

In conjunction with rising real-estate prices citywide, New York City's housing crisis is aggravated by the loss of formerly affordable housing stock. Between 1994 and 2012, the city suffered a net loss of approximately 150,000 rent-stabilized apartments. Today, approximately one million rent-stabilized or rent-controlled apartments remain. New legislation has sought to manage the rate of rent increases in rent-stabilized apartments, while also including a provision that increases the availability of these units to those in need; tenants whose income grows to exceed the threshold of the benefit are allowed to stay without penalty or increase in rent outside the permitted annual percentage. Furthermore, affordable units created through the city's 421-a program, which gives real-estate developers tax exemptions for including a certain percentage of affordable housing in new construction, do not create permanent affordability due to the existence of fifteen- to twenty-five-year rent control limits. Finally, as owners age and seek to capture high returns on New York City real estate, condos and co-op boards throughout the city increasingly opt out of their tax-incentivized, limited-equity status.

The scale of New York City's homelessness crisis is vast but, despite a homeless population the size of a small American city, those experiencing homelessness are largely hidden from view. The city's "right to shelter" policy, the reluctant result of consent decrees reached between 1979 and 2008, has created a patchwork system of hotels, privately owned residential buildings, and Tier II New York State-certified shelters[9] run either by nonprofits or the city itself. In 2018, nearly $2 billion of the city's homeless services budget of $3 billion went toward these impermanent solutions—approximately $16,000 per shelter occupant per year. These temporary housing alternatives and additional supportive programs are not enough to help stabilize families or reduce homelessness—more than half of the individuals entering DHS shelters in 2019 had experienced a prior episode of homelessness before. Initiatives that prioritize immediate "shelter" over long-term "homes" result in programs that have effectively transformed temporary stay facilities into de facto temporary houses, as hotels and shelters have

"Housing Is a Human Right": protest banner outside the Republican National Convention, New York City, 2004

become many families' place of residence for eighteen months on average.

Meanwhile, incentive- and market-driven proposals by the state, the city, and private developers have resulted in the construction of alternative housing projects that exclude homeless families, instead creating residences that are more akin to hotels and shelters than actual homes. Alternative housing models, including single-room occupancy units, co-living apartments, and micro-housing have been introduced into New York's rental market with no significant impact on rising housing costs and with no concern for the most vulnerable and at-risk population: families with young children. To make matters worse, the NYC Housing Authority's limited public housing stock is plagued by the concentration of poverty and by sub-standard living conditions across its properties. Citywide voucher programs, which encourage long-term depend-ability on government assistance, have found success with seniors but less with other groups of people experiencing homelessness. Furthermore, when families gain access to this form of assistance, they are often unable to find landlords who are willing to accept their housing vouchers, pushing them back to the shelter system once again.

In seeking to address the growing and interrelated crises of affordability and homelessness, New York City and State agencies acknowledge the challenges created by a large number of units leaving the affordable housing pool as more cooperatives convert to market rate and properties

built with 421-a tax credits begin to reach the term limits of their affordability restrictions. This exodus includes units created by the single most successful long-term family-oriented housing policy the country has ever seen: New York State's 1955 Mitchell-Lama Program, which financed the development of more than 150,000 afford-able units between 1955 and 1978. Today, the units that remain are the last bastion of affordable home ownership in New York City. And it is not a far-fetched idea to revive and modernize family-oriented housing programs that provide housing security to low-income New Yorkers. The city certainly has the resources to do so.

Alternative Equity Models in the Development and Preservation of Long-Term, Deeply Affordable Housing

The United States Department of Housing and Urban Development (HUD) stated in 2020 that one out of every four people experiencing homelessness in the United States did so in either New York City or Los Angeles and stated that a majority of New York City's homeless population were people in families with children.[10] This situation has the potential to be exacerbated by the coronavirus pandemic, which has taken a heavy toll on a city where, even before the pandemic, as many as 1.5 million people lived below the poverty line. City programs, aimed at addressing the "right to shelter," create a fragile and imperfect safety net of temporary

Twin Parks, a social housing project within a "community context"

shelters for those without permanent stable housing but do not address the greatest contributor to homelessness in the city: long-term affordability.

In recent years, the city has attempted a variety of models to address affordability, including the development of affordable housing, tax-based financial incentives, voucher programs, and a bevy of alternative housing models that attempt to reimagine our collective understanding of comfort under the misguided notion that square footage drives the cost of housing in NYC. Yet, scattered throughout the city are the remnants and legacy of the single initiative that had the greatest impact on sustainable affordable housing in the city: the Mitchell-Lama Program. Conceived as a limited profit program, Mitchell-Lama combined and directed many of the same tools that the city and state have access to and deploy to less effect today: low-interest loans, tax abatements, and direct subsidies. The result of this program was the creation of more than 150,000 long-term affordable housing units between 1955 and 1978, many of which remain affordable more than sixty-five years later.

Mitchell-Lama's success, like that of the Limited Dividend program of the 1920s,[11] was based on the program's ability to create an economic model that disincentivized the utilization of housing as an investment tool by stabilizing costs and returns for both the homeowner and the developer. The program resulted in limited equity co-ops, a resale-restricted homeownership model where a small

down payment and a monthly service charge afford residents the rights of shareholders who, when they move out, sell their unit back at the same price or at a marginally adjusted price, ultimately creating stable homes and communities.

Two such projects, Co-op City and Twin Parks, each in the Bronx, have remained bastions of affordability in the city. A two-bedroom apartment in Co-op City for income-qualified applicants costs only about $24,750[12]—roughly half of the approximately $48,000 the city spends on housing a three-person family in its shelter system. By taking the cost of shelter out of the equation, co-op residents can focus on building community, earning an education, developing careers, and saving toward retirement—all factors that can help keep them from entering or reentering homelessness in the future.

A modern version of Mitchell-Lama could allow existing buildings to opt in to the program, with similar incentives for bonds, tax breaks, access to low-interest loans for renovations, and direct subsidies for maintenance or housing assistance. The program could work at a smaller scale, adjusted to buildings with as few as four units to spur community-led and resident-owner-led infill development. It could work through the support of alternative lenders, including nonprofits and crowd-sourced investment vehicles, and it could reframe land ownership through the use of long-term leases, in lieu of land dispositions for city-owned properties, as a way to ensure

The social housing complex Co-op City in the Bronx, a "bastion of affordability"

permanent affordability. Together, these policy mecha-nisms could offer a pathway to expanding affordable housing across the city through preservation, conversion, and development. The question, then, becomes: What role do planning, urban design, and architecture play in supporting these initiatives?

From 1966 to 1973, the most ambitious of New York City's cooperative developments, Co-op City, rose on undevel-oped marshland along the Hutchinson River in the Bronx. A tower-in-the-park complex comprised of thirty-five megaliths ranging from twenty-four to thirty-three stories, Co-op City consists of 15,300 apartments housing more than 50,000 people. The towers, in the form of chevrons, Xs, and combinations of Xs, allow for a variety of unit types, supporting a broad and diverse community. The cruciform floor plans, favored by the architect Herman Jessor and reminiscent of Le Corbusier's Ville Contem-poraine, also make for highly livable apartments with a window to every room—a blessing for many families arriving from dark and airless tenements. Building foot-prints occupy only 20 percent of the overall site, the remainder of which takes the form of green spaces, athletic fields, buffers, paths, and streets. The buildings, pulled back from the streets and indifferently oriented to the open spaces, lack a human scale but also offer an ambiguity of ownership that supports a reading of the project as truly open and public.

Contemporaneously built, Twin Parks explores a radically different approach to the creation of affordable housing in the Bronx. Its 2,250 units were developed throughout multiple noncontiguous parcels in the early 1970s. The infill

strategy pursued by the New York State Urban Develop-ment Corporation engaged the services of rising architects in the city, including Richard Meier, James Polshek, and Lo-Yi Chan, among others. The developments managed to integrate small-scale, multiunit buildings, typically less than six stories in height, into the neighboring community context, while introducing new neighborhood amenities including commercial spaces, gardens, and courtyards.

Both approaches have had their challenges. Co-op City met its critics in Jane Jacobs and the thousands of daily commuters along I-95 who have mischaracterized the project as an example of urban renewal or slum dwellings. Meanwhile, the success of the infill strategy employed in Twin Parks was jeopardized by the management of its public spaces, which were neglected in the late 1970s and early 1980s, succumbing to the same pressures felt by the rest of New York City: the destabilization of economic, social, and demographic equity. Yet, each project has offered a glimpse of the long-term opportunities made possible and sustained by the Mitchell-Lama program.

In mid-2020, *The New York Times* noted that, "since 2013, there have been more than 25 million applications sub-mitted for roughly 40,000 [affordable] units,"[13] meaning that less than one in 600 qualifying applicants will have access to affordable housing through the city's lottery system. The pandemic has further exposed a mounting crisis of housing affordability in New York City, one that, if left unabated, could plunge millions into homelessness. It is time we look back to the ambitions and successes of the Mitchell-Lama program to build a framework of housing with proven long-term affordability.

1 The New York State Senate, Legislation, Section 42 of the Homeless Housing and Assistance Program, https://www.nysenate.gov/legislation/laws/SOS/42 (all URLs accessed in August 2021).

2 The Bowery Mission, "The Bowery Mission," https://www.bowery.org/homelessness/.

3 The numbers of estimated homeless per night (83,000) and the numbers of homeless accounted for in the NYC shelter system (55,000) are different as the shelter system numbers do not include those individuals who are on the streets, doubling up in temporary housing situations, or otherwise unable to receive housing in the shelter system.

4 Advocates for Children of New York, "New Data Show Number of NYC Students who are Homeless Topped 100,000 for Fourth Consecutive Year," October 28, 2019, https://www.advocatesforchildren.org/node/1403; David Brand, "NYC Has a Family Homelessness Crisis: Who are the Families?," City Limits, December 10, 2019, https://citylimits.org/2019/12/10/nyc-has-a-family-homelessness-crisis-who-are-the-families/.

5 NYC Department of Homeless Services, "Turning the Tide on Homelessness in New York City," https://www1.nyc.gov/site/dhs/about/tide.page.

6 The City of New York, "Turning the Tide on Homelessness in New York City," 2017, https://content.manhattan.edu/csfe-files/turning-the-tide-on-homelessness_mayor-diblasios_plan_march-2017.pdf.

7 Sarah Paynter, "Here's where NYC's real estate market stands right now," New York Post, July 20, 2021, https://nypost.com/article/nyc-real-estate-market-housing-prices/.

8 Family Homelessness Coalition, "Facts about Homelessness," https://fhcnyc.org/the-facts/.

9 Tier II shelters are those which have been certified by New York State and which also provide on-site social services to occupants. These shelters are typically run by nonprofit organizations in privately owned buildings and operate under contracts with the city or are directly run by the city itself. See "The Dynamics of Family Homelessness in New York City," https://www.icphusa.org/wp-content/uploads/2019/07/Shelter-DynamicsFinal07819.pdf.

10 The U.S. Department of Housing and Urban Development, "The 2020 Annual Homeless Assessment Report (AHAR) to Congress," January 2021, https://www.huduser.gov/portal/sites/default/files/pdf/2020-AHAR-Part-1.pdf.

11 A precursor to the Mitchell-Lama program, the Limited Dividend Company Act, as utilized by the Amalgamated Clothing and Textile Workers Union (ACTWU), pioneered the concept of cooperative housing.

12 Co-op City, "Real Estate Advertisement Co-op City," https://coopcitynyc.com/img/apply/apartments_residential_sales_ad.pdf.

13 Matthew Haag, "25 Million Applications: The Scramble for N.Y.C. Affordable Housing," The New York Times, June 15, 2020, https://www.nytimes.com/2020/06/15/nyregion/nyc-affordable-housing-lottery.html.

San Francisco

Population
1990: 723,959
2000: 776,733
2010: 805,235
2020: 882,519

Population of People Experiencing Homelessness
1990: 5,569
2000: 5,376
2010: 6,485
2020: 8,922 / 17,595 (unofficial)

How many people in the city are considered to be living below the poverty line by local standards?
1989: 12.4%
2000: 11.3%
2010: 10%
2018: 10%
2019: 9.5%

Unemployment Rates
1990: 3.6%
2000: 3.4%
2010: 9.9%
2020: 8%

Ownership Rate / Rental Rate in the Housing Market
1990: no data
2000: 35% (ownership)
2010: 35.8% (ownership)
2015: 37.6% (ownership)

The San Francisco Department of
Homelessness and Supportive Housing,
in the period between
July 2016 and December 2018,
maintained housing for over

9,500 people

living in permanent supportive housing.

Average Buying Price per Square Meter in 2020
$1,000 per ft² (€9,300 per m²)

Average Annual Income and Minimum Hourly Wage in 2019/2020
2019 per household: $114,696 (€97,953)
2019 per individual: $52,677 (€44,987)
2020 minimum hourly wage: $12.00 (€10.25)

Sources, see p. 270

A Tale of Two Bays:
San Francisco's Struggle with Inequality and Tech

Valentina Rozas-Krause and Trude Renwick

Overpasses and highways often encircle homeless encampments and make them a key part of the daily commute—
a state of tension that is reflected in the foreground sign.

In February of 2021, amidst the global coronavirus pandemic, local law enforcement agents dismantled an encampment located across the street from the global Facebook headquarters in Menlo Park, California. More than seventy houseless individuals had been living in a protected marshland area known as Ravenswood Triangle, separated from the 250-acre Facebook campus only by a highway.[1] The effects of the eviction were short-lived; *The Los Angeles Times* reported that, only a month later, thirteen people had started rebuilding the destroyed site.[2]

The Ravenswood encampment, like many other sites across the San Francisco Bay Area, reveals the acute housing crisis unfolding in what is currently one of the most unequal cities in the United States.[3] On one side of the road, people live between bushes and debris, under improvised tents and shelters with no running water, electricity, or sewage management systems. On the other side, a quarter of Facebook's 45,000 employees enjoy a paradise of never-ending superabundance: unlimited food, drinks, entertainment, lounging areas, and connectivity. While one side of the road controls the social networks of most of the world, the other side does not have access to the Internet.

The state of California is the fifth largest economy of the world, surpassing even the United Kingdom, and is celebrated as a center for counterculture and progressive politics. However, California also has the highest poverty rate in the United States.[4] According to a recent *Bloomberg* report, 41.6 percent of California households, representing both owners and renters, are cost-burdened, meaning that they spend more than 30 percent of their income on housing.[5] The situation in the Bay Area is even more dire: a 2016 Metropolitan Transportation Commission report states that 89 percent of renter households earning less than $36,000 per year are rent-burdened.[6] As a result, almost 900,000 Bay Area renters experience housing insecurity, making them increasingly vulnerable to displacement, overcrowding, and homelessness.

These conditions make it clear that poverty, the number-one cause for houselessness, does not result from a lack of political interest or resources.[7] In today's California, it seems easier to send commercial flights to space than to provide affordable housing for middle- and low-income families. How is it possible that the birthplace of tech companies like Google, Apple, Uber, Lyft, Twitter, Airbnb, Tesla, and SpaceX, to name a few, has so far failed to adequately provide its citizens with one of the most basic human needs? The answer to this question is tied to a national and regional history of houselessness.

Geography and climate, combined with the social history of the Bay Area and California, have more broadly shaped a unique context for the unhoused as compared to the rest of the United States. The state's Mediterranean climate means that the houseless in this region do not suffer from temperatures as low as those found in the country's Northeastern and Midwestern regions. In addition to this mild climate that can make life more tenable, San Francisco's specific geography, as well as its prevalence of natural disasters, has played a major role in the settlement of the region, beginning with the city's population boom during the California Gold Rush of 1849. To this day, the 1906 San Francisco earthquake, and the subsequent three days of fire that raged throughout the city, remains one of the most notable events in the city's history. The earthquake, which destroyed a shocking 80 percent of the city, not only led to massive displacement but also dramatically shaped San Francisco's urban landscape through the establishment of strict building codes, the promotion of densification, and the large-scale construction of Victorian homes across the city. Temporary shelters erected after the earthquake can still be found throughout the city today.[8] Meanwhile, in recent years, the warm and dry fall months have become "fire season," during which uncontrollable, large-scale wildfires turn many of the area's residents into climate refugees. Not only do these fires destroy thousands of homes, but the smoke and ash they distribute throughout California have a serious impact on well-being, and particularly on the health of the 150,000 houseless individuals scattered across the state.

The contemporary conditions of San Francisco's homelessness crisis, however, are much deeper than these environmental factors. In her ethnography on homelessness in San Francisco, the sociologist Teresa Gowan describes how the city was impacted by Euro-American constructs of poverty based around sin, sickness, and the system.[9] In San Francisco's social imaginary, the causes of poverty are rooted in the notion that to be poor is to possess inherent character defects that make one predisposed to vulnerability. According to Gowan, accumulation processes that have depended on the expropriation of native lands, slave labor, and racial domination have resulted in the United States government's punishment-oriented attitude toward impoverished populations.[10] Settlement and vagrancy laws are early examples, dating back to the late nineteenth century, of discriminatory policies against immigrants and mobile urban populations in American cities.

After the economic crash of 1929, a major shift occurred in the government's penal approach toward the poor and the unemployed. As a result of the unprecedented rates of unemployment during the Great Depression, the conception of the poor as morally flawed could no longer be sustained. In response to the economic crisis,

The art installation *Raygun Gothic Rocketship* is a product of lasting public interest in tech, art, and counterculture in San Francisco. In contrast, the houseless individual reflects the extreme income inequality that defines this city.

The neighborhood surrounding San Francisco City Hall is known for its large homeless population. The Simón Bolívar monument is often used as a place to gather, wait, sell, barter, and sleep.

President Franklin D. Roosevelt led a nation-wide expansion of social services through New Deal programs. Meanwhile, many of the unemployed moved westward to the agricultural regions of California to live in federal transient camps established for migrant families or otherwise found work through the New Deal's massive public work projects. This Keynesian approach to handling the country's impoverished populations continued through the Second World War, when war mobilization resulted in the deindustrialization of urban centers and the rise of the suburbs. Despite the shift in approach represented by the New Deal, it is important to note that most of the opportunities created by the program perpetuated and deepened discriminatory practices against communities of color through segregationist redlining and racist housing covenants that often remain in place to this day.[11] In response to the increasing segregation of cities, the decades following the war also saw many urban centers becoming hotbeds for the Civil Rights Movement. The Office of Equal Opportunity, the Economic Opportunity Act of 1964, and federal aid programs like food stamps, Medicaid, and Medicare were bolstered by this period of civic activism. Around this time, San Francisco became

famous for attracting flocks of young middle-class hippie dropouts, ultimately becoming the center of American counterculture amidst the Vietnam War (1955–75).

However, major budget cuts began to emerge by the end of this long and expensive era of war. Housing and other social services in cities across the country suffered the most, as federal programs implemented from the 1930s through the 1960s were largely dismantled by the neoliberal policies of the 1980s. For example, during the 1980s, 40,000 beds in state mental health institutions were shut down, rendering homeless many individuals with mental illness, virtually overnight.[12] Under President Reagan, the moral rhetoric against homelessness burgeoned once again, and many progressive organizations lost their lobbying power to homeowner associations and developers, who perceived the poor as threats. These vulnerable groups were no longer considered part of the social body but were instead viewed as "loitering teens" and "homeless addicts."[13] Social services, previously provided by the government, were instead doled out by fragmented networks of small-scale nonprofit organizations. In San Francisco, the Tenderloin neighborhood, with its affordable rents and single-occupancy hotels, became the epicenter for the city's homeless populations.

Tech and the Conundrum of Homelessness

While San Francisco's homelessness crisis has, like many cities, been deeply impacted by neoliberal policies pushed by the United States federal government, the specific dynamics between the tech industry and the nostalgia for San Francisco's counterculture past make this city an important case study through which to examine homelessness.

As San Francisco battled a rise in houseless populations in the final decades of the twentieth century, the tech industry was booming in neighboring Silicon Valley. In the 1990s, organizations like Religious Witness with Homeless People and the Coalition on Homelessness fiercely advocated for people experiencing "homelessness" as neighborhood associations and conservative politicians cracked down on the issue by reviving public nuisance laws and other legislation that restricted and controlled access to public space.

During this period, the city's politics toward homelessness became increasingly inconsistent. Mayor Willie Brown (1996–2004) continued an aggressive stance toward the city's houseless populations with the clearing out of parks (including, in 2001, the largest open public space in the city, United Nations Plaza), and by placing restrictions on individuals living out of their vehicles. However, Brown also spent hundreds of millions of dollars on affordable housing and drug treatment centers. Meanwhile, the dot-com bubble and the rise of startups in the region during the first decade of the twenty-first century resulted in an influx of money and tech workers seeking housing. As rents skyrocketed, homelessness surged to upward of 20,000 people across San Francisco, Oakland, Berkeley, and San Jose.[14]

The tech industry helped build a centrist democratic voting base in the city of well-meaning and educated young liberal millionaires and billionaires. As a businessman born and raised in San Francisco, Mayor Gavin Newsom (2004–11) was an ideal candidate to represent a city grappling with a surge in wealth brought about by Silicon Valley and the progressive politics that define the Bay Area identity. Centered around the slogans "Care not Cash" and "Housing First," Mayor Newsom's homelessness policies were widely backed by voters. Even though his administration saw the creation of emergency and affordable housing, some of Newsom's programs ultimately took away resources like treatment funding, while

promoting the gentrification of downtown San Francisco. Despite the progressive rhetoric, people experiencing homelessness were nonetheless treated as social outsiders and as a "blight" that had to be controlled and removed from the city's center.

And here we return to Menlo Park. Although Facebook did not intervene in the name of its neighbors in early 2021, a spokeswoman for the company declared that the company had not been directly involved in the eviction.[15] Not completely immune to their region's issues, some of the Bay Area's tech companies have recently started to openly address the housing crisis. In December of 2020, a few months before the eviction of the Ravenswood encampment, Facebook created a $150 million fund to develop at least 2,000 affordable homes for low-income families in the Bay Area.[16] That investment came after an earlier commitment of $1 billion to help address the affordable housing crisis in California as a whole. Similarly, in 2019, Apple pledged $2.5 billion while Google promised $1 billion to fight the Bay Area's crisis of affordability.[17]

Funding is crucial to address the crisis, as construction costs in California are the highest in the nation, with an approximate median cost of $450,000 per unit, a figure that increases up to $700,000 in San Francisco proper.[18] However, to quote Newsom, who has served as California's governor since 2019, "Solving our housing challenges will require more than just throwing money at the problem."[19] By their own estimates, Google and Facebook's housing funds together would build 40,000 homes. However impressive, this figure pales when compared to a 2016 report by the McKinsey Global Institute, which estimated that in order to meet the needs of California's fast-growing economy, 3.5 million new housing units would need to be completed by 2025, with a theoretical cost of $1.6 trillion.[20]

Alongside construction costs, most experts agree that a combination of two factors lie at the root of California's housing affordability crisis: restrictive local housing regulations and accelerated economic growth.[21] Despite their outward liberal politics, when it comes to building affordable housing Californians have consistently opposed propositions to increase density and allocate a percentage of new building space to low-income families.[22] Furthermore, new affordable housing projects face a myriad of obstacles including zoning restrictions, land use, and city permits. In Berkeley, for example, one of the most liberal areas in the Bay Area, a mixed-use affordable housing developer had to sue the city in order to obtain a building permit. Often in these cases, progressive environmental protection and historic preservation laws are used to thwart the development of affordable housing projects, effectively pitting social equity against environmental

"Human being, not human doing": being homeless is often seen as possessing a defect in character, because in the United States one is expected to "pull yourself up by the bootstraps."

sustainability—a liberal nightmare.[23] Berkeley city's response to densification echoes the journalist Ezra Klein's description of Californians as "symbolically liberal, but operationally conservative."[24]

Besides this operational conservatism, the biggest challenge to ameliorating houselessness in the Bay Area is growth. In the last decade, the Bay Area's population increased by 8.4 percent while the number of housing units rose by less than 5 percent. Simply put, the provision of housing cannot keep up with the accelerated growth of tech companies and their subsidiary service industries. Simultaneously, rent prices have increased a staggering 40 percent from 2010 to 2014, reflecting the new demographics of the region. An entry-level salary for a Silicon Valley software engineer is about $160,000, while a beginning high school teacher makes a little under $48,000 annually.[25]

Recent efforts by Bay Area-based tech companies to offer money and land to develop affordable housing represent a relatively late response to a cumulative housing shortage they helped to create. Long gone are the times of company towns that American twentieth-century industrialists built in places like Lowell, Massachusetts, and Norris, California, to name a few.[26] In today's Silicon Valley, work and living are disconnected. Tech employees are bused into their workplaces from across the Bay Area, stretching the housing shortage way beyond the bounds of the tech valley, a process only accelerated by remote working during the pandemic. Still, it is impossible to divorce Google, Apple, and Facebook from their contexts; even tech companies are rooted in space, and their employees need a place to live, as do the middle- and low-wage workers who keep running the cities they inhabit.

The image of the Ravenswood encampment perched against the colorful buildings of the Facebook campus makes the human costs of the Bay Area's tech boom painstakingly clear. So far, Silicon Valley's response to the negative externalities they have created is insufficient. A coordinated and sustained effort is necessary, alongside regulatory changes, tax incentives, and, more importantly, a permanent affordable and emergency housing fund for the cities of California's Bay Area.

1   Sue Dremann, "Fires Point to Risky Conditions in Ravenswood Triangle," *Palo Alto Weekly,* July 10, 2020, https://www.paloaltoonline.com/news/2020/07/10/fires-point-to-risky-conditions-in-ravenswood-triangle (all URLs accessed in August 2021).

2   Susanne Rust, "Near Facebook Headquarters, a Fire-Prone Homeless Camp Is Dismantled, and Springs Back," *Los Angeles Times,* March 4, 2021, sec. California, https://www.latimes.com/california/story/2021-03-04/silicon-valley-homeless-camp-near-facebook-returns.

3   Sarah Bohn, Dean Bonner, Julien Lafortune, and Tess Thorman, "Income Inequality and Economic Opportunity in California," Public Policy Institute of California, December 2020, https://www.ppic.org/publication/income-inequality-and-economic-opportunity-in-california/.

4   Kieran Corcoran, "California Economy Ranks 5th in the World, Beating the UK," *Business Insider,* May 5, 2018, https://www.business-insider.com/california-economy-ranks-5th-in-the-world-beating-the-uk-2018-5; Liana Fox, "The Supplemental Poverty Measure: 2019," Census Bureau, September 2020, p. 32.

5   Noah Buhayar and Christopher Cannon, "How California Became America's Housing Market Nightmare," Bloomberg, November 6, 2019, https://www.bloomberg.com/graphics/2019-california-housing-crisis/.

6   At the time, over 1 million jobs region-wide paid less than $18 per hour (or $36,000 a year for full-time work). See Bay Area Regional Health Inequities Initiative, "Housing Insecurity and Displacement in the Bay Area," San Francisco, CA: Metropolitan Transportation Commission, February 20, 2016, p. 1.

7   Erica Hallerstein, "It's Official: Bay Area Has Highest Income Inequality in California," *KQED,* January 31, 2020, https://www.kqed.org/news/11799308/bay-area-has-highest-income-inequality-in-california.

8   There were 5,500 shacks built for more than 20,000 refugees who had originally been placed in government-run camps located in the city's parks.

9   Teresa Gowan, *Hobos, Hustlers, and Backsliders: Homeless in San Francisco* (Minneapolis: University of of Minnesota Press, 2010).

10   Ibid., p. 29.

11   Richard Rothstein, *The Color of Law: A Forgotten History of How Our Government Segregated America* (New York: Liveright Publishing Corporation, 2017); Richard Rothstein, "Opinion: The Black Lives Next Door," *The New York Times,* August 14, 2020, sec. Opinion, https://www.nytimes.com/2020/08/14/opinion/sunday/blm-residential-segregation.html.

12   E. Fuller Torrey, "Ronald Reagan's Shameful Legacy: Violence, the Homeless, Mental Illness," *Salon,* September 29, 2013, https://www.salon.com/2013/09/29/ronald_reagans_shameful_legacy_violence_the_homeless_mental_illness/.

13   Gowan, *Hobos, Hustlers, and Backsliders,* p. 55.

14 Richard Walker, "Boom and Bombshell: New Economy Bubble and the Bay Area" *FoundSF,* https://www.foundsf.org/index.php?title=Boom_and_Bombshell:_New_Economy_Bubble_and_the_Bay_Area.

15 Rust, "Near Facebook Headquarters, a Fire-Prone Homeless Camp Is Dismantled, and Springs Back."

16 David Wehner, "Facebook Invests $150 Million in Affordable Housing for the Bay Area," *About Facebook* (blog), December 9, 2020, https://about.fb.com/news/2020/12/facebook-invests-150-million-in-affordable-housing-for-the-bay-area/.

17 "Apple Allocates More than $400 Million to Combat California Housing Crisis," Apple Newsroom, July 13, 2020, https://www.apple.com/newsroom/2020/07/apple-allocates-more-than-400-million-to-combat-california-housing-crisis/; Sundar Pichai, "$1 Billion for 20,000 Bay Area Homes," Google, June 18, 2019, https://blog.google/inside-google/company-announcements/1-billion-investment-bay-area-housing/; David Wehner, "Facebook Commits $1 Billion and Partners with the State of California to Address Housing Affordability," *About Facebook* (blog), October 22, 2019, https://about.fb.com/news/2019/10/facebook-commits-1-billion-to-address-housing-affordability/; Marisa Kendall, "Bay Area Housing Gets $500 Million Boost," *The Mercury News,* January 24, 2019, https://www.mercurynews.com/2019/01/24/bay-area-housing-gets-500-million-boost-from-local-tech-foundations/.

18 Conor Dougherty, "Why $4.5 Billion From Big Tech Won't End California Housing Crisis," *The New York Times,* November 6, 2019, sec. Business, https://www.nytimes.com/2019/11/06/business/economy/california-housing-apple.html.

19 Gavin Newsom, "The California Dream Starts at Home," *Medium*, October 21, 2017, https://medium.com/@GavinNewsom/the-california-dream-starts-at-home-9dbb38c51cae.

20 Dougherty, "Why $4.5 Billion From Big Tech Won't End California Housing Crisis."

21 Conor Dougherty, *Golden Gates: Fighting for Housing in America* (New York: Penguin Press, 2020).

22 Conor Dougherty and Thomas Fuller, "California Today: Lawmakers Shelve a Potential Remedy to the Housing Crisis," *The New York Times,* May 17, 2019, sec. U.S., https://www.nytimes.com/2019/05/17/us/california-today-housing-crisis-sb50.html; Marisa Kendall, "The Bay Area Is Fed Up with Homelessness, but Interest in Housing Is Flagging," *The Mercury News* (blog), May 4, 2021, https://www.mercurynews.com/2021/05/04/bay-area-residents-are-fed-up-with-the-homelessness-crisis.

23 Marisa Kendall, "Berkeley Rejects Controversial Project That Sought Fast-Track under New State Law," *The Mercury News,* September 5, 2018, https://www.mercurynews.com/2018/09/04/berkeley-rejects-controversial-project-that-sought-fast-track-under-new-state-law/; Frances Dinkelspiel, "Court Rules an Apartment Complex Can Go up on West Berkeley Shellmound," *Berkeleyside,* April 21, 2021, sec. City, https://www.berkeleyside.org/2021/04/21/court-rules-a-260-unit-apartment-complex-can-go-up-at-1900-fourth-st-a-site-the-ohlone-consider-sacred.

24 Ezra Klein, "Opinion: California Is Making Liberals Squirm," *The New York Times,* February 11, 2021, sec. Opinion, https://www.nytimes.com/2021/02/11/opinion/california-san-francisco-schools.html.

25 Dain Evans, "Amazon, Apple, Facebook and Google Are Spending Money to Address the Affordable Housing Crisis They Helped Create," CNBC, December 1, 2019, https://www.cnbc.com/2019/12/01/amazon-google-apple-seek-fix-for-housing-crisis-they-helped-create.html; California Department of Education, "Average Salaries & Expenditure Percentage – CalEdFacts (CA Dept of Education)," California Department of Education, 2019, https://www.cde.ca.gov/fg/fr/sa/cefavgsalaries.asp.

26 Margaret Crawford, *Building the Workingman's Paradise: The Design of American Company Towns,* Haymarket Series (London and New York: Verso, 1995).

Los Angeles

Population
1990: 3.48 million
2000: 3.69 million
2010: 3.79 million
2019: 3.97 million

Population of People Experiencing Homelessness in Los Angeles County
1990: 10,129 (unofficial)
2000: no data
2011: 23,539
2020: 66,433

How many people in the city are considered to be living below the poverty line by local standards in the City of Los Angeles?
1999: 18.3%
2007: 12.4%
2009: 14.2%
2012: 17.1%
2020: 20.4%

During the coronavirus pandemic, the poverty rate in Los Angeles reached 20.4%, with 1 out of every 4.9 residents of Los Angeles living in poverty.

Unemployment Rates in Los Angeles County
1990: 5.4%
2000: 5.5%
2010: 12.6%
April 2020: 18.2%
2021: 10.9%

In Los Angeles,
the median rent is **46.7%**
(nearly half) of the median income.
This is largely because LA is
509,404 units short of meeting
the current need for affordable housing.

Ownership Rate / Rental Rate in the Housing Market

1989: 48.3%
2000: not found
2010: 52.2%
2019: 51.6%
2020: 48.3%

Average Buying Price per Square Meter in 2020

$507 per ft² (€4,713 per m²)

Average Annual Income and Minimum Hourly Wage in 2019, 2021

2015–19 per household: $68,044 (€58,700)
2019 per individual: $34,156 (€29,500)
January 2021 average minimum hourly wage: $13.50 (€11.50)

Sources, see p. 270

Homelessness in Los Angeles: Systemic Racism and Segregation

María Esnaola Cano

Burning tent on Spring Street in Downtown Los Angeles, 2020

Los Angeles has come to be regarded as "the homelessness capital" of the United States.[1] Citizens, politicians, and advocates agree: the most serious challenge facing the city is homelessness. According to the "Greater Los Angeles Homeless Count" of the Los Angeles Homeless Services Authority (LAHSA), 66,436 people were unhoused in Los Angeles County in 2020.[2] Homelessness in the city has increased by nearly 50 percent over the last decade—and it grew by 12 percent in the year 2019 alone, a significantly higher rate of increase than that of the United States as a whole, where homelessness grew by approximately 3 percent over the same year.[3]

One characteristic that distinguishes homelessness in Los Angeles from homelessness in other cities is the fact that most unhoused people in LA are unsheltered, meaning that they live and sleep in the city's public spaces—on the streets, under freeways, and in parks. Nowhere in the US is homelessness a more visible part of life than in the "City of Angels": 76 percent of the city's homeless population is unsheltered, a striking contrast to the 5 percent in New York City.[4] While New York City has a year-round "right to shelter" mandate, requiring that the city find a bed for each person in need, in Los Angeles corporate-driven gentrification and decades of institutional neglect have left people with no other choice but to camp out on the street. Homeless people without shelter in Los Angeles County represent over half of this population in the nation, a group that much more vulnerable to severe health issues, violence, and criminalization.

There are two main factors that impact the unique presentation of homelessness in Los Angeles: firstly, the city's affordability crisis caused by insufficient housing supply and high unemployment, and, secondly, the persistence of structural and institutionalized racism combined with little assistance to tackle poverty and mental health issues. Furthermore, the labyrinthic structure of local government has led to years of uncoordinated policy responses between Los Angeles City and County, which has severely aggravated a deeply rooted problem decades in the making. While the city exercises policing and zoning power, the county is responsible for social welfare, but neither entity is actually responsible for providing housing. The result is a fractured response with a patchwork of welfare groups and nonprofit organizations trying to fill in the gaps.[5]

The affordability crisis in Los Angeles can be traced back to World War II, when the city became the second largest defense production cluster in the country, attracting Depression-weary migrants looking for jobs. Between 1940 and 1946, Los Angeles's population increased by 20 percent, leading to the first severe housing shortage in the city's history.[6] Los Angeles witnessed a comparable rise in the number of encampments shortly after in the 1950s, when thousands of veterans returned from the war and settled in Westlake Park, later renamed MacArthur Park.

During the 1960s, the city's once-prosperous downtown residential hotels began to close down and quickly fell into disrepair. Blinded by the dream of "urban renewal," the Community Redevelopment Agency tore down the multiethnic district of Bunker Hill, with the hopes of transforming the area into a high-end culture district.[7] Over 100,000 housing units were demolished, forcing many into a state of permanent economic insecurity[8] and setting the foundations for, arguably, one of the largest homeless encampments in the nation: Skid Row.

Regrettably, as Los Angeles came out of a devastating recession in the first decade of the twenty-first century, the city missed an opportunity to increase economic prosperity by investing in infrastructure and affordable housing. As jobs returned to Los Angeles, its middle class grew steadily and its population increased by 65,000. However, in this time, only 1,940 housing units were built. As a result, between 2000 and 2010 rents in LA increased by 28 percent, and $1,000 per month rents simply vanished.

Today, the housing crisis affects younger, white-collar Angelenos as well. In the late 1960s, the average California home cost about three times the average household income;[9] currently, that number has jumped to seven. While lower-income communities have struggled to afford homes for decades, the term "housing crisis" only really came into public use when high real-estate prices started affecting wealthier sectors of society. Furthermore, while polls show that "Ending Homelessness" is the highest priority for the public, it is difficult not to see this newfound urgency as a response to encampments encroaching on people's backyards.[10] Nonetheless, the public's growing concern served as the genesis for Measures HHH[11] and H,[12] local initiatives that increase taxes in order to address homeless housing and services in Los Angeles County and City. Implemented in 2017, the goal of these programs is to create 10,000 housing units, providing shelter for 45,000 people over a ten-year period.

Systemic racism has also made African Americans much more likely to experience homelessness. While Black Angelenos make up only 8 percent of the county's population, they are disproportionately impacted by housing instability, representing 33.7 percent[13] of the city's population of individuals experiencing homelessness.[14] In Los Angeles, African Americans are four times more likely to experience homelessness than White Angelenos.

In the early twentieth century, federal housing policy played a critical role in shaping Los Angeles communities, while building segregation into the urban fabric. In 1939, the federal government released residential security maps through the Home Owners Loan Corporation,[15] which were used to determine whether households were eligible for government-backed home loans. Households in high-risk areas, marked in red, which typically had higher minority populations, were prevented from accessing these loans in a practice known as "redlining." This institutionalized system of discrimination ultimately drew private investment away from diverse minority communities like Boyle Heights and Watts.

Meanwhile, between 1940 and 1970, the Black population in Los Angeles grew by a factor of ten.[16] Rampant employment discrimination, residential segregation, and financial demarcation confined the majority of Africans Americans to low-wage employment and densely populated areas. By 1960, Black neighborhoods had population densities around three times higher than the county average. Concurrently, efforts by the City Planning Department to reorient the metropolis around its swelling suburbs prioritized the highway over the provision of affordable housing, splitting predominantly Black and Latinx communities in the process.[17]

Today, heavy policing only serves to exacerbate the conditions of segregation and homelessness in the city. Data shows, for example, that 60 percent of individuals experiencing homelessness in Los Angeles have cycled through the penitentiary system, with a striking 30 percent of them being Black.[18] Furthermore, the criminalization of communities of color has coincided with the deinstitutionalization of mental illness, further increasing vulnerability in the city. In the early 1980s, during President Reagan's first few years in office, his administration slashed Medicaid expenditures by more than 18 percent and ended the federal government's role in providing services to the mentally ill. In California, mental health institutions discharged more than half a million patients, over 100,000 of whom lived in Los Angeles.[19] By 1990, 30 percent of the city's unhoused population were afflicted with mental disorders.

The LA homeless represent the most flagrant physicalization of systemic racism and segregation policies embedded across systems within the fabric of American society. Furthermore, Covid-19 and climate change are significantly aggravating an already insurmountable disaster. Los Angeles is now bracing for another, more immediate surge of unhoused people, with the state's eviction moratoriums set to expire in September 2021. A rent-relief plan of $5.2 billion, recently proposed by

California's governor, Gavin Newsom, will soften the blow, but it may not be sufficient.

Climate Change and Equity for the Los Angeles Homeless

"LA has great weather, yet more homeless die of the cold here than in New York."[20] Through this headline, the *Los Angeles Times* challenges a pervasive myth about the homelessness crisis in Los Angeles: that the city's homeless population got there by choice, migrating from the Midwest and the East Coast, lured by its climate and the promise of improved health. But as the crises of climate change and inequality converge in the city,[21] no one is more vulnerable than people who experience homelessness.

More than 75 percent of the homeless population in Los Angeles is unsheltered,[22] a figure up to ten times higher than in other big cities, and one that represents 40 percent of the total unsheltered homeless population of the entire United States.[23] This defining characteristic of homelessness in Los Angeles also makes this population far more vulnerable to weather events and changing climate conditions. According to the Los Angeles County Medical Examiner-Coroner's Office, on September 6, 2020, alone, the warmest[24] and deadliest day of the year, ten unsheltered people died in the city from heat-related causes.[25] As the effects of climate change intensify, the well-being of those without the protection of a roof, nor access to water or a climate-controlled environment, is highly at risk. The issue is further intensified by the fact that Southern California is one of the most climate-challenged regions of North America. Projections developed for the state's Fourth Climate Change Assessment[26] focus on two urgent climate-related events that directly impact health: heat and fire.

Heat waves cause more deaths in the US each year than floods, storms, and lightning combined.[27] Researchers at the University of Southern California found that for every 10-degree-Fahrenheit increase in temperature, there is a 2.6 percent increase in cardiovascular deaths.[28] Alarmingly, if greenhouse gas emissions remain at current rates, by 2070 the daily average temperatures in Los Angeles will rise by 8.5 degrees Fahrenheit and the city will experience three times as many days with temperatures over 95 degrees Fahrenheit, reaching one hundred days per year by 2050.[29] The report also forecasts that back-to-back extreme heat days, which lead to a 30 percent increase in all-cause deaths, will occur with greater frequency.[30] Combined, these forecasts paint a future of unprecedented risk to the public health of the city, and particularly to its most vulnerable populations.

People sleeping at Pershing Square in Downtown Los Angeles, 2013

Tents on a freeway overpass near Wilshire Grand Center in Downtown Los Angeles, 2016

One reason why vulnerable populations, especially African Americans, are more susceptible to the increased frequency of extreme heat events has to do with the urban distribution of poverty. Low-income neighborhoods are often segregated in the inner city,[31] which is more likely to suffer the consequences of the urban heat island effect.[32] This term is used to account for the fact that urbanized areas tend to experience higher temperatures due to the prevalence of built structures that absorb and reemit the sun's heat, as well as to the absence of natural shade and landscaping to mitigate heat. Studies in Los Angeles show a positive correlation between the presence of impervious, heat-trapping surfaces and community poverty[33] and a negative correlation with the density of the tree canopy.[34]

Meanwhile, wildfires have intensified so much in Southern California that they have become a primary cause for displacement. 2,054,900 structures in California are in "Very High Fire Hazard Severity Zones," a number that includes an estimated 15 percent of the state's households.[35] Predictions are even more bleak: according to a study published in 2019 by the American Geophysical Union, the area burned by wildfires in California has increased fivefold since the 1970s.[36] Los Angeles alone is expected to experience wildfires that could burn up to 178 percent more acres per year than current averages.

Fire presents a two-way problem with regard to homelessness in California. On the one hand, fire impacts housing affordability, as recent wildfires have burned homes at almost a greater pace than the state can rebuild.[37] On the other hand, many of the fires actually start in homeless encampments. These precariously built settlements, which often take over hillsides or key infrastructure sites, are likely to fuel fires due to their high concentrations of human activity and the massive amounts of debris produced by their inhabitants. In 2018, Los Angeles encampments experienced an average of seven fires a day; in 2021, that number has more than tripled to twenty-five.[38] This connection between encampments and fires has aggravated an already widespread stigma against the homeless settlements of Los Angeles.[39]

Research also shows that the effects of global warming have a disproportionately unequal impact on communities of color, which are often located in low-income neighborhoods. African Americans and Latinx are also some of the groups most severely impacted by homelessness, a situation that compounds the vulnerability of these populations. Strikingly, Black people make up 8 percent of the population of Los Angeles, but 34 percent of its homeless population.[40]

Years of inequitable urban policy, redlining, and predatory private investment have segregated poorer communities,

"Homeless Republic" billboard in Los Angeles, 2020

primarily African American and Latinx neighborhoods, limiting their access to climate-resilient urban infrastructure and making them more vulnerable to the effects of climate change. These city-level interventions should happen in areas such as institutional development, land use planning, flood management, emergency response systems, and ecosystem strengthening to anticipate and adapt to changing climate conditions.

The impact of poverty reaches beyond individuals and communities; it has a direct financial impact on local government. High-poverty communities have above-average per capita costs for public safety and other municipal services such as courts or fire protection. These costs exceed those for services directly linked to poverty such as emergency health care, affordable housing, and infrastructure. Furthermore, they have increased over time, making the implementation of a resiliency plan unaffordable and aggravating the impact of fire in such communities. While the number of people living in acute poverty has declined across the United States, in Los Angeles areas of concentrated poverty have become more prevalent over the last ten years.[41]

A hallmark example of climate-resilient urban infrastructure is shade, a crucial yet sometimes-criminalized resource in Los Angeles. Sidewalks, parks, bus stops, freeway underpasses, and the Los Angeles River are all sites where the presence of shade is problematized and often explicitly made illegal due to bureaucratic mismanagement, surveillance, and issues of profit. "The name of the game is to maximize floor area."[42] According to current zoning regulations, open areas beneath habitable space—like an arcade cut out of a building, or a patio beneath a balcony—can be counted as floor space in the density ratio. A ballot approved in 1986 changed the zoning code, severely limiting the floor-area ratio and making it hard for architects to justify such spaces to their clients. This significantly limited areas of shade in new commercial developments and created public spaces with no shelter from the sun.

Access to clean water, an essential necessity for health, is a similarly disputed form of resilient infrastructure. As a result of water insecurity,[43] cases of hepatitis A and murine typhus outbreaks have been reported in Skid Row, diseases that are associated with inadequate access to basic water, sanitation, and hygiene services.[44]

While municipal programs such as Million Trees LA[45] or local community movements like Water Drop LA[46] work to provide immediate solutions to these infrastructural inequalities, Los Angeles finds itself in need of responsive, incremental, and decentralized solutions that can effectively provide basic urban infrastructure and services to palliate the threats of climate change at a citywide scale.

Unfortunately, current local investment efforts are directed to solve homelessness and not the vulnerability of the homeless. Expenditure is almost exclusively directed toward building housing (Prop. HHH, H), meaning that thousands of Angelenos are left to combat extreme heat with nothing but a tent.

Climate change could pose the biggest challenge to ending homelessness in Los Angeles and make an already vulnerable group even more vulnerable. It is a crisis that exacerbates the lack of housing stock and widens the racial injustice in the city, and it demands a renewed mindset about urban and social policy to avoid a harrowing loss of human life.

1 Steve Gorman, "Los Angeles Homelessness Rises Sharply as Housing Crisis Deepens," Reuters.com, June 4, 2019.

2 Los Angeles Homeless Services Authority, "The Greater Los Angeles Homeless Count: 2020 Homeless Count by Community/City," https://www.lahsa.org/news?article=726-2020-greater-los-angeles-homeless-count-results (all URLs accessed in August 2021).

3 Benjamin Oreskes and Doug Smith, "Homelessness Jumps 12% in the County and 16% in the City; Officials Stunned," Los Angeles Times, June 4, 2019.

4 This data was accessed from the U.S. Department of Housing and Urban Development's Point-In-Time (PIT) counts. See "The 2019 Annual Homeless Assessment Report (AHAR) to Congress: Point-in-time estimates," U.S. Department of Housing and Urban Development, January 2020.

5 Gary Blasi, "UD Day: Impending Evictions and Homelessness in Los Angeles," UCLA Luskin Institute on Inequality and Democracy, May 28, 2020.

6 Los Angeles Mayor Eric Garcetti cited this information while addressing Panel 1 at the 2018 USC Homelessness Initiative Research Summit, "Vision 2018: Why We Must Succeed," on May 10, 2018.

7 Mara A. Marks, "Shifting Ground: The Rise and Fall of the Los Angeles Community Redevelopment Agency," Southern California Quarterly 86, no. 3 (2004), pp. 241–90.

8 Gilda Haas and Allan David Heskin, "Community Struggles in Los Angeles," International Journal of Urban and Regional Research 5, no. 4 (1981), pp. 546–63.

9 "The affordable housing crisis, rising unemployment rates, the deinstitutionalization of the mentally ill, and the deterioration of the social safety net over the 1980s contributed to this new wave, The New Homelessness." See Kirsten Moore Sheeley, Alisa Belinkoff Katz, Andrew Klein, Jessica Richards, Fernanda Jahn Verri, Marques Vestal, and Zev Yaroslavsky, "The Making of a Crisis: A History of Homelessness in Los Angeles," report by the UCLA Luskin Center for History and Policy, January 2021, p. 28.

10 "Perhaps more surprising than this urban hipster upgrade has been another consequence of the vanishing buffer zone between Skid Row and the rest of L.A.: It seems, finally, to be forcing Angelenos to open their eyes to how the city treats its most vulnerable residents." See Ed Leibowitz, "Reinventing Skid Row," Los Angeles Times, December 14, 2017.

11 "Proposition HHH, approved in 2016, provides funds for the development of supportive housing for homeless individuals and families throughout the city. The program provides an average HHH loan commitment of $140,000 per unit and total development costs of $4,086,292,454." This data was accessed from the LA City Housing and Community Investment Department, Prop HHH Report, June 2021.

12 "Measure H, approved in 2017, is a 1/4-cent sales tax to raise a projected $3.5 billion over 10 years for preventing and combating homelessness." This data was accessed from the LA City Housing and Community Investment Department, *Prop HHH Report*, June 2021.

13 "Los Angeles Homeless Services Authority: 2020 Greater Los Angeles Homeless Count Presentation," Los Angeles Homeless Services Authority, June 12, 2020.

14 "Black people make up 8% of L.A. population and 34% of its homeless. In Los Angeles Unified, the second-largest school district in the country, about 90% of those who attend district schools are students of color, and 80% of LAUSD students fall below the poverty line. A Times study published [in 2020] determined that of the nearly 900 people killed by police in L.A. County since 2000, 80% were people of color." See Steve Lopez, "Column: Black people make up 8% of L.A. population and 34% of its homeless. That's unacceptable," *Los Angeles Times*, June 13, 2020.

15 "The 1939 Home Owners Loan Corporation's map of central Los Angeles has long been seen as both a savior to the housing sector and a force for racial segregation. As the economic collapse of the 1930s recedes beyond living memory, historians have focused more on the segregationist nature of housing policy—how racism helped save the American economy." See Ryan Reft, "Segregation in The City of Angels: A 1939 Map of Housing Inequality in L.A.," *KCET*, November 14, 2017.

16 Poverty Areas in Los Angeles County, "Welfare Planning Council, Los Angeles, records Collection no. 0434," *USC Libraries*, April 1964.

17 Kirsten Moore Sheeley, Alisa Belinkoff Katz, Andrew Klein, Jessica Richards, Fernanda Jahn Verri, Marques Vestal, and Zev Yaroslavsky, "The Making of a Crisis: A History of Homelessness in Los Angeles," UCLA Luskin Institute, p. 25.

18 Peter Lynn (Executive Director of LAHSA), "Examining the homeless crisis in Los Angeles," field hearing committee on financial services, U.S. House of Representatives, 116th Congress, First Session, August 14, 2019.

19 This data was accessed from the "Homeless Task Force Draft Report: Planning and Recommendations for the Homeless Mentally Ill," Los Angeles County Department of Mental Health, *USC Archives*, June 1985.

20 Gale Holland, "L.A. has greater weather, yet more homeless die of the cold here than in New York," *Los Angeles Times*, February 17, 2019.

21 Rachel Morello-Frosch, Manuel Pastor, James Sadd, and Seth B. Shonkoff, *The Climate Gap: Inequalities in How Climate Change Hurts Americans & How to Close the Gap*, University of Southern California, May 2009, p. 5, https://dornsife.usc.edu/assets/sites/242/docs/The_Climate_Gap_Full_Report_FINAL.pdf.

22 U.S. Department of Housing and Urban Development 2019 point-in-time data (see note 4).

23 Samantha Batko, Alyse D. Oneto, and Aaron Shroye, "Unsheltered Homelessness Trends, Characteristics, and Homeless Histories," Urban Institute, December 2020, p. 8, Table 2.

24 Temperatures that day reached 113 degrees Fahrenheit according to the NASA Earth Observatory.

25 Anna Scott, "LA's heat wave is deadly for the county's unhoused population," *KCRW*, September 16, 2020.

26 Estate of California Energy Commission, "California's Changing Climate 2018," *California's Fourth Climate Change Assessment: Statewide Summary Report*, 2018.

27 County of Los Angeles Public Health, "Stay Healthy in the Heat," LA County Public Health in Action: Extreme Heat in Los Angeles County.

28 Morello-Frosch et al., *The Climate Gap,* p. 9.

29 County of Los Angeles Public Health, "Days Over 95F Annually: UCLA Institute of the Environment and Sustainability, Center for Climate Science," County of Los Angeles Public Health, Figure 1.

30 Edith de Guzman, Laurence Kalkstein, David Sailor, David Eisenman, Scott Sheridan, Kimberly Kirner, Regan Maas, Kurt Shickman, David Fink, Jonathan Parfrey, and Yujuan Chen, "Rx for Hot Cities: Climate Resilience Through Urban Greening and Cooling in Los Angeles," TreePeople, Los Angeles Urban Cooling Collaborative (2020), p. 4.

31 Jessie Daniels and Amy J. Schulz, "Constructing Whiteness in Health Disparities Research," in *Health and Illness at the Intersections of Gender, Race and Class*, ed. Amy J. Schulz and Leith Mullings (San Francisco: Jossey-Bass Publishing, 2006), pp. 89–127.

32 United States Environmental Protection Agency, "Heat Island Community Actions Database," January 8, 2020.

33 "African-Americans were 52% more likely, Asians 32% more likely, and Hispanics 21% more likely than Whites to live in areas where impervious surfaces covered more than half the ground, and more than half the population lacked tree canopy." See Bill M. Jesdale, Rachel Morello-Frosch, and Lara Cushing, "The racial/ethnic distribution of heat risk-related land cover in relation to residential segregation," *Environmental Health Perspectives* 121, no. 7 (July 2013), pp. 811–17.

34 "LAUCC quantified how increasing tree cover and solar reflectance of roofs and pavements in Los Angeles could reduce summer temperatures, decrease the number of oppressive air mass days leading to higher heat-health risks, and prevent heat-related deaths." See Los Angeles Urban Cooling Collaborative, *Tree People*, 2020. Also see "Land cover characteristics by percent of households living below the poverty line," in Morello-Frosch et al., *The Climate Gap,* p. 9, Figure 3.

35 FireLine Data, "Wildfire risk management tool: FireLine evaluates wildfire risk at the address level using advanced remote sensing and digital mapping technology," *Verisk Wildfire Risk Analysis Report*, 2020.

36 "Since the early 1970s, California's annual wildfire extent increased fivefold, punctuated by extremely large and destructive wildfires in 2017 and 2018." See A. Park Williams, John T. Abatzoglou, Alexander Gershunov, Janin Guzman-Morales, Daniel A. Bishop, Jennifer K. Balch, and Dennis P. Lettenmaier, "Observed Impacts of Anthropogenic Climate Change on Wildfire in California," *Earth's Future* 7, no. 8 (August 2019), pp. 892–910.

37 Gina Ferazzi, "LA already has a housing crisis," *Los Angeles Times*, 2020.

38 Josh Haskell, "Los Angeles experiencing alarming jump in fires at homeless encampments," *KABC 7*, May 13, 2021.

39 Homeless Hub, "NIMBY, an acronym for 'Not in My Backyard,' describes the phenomenon in which residents of a neighborhood designate a new development or change in occupancy of an existing development as inappropriate or unwanted for their local area," Canadian Observatory of Homelessness, 2021.

40 This data was accessed from the Los Angeles Homeless Services Authority, "2020 Greater Los Angeles Homeless Count Presentation," LAHSA, June 12, 2020.

41 Michael Matsunaga, "Concentrated Poverty Neighborhoods in Los Angeles," *Economic Roundtable Report*, February 2, 2008, p. 5.

42 "The city exempts 5 feet of open space beneath a cantilevered balcony, but space that is larger than that or supported by columns is considered part of the building. In an interview, Simon Ha said the Building Department has a 'strict' and 'detailed set of rules' that counts any space that could potentially be enclosed in the future as part of the floor area. So, for example, shaded space beneath a skybridge can be counted as habitable space or even space beneath a rooftop solar panel array." See Sam Bloch, "Shade," *Places Journal*, April 2019.

43 Juliet Eilperin, Brady Dennis, and Josh Dawsey, "EPA tells California it is 'failing to meet its obligations' to protect the environment," *The Washington Post*, September 26, 2019.

44 Lourdes Johanna Avelar Portillo, Yao-Yi Chiang, Robert O. Vos, Jose Jesus Rico, Yanyi Qian, Xiaozhe Yin, and Kate Vavra-Musser, "Los Angeles Homelessness and the Access to Water, Sanitation, and Hygiene (WASH)," University of Southern California, 2019.

45 E. Gregory McPherson, "Monitoring Million Trees LA: Tree Performance During the Early Years and Future Benefits," *Arboriculture & Urban Forestry* 40, no. 5 (2014), pp. 286–301.

46 "Water Drop LA is a 100% volunteer-run community organization whose mission is to provide clean water and other necessities to communities facing water inaccessibility." See Water Drop Los Angeles, https://www.waterdropla.org/.

São Paulo

Population (São Paulo City)
1991: 9.62 million
2000: 10.40 million
2010: 11.25 million
2020: 12.32 million

Population of People Experiencing Homelessness
1991: no data
2000: 8,706
2011: 14,478
2019: 24,344 (sleeping in shelters: 11,693 / rough sleeping: 12,651)

According to official statistics, there were [about] 24,000 homeless people in São Paulo before the pandemic, the result of a 65 percent rise in the preceding four years. Aid organizations believe the official numbers are far lower than the reality.

How many people in the city are considered to be living below the poverty line by local standards?
In 2010, 31.6% of the population of São Paulo lived below the poverty line. (The poverty line is drawn when monthly income is half of the monthly minimum wage of around R$1,000 or €160.)

Unemployment Rates (São Paulo Metropolitan Region)
1991: 10.3%
2000: 17.6%
2010: 11.9%
2018: 16.6%

Volunteers estimate that the number
of homeless people in São Paulo,
the largest and economically
most powerful city in South America,
has jumped by 60 to 70
percent [in 2021].

Ownership Rate / Rental Rate in the Housing Market
Rental rate in São Paulo in the 2010 census: 24.8% (households)

Average Buying Price per Square Meter in 2020
R$6,970,00 (around €1,120)

Average Monthly Salary and Minimum Monthly Salary in 2019/2020
2019 per household: R$3,443.00 (€553)
2019 per individual: R$1,438.67 (€231)
2020 minimum monthly salary: R$1,039.00 (€167)

Sources, see p. 270

São Paulo through the Lens of Homelessness

Clara Chahin Werneck and João Bittar Fiammenghi

"Tonight, over 25 thousand people will sleep on the streets of the richest city in Latin America." Projection on a blind wall in São Paulo's downtown, on a night when the thermometers marked 10 degrees centigrade. Organized by the activist group Coletivo Projetemos.

In 1954, as São Paulo celebrated its fourth centenary, the city was on the verge of surpassing Rio de Janeiro as the most populous city in Brazil. By then, São Paulo had already established itself as the country's economic center and was firmly competing with the former federal capital to become the cultural center of the country as well. The city, however, was yet to experience its most unprecedented period of urban growth. After going from a town of 60,000 inhabitants, home of the country's coffee-farming elites, to an industrialized city, mid-twentieth-century São Paulo was now primed for its transformation into the 22-million-inhabitant global financial metropolis it is today.

São Paulo is the largest city in South America, a complex and heterogeneous social kaleidoscope that faces a slew of urban and social challenges. This city's growth has been characterized by urban sprawl, prompted by the developmental policies of an authoritarian military regime (1964–85) that disregarded the importance of densification and reinforced social segregation through car-centric expansion.[1] Brazil's modernization processes were deeply impacted by the country's history of slavery, which still reverberates across today's structurally racist society, marked by a strongly conservative bias. As a result of the reproduction of historic and archaic social inequalities, a considerable contingent of the country's population is maintained as a cheap and unskilled labor force.

During the country's so-called "economic miracle" in the midst of the military dictatorship in the early 1970s, the civil construction industry boomed. The numerous public infrastructure projects that were built across the country generated enormous amounts of undervalued jobs while also propelling the concentration of wealth. Like many economic bubbles, however, the "miracle" rapidly burst, leaving the country economically destroyed by the end of the regime in 1985. Unprecedented inflation, growing unemployment, and a shattered political apparatus set the tone for the 1980s, a decade that was marked by rising social inequalities. During this time, bottom-up organizations that had fought for democracy during the dictatorship occupied a central role in civic society, demanding social justice and wealth redistribution.

Until the fall of the military regime, the discourse on urban inequality and poverty had focused mainly on the expanding peripheries and the issue of internal migration, largely overlooking the homeless population that inhabited central territories of the city.[2] At this time, homelessness was not framed as a structural problem, meaning that it fell outside of the purview of politics; as such, ameliorating housing vulnerability was exclusively the concern of often-paternalistic charitable organizations and nonprofit

organizations with a paternalistic bias. However, the gradual decline of the military regime set into motion a politicizing shift within progressive religious entities that worked with marginalized populations, leading to what we could refer to as a "utopian turn" that went hand in hand with Brazil's process of redemocratization.[3] From this point on, the country's homeless population started to be understood as a constitutive part of Brazilian capitalism. People experiencing homelessness were no longer seen as individuals who were personally incapable of properly inserting themselves into society, but as a social segment, also composed of unemployed workers, many of whom had literally built the country's massive infrastructure systems of the 1970s. It is this shift in the conceptualization of homelessness that rendered it visible, allowing the issue to be measured and addressed in wholly different ways.[4]

Some of Brazil's first bottom-up organizations that tackled homelessness under this new conceptualization of the issue were cooperatives of recyclable material collectors, such as Coopamare. These organizations positioned collectors and the homeless as excluded and exploited workers, a specific segment of the Brazilian working class far from the lumpenproletariat.[5] Another important nongovernmental entity that worked with marginalized and homeless populations during this period was the Fraternal Aid Organization (OAF),[6] whose restructuring at the turn of the 1970s, influenced by liberation theology and Paulo Freire's popular education movement, illustrates how the notion of homelessness in the country was being transformed.[7] At OAF, homelessness was posed as a structural issue that required community-based organizing to formulate solutions, in stark contrast to the individualized, meritocratic, and essentially depoliticized conception of the issue that had been prevalent in the past decades.

The reconceptualization of homelessness also necessitated the development of new terminology to further and reframe public discourse. Originally referred to as *mendigos* (beggars) or *sem-teto* (roofless), and later known as *moradores de rua* (street dwellers), Brazil's homeless population finally came to be identified as *pessoas em situação de rua* (persons living in a street condition), a term that reinforces their position as a social class while also evoking a sense of transitory temporality.[8] Rather than being branded as individuals who do not have a home, a house, or a roof over their heads (homeless, *sans-abri*), the term centers the identity of this population on the street. The street is the place where they live out their lives; it also functions as their source of income, resources, and entertainment, and as the site where they gather to organize socially and politically. Instead of being

Induction ceremony of the Pop.Rua Committee, March 2020

seen as dispossessed of a fixed shelter, the term emphasizes the street as a symbolic locus, as the source of their deprivations and violations, but also as a space over which they have a claim.

The city government first began to directly address the issue of homelessness in São Paulo under the municipal administration of Luiza Erundina (Workers Party, PT), from 1989 to 1992. The manifold experiences of bottom-up organizations during the 1980s were taken into consideration during this period of public policy-making, creating a participatory forum that served as a political arena for debate and action on homelessness.[9] The administration implemented important policies and initiatives, including the *Casas de Convivência*, multi-programmatic community centers that were managed in partnership with existing and established grassroots organizations. The city also formed a partnership with the Documentation and Communication Center for the Marginalized, which reorganized into Rede Rua in 1991. The entity is responsible for *O Trecheiro*, a newspaper published by and for the city's homeless population for the past thirty years. However, despite the many programs and policies enacted by this administration to aid the homeless, it was not able to enact broader laws to guarantee the legal protections of the city's homeless population.[10]

Today, the network of grassroots organizations dedicated to addressing homelessness also brings awareness to the systematic violations of human rights that unstably housed individuals continue to experience, particularly through the state's deployment of a repressive police apparatus. In Brazil, where there is sometimes an abyss between written laws and their rightful implementation, legislation meant to protect vulnerable groups has not always been successful at doing so. The Bill for the Protection of Homeless People (Lei de Atenção à População em Situação de Rua), for example, was considered an important legal achievement when it was enacted in 2001, but, in reality, it did not provide sufficient guarantees or protections for individuals. In August 2004, only a few years after the signing of the bill, a massacre in Praça da Sé, the main plaza in central São Paulo charged with symbolic and historical meaning, led to the deaths of seven homeless people at the hands of the military police. The massacre, and the failure to prosecute those responsible, triggered a massive outcry from homeless rights groups, who ultimately declared August 19 the National Day of the Fight for the Homeless.[11]

Homelessness became an issue of national prominence during the Lula administration (Partido dos Trabalhadores, PT). Lula's government initiated and implemented several measures to address the homelessness crisis, including administrating the first national census of the homeless population, providing the country with technical and demographic data to better develop policies aimed at this segment of the population. In 2009, the government

Street in "Cracolândia," an area near Luz central train station, where the conflation and complex entanglement of crack cocaine users and homeless people in urban space is visible.

promulgated the National Policy for the Inclusion of Homeless People, which established a committee to monitor and assess the policy's effective implementation.[12] Recognizing that popular participation is an essential pillar for the development of public policies to address homelessness, the Fernando Haddad administration founded the Comitê Pop.Rua (Homeless Population Committee) in 2013, which utilizes a participatory model to develop and evaluate homelessness policies at the municipal level. But while the state's homeless aid apparatus and its legal framework have consolidated over the past four decades, the issue of homelessness still seems to be at the mercy of fluctuating political orientations, subject to the interests, priorities, and ideologies of changing right- and left-wing administrations.

Alongside the growing presence of homelessness in the national political discourse, the dawn of the twenty-first century deepened historically rooted prejudices and public perceptions, bringing forth new stereotypes of this sector of the population. For one part, since the drug's popularization in the early 2000s, people experiencing homelessness have been increasingly conflated with users of crack cocaine. This conflation has also served to justify the criminalization of homelessness, engendering hygienist policies that allow for the deployment of police repression against "undesirable" populations. The main stage of this conflict is Cracolândia, an area surrounding Estação da Luz, the central train station,

which has been the target of successive attempts at dispersion over the past twenty years.[13] It is worth noting that, although people experiencing homelessness are present all over the city, almost half live in the Sé sub-prefecture (45.4 percent, according to official 2019 data), where Cracolândia is located. Even more alarming is the fact that 60 percent of all rough sleepers, unsheltered homeless individuals who sleep on the street, are also concentrated in this area.[14]

Tensions in the central city have deepened over the last decade, due to the proliferation of public-private partnerships that aim to rebrand the Luz district as a cultural and business hub, in accordance with the neoliberal global playbook of large-scale urban "revitalization" projects. It would not be an overstatement to say that the district is a symbolic—and many times a literal—battlefield. While the neighborhood may be home to elite cultural institutions that help cement São Paulo's image as a global capital, Luz is also located next to the greatest concentration of homeless people in the city and is often the target of police operations.[15] As with many Latin American cities, this phenomenon cannot be simply categorized as a case of gentrification in its classical terms, as the area was never truly abandoned and still retains its popular, working-class character.[16] This supposedly necessary reclamation of the central city by real-estate developers and other market agents flanked by the state illustrates the escalating process of financialization in the city, which

Asdrúbal do Nascimento II housing complex. Located near Praça da Sé, it offers thirty-four units based on the Housing First model, providing affordable, rent-controlled housing in retrofitted, formerly vacant, or underutilized buildings.

aims to frame São Paulo as a global metropolis, weaving an interlaced ideological narrative marked by racism and conservative "moral standards" that supports the extremely profound violations of the bodies that inhabit the streets.

Toward a New Agency: Notes on Architecture and Homelessness in São Paulo

What is the role of the architecture profession when it comes to finding solutions to the many issues surrounding homelessness? In Brazil, and particularly in São Paulo, the right to property seems to have overridden the right to live, making it imperative that we approach the crisis of homelessness from a multidisciplinary standpoint that rethinks the role of the architect and relies on the development of non-alienating design practices. It is pressing that the profession go through a period of reflection in order to truly understand the privileged position of architectural praxis, particularly in the context of Brazil's modernization process, during which a significant portion of the homeless population actually served as part of the country's construction workforce,[17] playing an integral role in the creation of the society that now excludes them. New forms of agency will require a better understanding of both the limits and potential opportunities of the architectural discipline. So long as architectural production continues to reproduce the precariousness of life in its own processes, it will never be truly inclusive or democratic—from the design process to the construction site.[18]

In Brazil, being able to comprehend, critique, and propose policies aimed at the provision of housing is considered an integral part of architectural pedagogy. This requisite has become even more urgent as the country comes face to face with its housing issues. Another vital locus of action for housing policy can be found in insurgent practices, as exemplified by the many organizations that advocate for universal housing rights, squatting rights, the re-urbanization of favelas, mutirões (joint community construction efforts), and other bottom-up initiatives. In the 1990s and early 2000s, in response to the growing number of vacant properties in the central city and in the wake of the pioneering initiatives of tenement residents, it was these organizers who advocated for the formalization of São Paulo's downtown squats.[19] While the relationship between squatters' rights and the rights of the homeless is complex and full of tensions,[20] the advocacy efforts of both groups rely on questioning and inverting the current logic of the housing system. In a city of São Paulo's scale—where two-hour work commutes are not uncommon and where health-care, educational, and cultural facilities are unevenly distributed—sociospatial segregation is accentuated by the construction of housing complexes at the periphery. Sleeping on the streets, squatting on an empty property in the center of the city, and living in a favela or housing complex on the fringes of the city ultimately represent different forms of housing insecurity in São Paulo's spectrum of vulnerability, a gradient of conditions involving multiple networks of sociability and influenced by several specific factors.

The need to acknowledge complexity is demonstrated in the fact that, in São Paulo, there is not a direct relationship between evictions and homelessness; according to the 2019 census, 41 percent of individuals experiencing homelessness claimed that their housing instability stemmed from family conflicts, as compared to only 13 percent who cited evictions as the primary cause. This situation is quite different from what appears to be the general rule in countries such as the United States, where these phenomena seem to have a more direct correlation.[21] In São Paulo, homelessness is not a housing problem, or, at least, it is not exclusively a housing problem. The lack of affordable housing in the city is not the primary cause of the crisis, meaning that the provision of housing is not necessarily the only solution. Likewise, when analyzing the historical processes that shaped homelessness in Brazil, it is not sufficient to merely frame the homeless population as a group that has been overlooked by social housing policies and that has thus far been excluded from the real-estate market.

Despite the impressive housing provision programs implemented by the government over the past years (the Minha Casa Minha Vida program[22] being a prime example), the pathways of access to housing have not directly targeted people experiencing homelessness. Framing homelessness exclusively as a housing issue fails to address its inherent complexity, including how the condition is impacted by the disaggregating and destructuring processes promoted by Brazilian capitalism, or how the amalgam of precarious living conditions that can be found in the São Paulo metropolis can be acknowledged. These massive, state-subsidized housing projects, almost exclusively concentrated on the peripheries and based on the notion of private property, thus overlook a Brazilian society that is characterized by multifactorial socioeconomic vulnerability, where a vast number of people live on the verge of homelessness as a result of a complex set of factors caused by varied social disaggregation processes for which many times there is little to no protection.[23]

Rather than develop housing policies that simply provide houses, placing architecture as a heroic gesture that is capable of tackling profound social issues on its own, housing programs should be considered one of the many tools created to address sociospatial segregation and alleviate socioeconomic vulnerability, allowing for the development of an inter-sectoral approach that provides centrally located and rent-controlled housing as well as continued assistance—an approach where aid does not end with the handing over of a set of keys.[24]

To this end, in early 2019, São Paulo inaugurated a social rent pilot project specifically aimed at the city's homeless population, following discussions on the provision of affordable rents to the homeless that took place within the Comitê Pop.Rua. This program, based on the Housing First model, provides affordable, rent-controlled housing in retrofitted, formerly vacant, or underutilized buildings, targeting low-income families with up to three minimum wages per household, of which a maximum of 15 percent would be allocated to rent. The Asdrúbal do Nascimento II housing complex, located near Praça da Sé, offers thirty-four such units for a variety of family configurations.[25]

Exemplary collaborative work is also being conducted by the collective Co-Criança, formed by a group of young architects who focus their practice on establishing participatory design processes. At the Asdrúbal complex, the collective is working with residents in order to rethink the building's existing common areas, seeking to strengthen the bonds between tenants and their collective spaces. As is seen in their work, collaborative practices can implement architecture as a device to reinforce interpersonal relationships and enhance the subjective connections between residents and their shared spaces.

Participatory design methodologies could foster new possibilities for the architectural field, leveraging the interplay between architects and users to transform players into co-designers.[26] From this point of view, architectural praxis could come to occupy a proactive and collaborative role in the provision of solutions to the homelessness crisis, not by acting as an isolated discipline loaded down by paternalistic bias, but as one of many in a joint effort toward the active and ongoing construction of social justice.

1   Heitor Frúgoli Jr., *Centralidade em São Paulo: trajetórias, conflitos e negociações na metrópole* (São Paulo: Cortez; Edusp, 2000); Teresa Pires do Rio Caldeira, *Cidade de Muros: crime, segregação e cidadania em São Paulo* (São Paulo: Edusp, 2000); Flávio Villaça, "São Paulo: urban segregation and inequality," *Dossiê São Paulo, hoje - Instituto de Estudos Avançados da USP* 25, no. 71 (January–April 2011), pp. 37–58.

2   Luciano Oliveira, "Circulação e fixação: o dispositivo de gerenciamento dos moradores de rua em São Carlos e a emergência de uma população" (PhD diss., Graduate Program in Sociology at UFSCar, São Carlos, 2013); Daniel De Lucca, "A Rua em Movimento: experiências urbanas e jogos sociais em torno da população de rua" (PhD diss., FFLCH, University of São Paulo, 2007).

3   Joana da Silva Barros, "Moradores de rua, pobreza e trabalho: interrogações sobre a exceção e a experiência política brasileira" (PhD diss., FFLCH, University of São Paulo, 2004), p. 22.

4   De Lucca, "A Rua em Movimento," pp. 115–25.

5   For the lumpenproletariat, see Igor Martins Medeiros Robaina, "Entre mobilidade e per-manências: uma análise das espacialidades cotidianas da população em situação de rua na área central da cidade do Rio de Janeiro" (PhD diss., Dep. de Geografia, Federal University of Rio de Janeiro, 2015), p. 26.

6   The OAF is a religious entity founded in 1958. Historically, many of the central actors advo-cating for the homeless in São Paulo were religious leaders who worked closely with vulnerable populations. See De Lucca, "A Rua em Movimento," pp. 43–114; Barros, "Moradores de rua, pobreza e trabalho," p. 17.

7   Liberation Theology was a social and ecclesi-astical movement that emerged from a pro-gressive sector of the Catholic Church in the 1960s. They proposed a critical analysis of social reality and fought for the poor and other oppressed populations. See Michael Löwy, *O que é cristianismo de libertação: religião e política na América Latina* (São Paulo: Fundação Perseu Abramo / Expressão Popular, 2016). Paulo Freire (1921–1997) was a Brazilian educator, philosopher, and leading advocate of critical pedagogy. He is best known for his work *Pedagogy of the Oppressed*.

8   There are no accurate translations into English for the Portuguese term *pessoa em situação de rua* because its meaning is dependent on the differentiation between the verbs *ser* and *estar*—"to be" in a permanent, existential sense and "to be" in a certain moment in time. In our opinion, this nuanced temporal differ-entiation indicates that living on the streets is not a timeless, permanent condition, but a circumstance that can be overcome. See Barros, "Moradores de rua, pobreza e trabalho," pp. 14–16.

9   The Forum Coordenador dos Trabalhos, for example, created by the Social Welfare Secretary, brought together different entities, such as the OAF, the Gaspar Garcia Center for Human Rights, and the Comunidade dos Sofredores de Rua, among others. One of its

most significant achievements was commissioning the first-ever censual report of the city's homeless population in 1991. See De Lucca, "A Rua em Movimento," pp. 115–35.

10 Rede Rua is a ground-up organization whose mission is to establish a network of relationships between the homeless population and other entities. See De Lucca, "A Rua em Movimento," pp. 88–92. See also Maria Antonieta da Costa Vieira, Eneida Maria Ramos Bezerra, and Cleisa Moreno Maffei Rosa, *População de rua: quem é, como vive, como é vista* (São Paulo: Hucitec, 1994).

11 After the massacre, August 19 became a day of public demonstrations for justice and reparations. See De Lucca, "A Rua em Movimento," pp. 124 and 135–37.

12 The committee created by the national policy is called the Comitê Intersecretarial de Acompanhamento e Monitoramento da Política Nacional para População em Situação de Rua (CIAMP Rua).

13 According to the country's Homeless Population Census (2019), 18.9 percent of the homeless population uses crack regularly. See also Taniele Rui, "Fluxos de uma territorialidade: duas décadas de 'cracolândia' (1995–2014)," in *Pluralidade urbana em São Paulo: vulnerabilidade, marginalidade, ativismos,* ed. Lúcio Kowarick and Heitor Frúgoli Jr. (São Paulo: Editora 34, 2016), p. 237.

14 Prefeitura do Município de São Paulo, *Pesquisa Censitária da População em Situação de Rua* (São Paulo, 2020), p. 9.

15 Diane Helena, "A guerra dos lugares nas ocupações de edifícios abandonados no centro de São Paulo" (PhD diss., Faculty of Architecture and Urbanism, University of São Paulo, 2009), p. 99; Heitor Frúgoli Jr., *Centralidade em São Paulo: trajetórias, conflitos e negociações na metrópole* (São Paulo: Cortez; Edusp, 2000), pp. 72–73.

16 Heitor Frúgoli Jr. and Jessica Sklair, "O bairro da Luz em São Paulo: questões antropológicas sobre o fenômeno da gentrification," *Cuadernos de Antropología Social* 30 (2009), pp. 119–36, esp. pp. 122–32; Heitor Frúgoli Jr., "Territorialidades e redes na região da Luz," in Kowarick and Frúgoli Jr., *Pluralidade urbana em São Paulo,* pp. 249–71.

17 The 18.9 percent of people interviewed during the 2019 Homeless Population Census noted that they were unemployed construction workers, the highest percentage category (2019 Census). The historical connection between homelessness and construction work was discussed by Luiz Kohara during an interview with the authors on March 18, 2021.

18 Sérgio Ferro, *Arquitetura e trabalho livre* (São Paulo: Cosac Naify, 2006).

19 Ana Gabriela Akaishi, "O 'problema' do centro de São Paulo não está nas ocupações de prédios vazios, mas nos prédios vazios em si," *Cidades para que(m)?* (May 24, 2019); Helena, "A guerra dos lugares"; Bárbara Mühle, "Ocupações de Moradia no Centro: possibilidades do morar" (master's thesis, Faculty of Architecture and Urbanism, University of São Paulo, 2020).

20 As proposed by both Giulia Patitucci, coordinator of public policy for the homeless at the Municipal Secretariat of Human Rights and Citizenship, and Luiz Kohara, founder and researcher at the Gaspar Garcia Center for Human Rights, during interviews with the authors conducted on March 13, 2021, and March 18, 2021, respectively.

21 This difference was discussed by Karina Leitão, an urban planning professor in the Faculty of Architecture and Urbanism, University of São Paulo, during a research interview conducted on March 11, 2021. The data is corroborated by Brazil's latest Homeless Population Census (2019). See Prefeitura do Município de São Paulo, *Pesquisa Amostral da População em Situação de Rua* (São Paulo, 2020), p. 22.

22 Minha Casa Minha Vida is a social housing program created by the federal government in 2009 under the Lula administration.

23 Robaina, "Entre mobilidade e permanências," pp. 39–41.

24 As proposed by Luiz Kohara, founder and researcher at the Gaspar Garcia Center for Human Rights, during an interview with the authors conducted on March 18, 2021.

25 It is important to highlight, however, that this pilot project is not a Housing First program in the strict sense, as the pathways to access, as well as the program's target audience, are based on assumptions established by the São Paulo City Social Rent Program, which was launched in 2002. See Prefeitura do Município de São Paulo, *Relatório II* (São Paulo, 2020), p. 2; Camila D'Ottaviano, *Política habitacional no Brasil e Programa de Locação Social paulistano* (Cad. CRH, Salvador, 2014), pp. 255–66.

26 Research interview with Anna Ayumy Pompéia, Beatriz Martinez, Camila Sawaia, Camila Audrey, members of Coletivo Co-Criança, conducted on March 18, 2021.

Moscow

Population
1990: 8.94 million
2000: 10.02 million
2010: 10.56 million
2020: 12.67 million
2021: 12.65 million

Population of People Experiencing Homelessness
1990: no data
2000: no data
2010: 6,067
2017: 14,945
2018: 30,000
2020: 14,000 (official) / 20,000–150,000 (unofficial)

How many people in the city are considered to be living below the poverty line by local standards?
1995: 19.2%
2000: 23.6%
2010: 10%
2020: 6.3%

Unemployment Rates
No data

Ownership Rate / Rental Rate in the Housing Market
These terms can hardly be applied in the Russian context, and numbers barely reflect the reality of the housing situation. Land in Russia has never been fully privatized, and Moscow is the city that has the majority of what has been privatized. Practically all housing in Moscow (almost exclusively multistory tenant buildings) can be considered social housing.

There are currently

68,946 families on the list

for free accommodations designated

for low-income people in Moscow,
but only **3,600** families

could be housed in 2019.

Average Buying Price per Square Meter in 2020

13,500 RUB (€157) in "New Moscow" (recently annexed territories)

240,000 RUB (€2,790) in "Old Moscow"

Average Monthly Salary and Minimum Monthly Salary in 2020

Average monthly salary: 91,420 RUB (€1,063)

Average minimum monthly salary: 20,361 RUB (€237)

Sources, see p. 270

Homelessness in Moscow: Between Negation and Civic Initiatives

Tatiana Efrussi

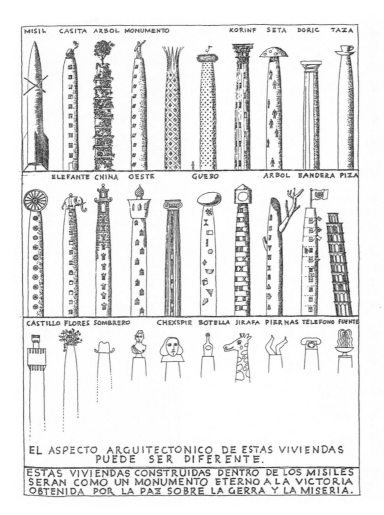

Sergei Barkhin, *Housing for Homeless People,* 1987, paper, ink, four sheets, 42 × 30 cm each

Searching for Soviet or Russian architecture projects that address homelessness yields surprisingly few results. One of the earliest is Sergei Barkhin's 1987 proposal "Housing for Homeless People," originally a submission to a competition organized by UNESCO. An example of the late Soviet Paper Architecture movement,[1] the conceptual project imagines a timely and global solution to homelessness: with the end of the Cold War and the disarmament of world powers in sight, missiles could be adapted into skyscrapers to house people experiencing homelessness.

While Barkhin's project responded to broad geopolitical changes, it nonetheless seems detached from the social realities of the Soviet Union, where homelessness, considered a consequence of capitalism, was not officially recognized as a local concern. Several measures also rendered invisible the condition. Land belonged to the state, which allegedly provided all working citizens with housing. Since 1932, *propiska*, a system of compulsory registration, had controlled access to benefits and tied together work, housing, and movement. Furthermore, in 1961, the USSR criminalized "parasitism" (*tuneiadstvo*), or long-term unemployment, along with vagrancy and panhandling. In 1967, the state also introduced labor treatment centers (LTPs), where individuals suffering from addictions were detained.

However, homelessness did, in fact, exist in the Soviet Union, spurred by criminal sentences that led convicts to lose housing,[2] by mental health issues, and by interfamilial conflicts, which often became intolerable in extremely dense living conditions.[3] The downfall of the Soviet Union in 1991 provoked a profound economic and social crisis, dismantling the state's welfare system. It also brought a new wave of homelessness that could not be hidden away, with no mechanisms in place to prevent it.

Today, homelessness is a low-priority issue for Russian officials and legislators, to the point that a law meant to address the issue, first drafted in 2000, has yet to be finalized.[4] Moreover, an official term for the condition does not even exist. Some institutions, like the Moscow shelter system, use the term *bomzh*, an acronym for *Bez Opredelennogo Mesta Zhitel'stva* (without a specific place of residence), which was first used by Soviet policemen in the 1970s to refer to people who were not registered at a permanent address.[5] While the term might seem neutral, it has become highly derogatory, acquiring a meaning similar to "dirty drunkard with lice" and replacing all other colloquial designations.[6] Its usage by government agencies demonstrates their disregard toward the homeless population in general. Furthermore, the term, which is historically tied to the *propiska* system, hardly describes homelessness today. Hundreds of thousands of people move to Moscow from other regions and do not bother to become formally registered until, for example, they have children that need to be placed in the school system. Violators of registration laws are not persecuted—and most can hardly be called homeless.

Homelessness, of course, does exist in Moscow, which, with a population of 12 million, is the largest city in Europe, let alone Russia. Many of the city's homeless population are men aged thirty-five to forty, who come to the capital in search of work, become victims of predatory employers, and are unable to return home due to lack of funds or the shame of failure. The second largest group, which includes men and women of all ages, experience housing instability as a result of interfamilial conflict. Another 15 to 20 percent fall prey to fraudulent real-estate transactions. These victims are often the elderly, orphanage graduates, or simply people who are not well versed in financial and legal matters.[7]

While the Moscow Department of Labor and Social Protection registers the city's homeless population as 14,000, homeless aid organizations estimate the actual number to be between 20,000 and 150,000. Under the pressure of these nonprofits, the Department of Labor and Social Protection has undertaken several important initiatives aimed at the city's homeless population. In 2009, the city launched a municipal "social patrol" van that searches for unsheltered individuals and provides them with medical care and rides to the city's official shelter located in the far-off Lyublino district. This initiative is of crucial importance during Moscow's winter months: while 1,223 homeless people froze to death during the winter of 2002, only 11 unsheltered individuals met that fate in 2017.[8]

The social patrol, however, only provides an immediate emergency service; the city still lacks long-term programs aimed at ameliorating homelessness. Moreover, Moscow's official shelter, which has a capacity of about 400 beds, can only host a (sober) person for a single night. Only proven Muscovites (or former Muscovites) have the right to stay in shelters for longer and can gain access to medical and social assistance. Even so, assembling the necessary paperwork is a tremendous hurdle for an unsheltered person. This condition deprives the majority of people who experience homelessness in Moscow from accessing aid.

The Russian government fails to address the issue of homelessness, in part because the state has not reassessed its attitude toward homelessness since the fall of the Soviet Union. However, the government is sometimes willing to provide funding, such as in 2020, when the

Ministry of Labor and Social Protection distributed grants totaling 220,000 euros to five homeless aid nonprofits.[9] During the coronavirus crisis, it was the nonprofit Dom Druzei, and not Moscow's municipal government, that rented hostels to provide homeless people with shelter during lockdown.[10] While the Moscow shelter system organized medical assistance and transportation to the hostels, they did not offer extra beds, nor did the city help finance the rental rooms.

Nonprofit organizations, however, cannot make large-scale investments in the provision of housing. In 2019, the nonprofit Caritas launched a housing program for the homeless, but the initiative was only able to house thirty individuals.[11] Meanwhile, millions of square meters of housing are currently being built in the city, with officials proudly declaring that Moscow is building faster than ever before, even surpassing the construction boom of the 1960s following Nikita Khrushchev's call for solving the housing crisis.[12]

Housing construction is happening at full speed, yet people still suffer from homelessness. How can we explain this paradox? Land in Russia has never been fully privatized, and most land in Moscow is actually city owned.[13] After 1991, property laws simply translated into new language the existing practices of compulsory registration at the municipal level—now these apartments could be sold, bought, and inherited. The privatization process was free for individual units, and today owners of these units pay only utility and maintenance charges.[14] This extremely privileged situation has a reverse side: only a tiny proportion of social housing is allocated by the city, limited to very specific categories of Moscow residents who usually spend years waiting for accommodations. Homeless people are not even listed in the categories of people who are eligible for municipal social housing. This extremely inflexible attitude to the housing question ignores the fact that real-estate prices are extremely high.[15]

Homelessness in Moscow is, in part, conditioned by certain engrained Soviet attitudes, including the negation and criminalization of homelessness and the rigidness of the Russian housing system. The crisis, however, is also aggravated by the city's current prospering economy. But how, then, do individuals at risk of homelessness find shelter? One productive way through which to examine homelessness and housing instability in Moscow is through the lens of work.

Experiencing and Dealing with Homelessness in Moscow: Work as Reason, Exploitation, Salvation, and Solution

1. Work as a Reason to Migrate to Moscow

Russian migrant laborers constitute the group that is most at risk of experiencing homelessness in Moscow. Unlike much of the rest of the country, the capital has a very low unemployment rate and is in constant need of unskilled workers, drawing migrants from the rest of the country and beyond. While the city's budget has steadily increased over the past ten years, representing one third of the national budget,[16] these funds are primarily directed toward improving the city's urban fabric rather than developing social infrastructure.[17] Through the city's My Street program, for example, the city invested a total of €2 billion from 2015 to 2018 to carry out street renovations. The city has also launched Renovatsia (Renovation), a densification program that replaces Soviet-era, low-rise prefabricated buildings with taller, contemporary structures. Construction sites are literally on every corner of the capital, attracting floods of migrant workers. According to experts, however, it is mostly national migrants who become the victims of homelessness, often after experiencing complications that crush their hopes of making a new life in the city.[18]

As Moscow undergoes these urban renovations, we find increasingly fewer public spaces that people experiencing homelessness can inhabit. Alongside built environment improvements, the city also boasts brand new examples of hostile design, including bus stops featuring benches that prevent people from lying down. Similarly, in preparation for the 2018 FIFA World Cup, an official shelter, strategically located in the city center behind three train stations, was moved next to the city's main shelter in distant Lyublino. Despite petitions, the shelter was not relocated to its original site after the games. And while nonprofits and volunteers continue to distribute food there, they do so without any legal protections.[19]

2. Work as Exploitation

Despite these measures to render homelessness invisible, vulnerability is still present on Moscow's streets. Every other lamp pole is plastered in advertisements:

WORK. Free accommodation and food, cigarettes, daily salary.
For citizens of Russia and Belarus.

"Smart" bus stop in Moscow with its unwelcoming design in order to keep people from staying, 2021

An example of an illegal workhouse advertisement on the streets of Moscow

An adjoined phone number directs inquiries to a workhouse. Today, workhouses usually take the form of an apartment or a country house in the suburbs where individuals receive room and board in exchange for part of their salary. People who live in workhouses are hired mostly as construction workers or loaders—jobs that offer no contracts, no benefits, no protection, and no security. Workhouses are also frequently run by former criminals, who often confiscate identification papers and beat people for misconduct or for attempting to leave. Typically, advertisements are addressed to citizens of Russia or Belarus[20] because hiring illegal foreign workers is a punishable offense.

Workhouses function in an economic and legal gray zone. According to the nonprofit Alternative, which works to liberate people from different forms of slavery, over the past seven years or so, workhouses have proliferated across all of Russia's larger cities. Daria Baibakova, director of the Moscow branch of Nochlezhka, the oldest nonprofit organization in the country that works to aid the homeless, estimates that between one in two or one in three of their clients have experienced the trauma of living in a workhouse.[21] Emelian Sosinskiy, head of the Noah Labor Commune, estimates that there are between several hundred to 1,500 workhouses in the Moscow region, each of them housing between ten and forty people. If these numbers are correct, it could mean that several tens of thousands of individuals have been roped into these schemes.

3. Work as Salvation

Apart from criminal workhouses, Moscow is also home to religious workhouses. Sosinskiy is the founder of one of the first of these: the Noah Labor Commune, which was established in 2011. Inspired by nineteenth-century labor communes, his homes aim to help individuals overcome their addictions and repent their "parasitism" through discipline and labor.[22] Religious workhouses function similarly to their "commercial" counterparts—and both are technically illegal—but boarders can come and leave as they please, so long as they follow strict behavioral rules. At the Noah Labor Commune, it is the boarders themselves who find employment options by taking advantage of their networks.

In 2021, Sosinskiy's organization provided shelter to 1,050 people across seventeen houses in the Moscow region.[23] Only 40 percent are employed, supporting the remaining 60 percent who are too old or are otherwise physically unable to work. Sosinskiy claims that his brigades, and others like his, have worked on all of Moscow's major construction sites, from street renovations to the prestigious Zaryadye Park by Diller Scofidio + Renfro and George Hargreaves.[24] During the pandemic, as the city's foreign migrant worker population decreased by 40 percent, the demand for unskilled laborers increased substantially. 2021 was actually the first year in which Sosinskiy's boarders were able to find work during the traditionally "dead" winter months, when construction usually stops due to inclement weather.

One of many residential complexes recently built in Moscow, 2021

4. Work as a Solution

In the absence of any other systematic approach to addressing homelessness in Russia, the government chooses to tolerate the existence of the workhouses. (Sosinskiy also claims that criminal workhouses pay their share to corrupt government officials).[25] But perhaps the very idea of a workhouse as a place where people experiencing homelessness are removed from public view also appeals to authorities. After all, even Sosinskiy's model is based on the assumption that people who are unstably housed are inherently different from the rest of society.[26] Although religious ideology serves as the foundation for the Noah Labor Commune, it is hard not to be reminded of Soviet-era attitudes toward homelessness.

The legacy of the Soviet conception of homelessness haunts Russian policymakers to this day. Today, we even see signs of a return of the belief in the "reforming powers" of labor. In 2019, a member of parliament, former Chief Sanitary Inspector Gennadiy Onishchenko, proposed the reintroduction of Soviet-era LTPs, punitive labor treatment centers for addicts that still exist in Belarus. And during the spring of 2021, as a result of the decrease in foreign migrants, lawmakers floated the idea of deploying the forced labor of convicts at construction sites.

As workers flee the peripheries to find employment in larger cities—first and foremost in the capital—many face housing instability. While authorities remain passive in the face of their plight, unstably housed migrant workers risk falling prey to criminal workhouses, which are integrated into Moscow's shadow economy. And while nonprofit religious organizations provide similar services, these total institutions are not a suitable alternative for individuals who wish to find their own independent housing. Soviet-style measures that inculpate unsheltered people and force them to work do not serve this aim either. Clearly, only a revision of economic and social policy at the national level can fundamentally change the situation.

1 The term "Paper Architecture" was coined by Yuri Avvakumov in 1984. The movement served as a form of protest against the de-humanizing nature of the concrete, mass housing that constituted Russian architecture at the time. Yuri Avvakumov, *Bumazhnaya Arkhitektura: Antologiya / Paper Architecture: An Anthology* (Moscow: Garage, 2021).

2 After arrest, ex-convicts would often lose their *propiska,* thus losing their access to housing. This discriminatory law was not abolished until 1995. See E. Kovalenko and E. Strokova, *Bezdomnost: Est li Vyhod?* (Moscow: Institut Ekonomiki Goroda, 2013), pp. 96–98.

3 As the sociologist Tova Höjdestrand explains, "... dense living remained the rule; to this day, despite the sanitary norm, even single-family apartments tend to imply collective living since two or more generations of one family (including different branches of lateral kin such as siblings with families of their own) are often crowded together in one apartment." Tova Höjdestrand, *Needed by Nobody: Home-lessness and Humanness in Post-Socialist Russia* (Ithaca, NY: Cornell University Press, 2009), p. 32.

4 Ibid., pp. 39–40.

5 Svetlana Stephenson, *Bezdomnye v sotsial' noi strukture bol' shogo goroda* (Moscow: INION RAN, 1997), p. 8.

6 Höjdestrand, *Needed by Nobody,* p. 9.

7 Estimates provided by nonprofit organizations cited in Daria Litvinova and Anna Romshchenko, "Ia – bezdomny: kak v Moskve ustroena zhizn' tekh, komu nekuda poitii," *Coda.ru,* January 29, 2019, http://codaru.com/war-on-reason/bezdomny/ (all URLs accessed in August 2021).

8 Andrei Pentiukhov, head of the Moscow Department of Labor and Social Protection, to RIA News Agency: "Smertnost' bezdomnykh ot kholoda sokratilas' v Moskve v 10 raz za 8 let," RIA Novosti, February 21, 2011, https://ria.ru/20110221/336987369.html.

9 Dmitrii Bezuglov, Artem Beresnev, Maria Makarova, Nikita Malolkin, and Julia Senina, "Putting a figure on the cost of homelessness in Russia, and discussing ways to collect reliable data in the future," Oxford Russia Scholarship student project, March 15, 2021, pp. 16–17.

10 "Hostely dlja vsekh bezdomnykh v Moskve na vremja karantina oplachivajut blagotvoriteli," *Miloserdie.ru,* April 25, 2020, https://www.miloserdie.ru/news/blagotvoriteli-oplachivayut-hostely-dlya-vseh-bezdomnyh-v-moskve-na-vremya-karantina/.

11 Nadezhda Klueva, head of Caritas Homeless Services, "Housing First v Moskve: Sociologi-cheskoe issledovanie nuzhd, zhelanij i idej bezdomnykh lyudej," presentation at the Annual International Conference on Homelessness organized by the NGO called Nochlezhka, Moscow, October 28–29, 2019, https://www.youtube.com/watch?v=7BLUcTkddek.

12 Ignat Bushukhin, "'Stol'ko v Moskve ne stroili nikogda': itogi Stroikompleksa 2019 goda," *RBK.Nedvizhimost,* December 27, 2019, https://realty.rbc.ru/news/5e05bf029a7947d58ee47d1b.

13 United Nations Economic Commission for Europe, "Country Profiles on the Housing Sector: Russian Federation," United Nations, 2004, pp. 97–104.

14 Yuliya Sudakova, "Skol'ko stoyat uslugi ZhKH v raznykh stranakh?," CIAN, July 16, 2019, https://www.cian.ru/stati-skolko-stojat-uslugi-zhkh-v-raznyh-stranah-294566/.

15 While the city's 2021 subsistence minimum was 224 euros, the cheapest rent for a one-bedroom apartment was estimated at 250 euros. Information published by the Moscow Department of Labor and Social Protection, https://dszn.ru/deyatelnost/Socialnye-vyplaty-i-posobiya/Prozhitochnyy-minimum-v-gorode-Moskve; see Ignat Bushukhin, "Rieltory nazvali srednuu stoimost' arendy zhil'ia v Moskve," RBC, January 20, 2020, https://realty.rbc.ru/news/5e25537a9a794760c311cc49.

16 Yulia Apuktina in collaboration Maria Abaku-lova, "Zolotaia moia: Reiting glavnykh benefit-siarov pokhoroshevshei Moskvy," *Proekt,* https://www.proekt.media/guide/moskva-sobyanina/.

17 Ibid.

18 Evgeni Varshaver, head of the Group for Mi-gration and Ethnicity Research at the Russian Presidential Academy for National Economy and Public Administration, confirmed via a personal email from April 8, 2021, that foreign migrant workers in Moscow have solid net-works of solidarity and try to leave in a critical situation—as proved by the coronavirus crisis. See also A. L. Rocheva, E. A. Varshaver, and N. S. Ivanova, "Vulnerable Groups in Disas-ters: Solidarity and Trust in Government as the Basis for Migrant Strategies in Russia During the COVID-19 Pandemic," *Monitoring of Public Opinion: Economic and Social Changes* 6 (2020), pp. 488–511.

19 Loretta Marie Perera, "A Moscow Homeless Shelter Moved to Accommodate the World Cup: One Year Later It Has Not Returned," *The Moscow Times,* June 27, 2019, https://www.themoscowtimes.com/2019/06/27/a-moscow-homeless-shelter-moved-to-accommodate-the-world-cup-a-year-later-it-has-not-returned-a66191.

20 The countries are bound by treaties to the Union State of Russia and Belarus.

21 Conversation with Daria Baibakova, Moscow, March 19, 2021.

22 See the Noah Labor Commune website, "Dom Trudolubiya Noi," https://dom-noi.ru.

23 Information published on the Noah Labor Commune website (ibid.).

24 Conversation with Emelian Sosinskiy, founder, Noah Labor Commune, March 25, 2021.

25 Ibid.

26 During his interview, Sosinskiy expressed his belief that his communes should function as permanent, lifelong shelters, where people marry, have children, and die. Conversation with Emelian Sosinskiy (ibid.).

Mumbai

Population
 1991: 9.9 million
 2001: 11.9 million
 2011: 12.4 million
 2020: 16 million

Population of People Experiencing Homelessness
 1991: no data
 2001: 39,074
 2011: 57,415
 2020: 11,915 (official) / 250,000 (unofficial)

How many people in the city are considered to be living below the poverty line by local standards?
 1998-99: 68,000
 2005-06: 2,500,000

Unemployment Rates (India)
 1999: 5.69%
 2000: 5.66%
 2010: 5.64%
 March 2020: 8%
 April 2020: 24%
 November 2020: 6.5%

In 2020, there were

2.12 million people
in Mumbai living
below the poverty line.

Ownership Rate / Rental Rate in the Housing Market (Maharashtra Region)
2019 housing vacancy rate: 15.3%
Ownership: 70%
Rental: 27%

Average Buying Price per Square Meter in 2020
2020: 198,278 INR (€2,299) per m²

Average Monthly Salary in 2020
2020 average monthly salary: 35,000 INR (€406)

Sources, see p. 270

Mumbai: Shifting the Paradigm to a Homelessness Vulnerability Spectrum

Aditya Sawant

Migrant workers waiting on a sidewalk in Mumbai

As per the city's most recent census, conducted in 2011, Mumbai has a total population of approximately 12.4 million people. Meanwhile, according to a survey conducted by the Municipal Corporation of Mumbai in 2019 and 2020, the city's total homeless population is about 12,000 people. However, nongovernmental organizations (NGOs) working with the homeless communities claim that the survey represents a severe undercounting of the population, estimating that the number could actually be as high as 250,000 people.[1] Though NGOs have questioned the efficiency of the methods used by the city to determine its homeless population, part of the undercount may also be due to the city's narrow definition of homelessness: in Mumbai which uses the definition provided by the census, an individual is officially defined as homeless "if they do not live in a census house, which refers to a 'structure with a roof.'"[2] But not every "structure with a roof" is able to provide a basic level of security and access to amenities. Furthermore, many of these structures, while technically homes under the city's definition, make the individuals who reside in them extremely vulnerable to housing instability and eviction. As such, Mumbai's official definition of homelessness does not account for the gradated vulnerabilities to which many of Mumbai's inhabitants are subject.

The term "home" is generally understood to refer to a physical space where a person can meet their basic needs and feel a sense of security. "Homelessness" can be defined as the absence of access to such a place. However, in Mumbai the idea of a home itself is a negotiated one, often requiring tradeoffs between factors such as employment opportunities, housing stability, living conditions, and access to amenities. To understand homelessness in Mumbai, we must therefore look beyond the binary of having a home versus being homeless. Here, individuals make or occupy different kinds of homes, each of which may come with its own set of risks and vulnerabilities, depending on the economic situation and political power of its inhabitants. In order to get a better understanding of homelessness in Mumbai, we must understand the condition as a spectrum of vulnerability.

The need to understand not just whether people have access to shelter but the risks associated with becoming shelter-less in Mumbai became increasingly urgent during the coronavirus pandemic. As the pandemic hit India in March 2020, a nation-wide lockdown was suddenly announced by Prime Minister Narendra Modi in order to reduce the speed of infection among the country's inhabitants. As it became clear that there was no end in sight to the lockdown, Mumbai began to see huge numbers of workers gather around the city's main railway stations and major exit points.[3] Referred to as "circular

migrants" by some experts, these workers had migrated from the rural hinterlands around Mumbai or from the less wealthy states of Bihar and Uttar Pradesh, located hundreds of kilometers away, in search of work opportunities in Mumbai's informal manufacturing or service sectors. While temporarily based in Mumbai, these transient workers do not set down permanent roots in the city and instead retain ties with their native villages where their families continue to live and where many of them return during the agricultural season to tend to their farmlands.

It is estimated that circular migrants could represent as many as 3 million people in Mumbai, most of whom find shelter accommodations in informal settlements or live in their workplaces—an informal factory, a shop or a restaurant, or even the taxis and rickshaws they drive through the city serve as their homes. Circular migrants are dependent on daily wages and have very little savings as they send most of their incomes to families back in their villages. Circular migrants also fall through the cracks of official census counts, as they are neither residents of the city with a permanent home address, nor are they technically "homeless," according to the city's official definition. However, their circumstances make them extremely vulnerable to changes in the city, as the pandemic made very clear. Not only did the sudden pause to all economic activities have a devastating effect on these transient workers, but their absence from any government database in Mumbai excluded them from accessing any emergency welfare benefits provided by the state.

Circular migrants are just one group of people on this "homelessness vulnerability spectrum," who are not officially recognized as homeless but are subject to extreme housing vulnerability and precariousness. The spectrum also includes communities living on hills that are prone to landslides during heavy monsoons, people living in low-lying areas that flood, and many who will be displaced with sea level rise and climate change. At times, the government itself also makes people homeless through eminent domain in order to build infrastructure projects, or otherwise fails to protect and provide aid to at-risk minorities like the transgender community. We must therefore ask, in a city like Mumbai, where about 40 percent of the population lives in high-risk, slum-like conditions, what does it really mean to be homeless? What should homelessness initiatives actually address? If it is solely a matter of providing shelter or adequate housing to individuals who are currently experiencing homelessness, what about the millions who are not on the street but are nonetheless living in very precarious and inadequate housing conditions?

An informal manufacturing unit in Mumbai

In Mumbai, we must redefine the paradigm of homelessness, taking into account the precariousness of living conditions as well as the vulnerability of individuals who access shelter. By doing so, we can understand housing instability in the city as a spectrum of gradated vulnerabilities and needs. By government standards, the city's existing homeless populations is, no doubt, the most vulnerable group in this spectrum and requires urgent support. However, addressing only the city's official definition of homelessness in a silo will not help a much larger but still extremely vulnerable sector of the population, one that, while not currently homeless, is at very high risk of becoming homeless at any moment.

Homelessness and the Image of the City

Under the direction of the Supreme Court of India, the Mumbai Municipal Corporation conducted a survey in 2019–20 to count the city's homeless population in order to determine the number of night shelters that needed to be constructed to adequately meet demand. It is only in recent years that the Supreme Court has started intervening and directing the government to provide shelters and other services to the country's homeless population.

And despite these recent rulings, many states still have in place anti-begging laws, giving authorities the power to arrest people simply for being homeless and detain them in detention centers. One of the ways in which the government deals with homelessness is through its criminalization. To understand the origins of this practice, we must take a historical approach, going back to the city's colonial period.

Mumbai's anti-begging laws have their origin in the European Vagrancy Act of 1869, which was enacted in the city when it was under British rule. The act received this name because it was meant to target the city's poor European population, a group that became more ubiquitous in the city following the takeover of the East India Company by the British Crown in 1857. The presence of these impoverished bodies on the streets of Mumbai challenged the self-declared premises of the racist colonial project and were perceived as a threat to the legitimacy of British rule in India. In order to quell this source of anxiety for the colonial state, it instituted the practice of rendering this group invisible, arresting and detaining poor European individuals in custodial institutions built far away from the city, with little or no contact with the outside world.

The unit acts as both working and living space for the migrant workers

The colonial state responded in a similar fashion following the Great Famine of 1876–78 and the Bombay (now Mumbai) plague epidemic of the late nineteenth century. Plague victims among the native populations of the city asking for alms and finding shelter on the streets, polluting public space in the colonial town, were perceived as a threat to the public health of residents in the European part of the city. These concerns were later materialized into the 1902 Police Act and subsequent anti-begging laws, which included within the definition of begging activities such as "singing, dancing, fortune telling, performing, or offering any article for sale."[4] The Bombay Beggars Act was first passed under colonial rule in 1945. Following Indian independence, the act was modified, reenacted, and finally passed on December 8, 1959, as the Bombay Prevention of Begging Act, which included the provision of "certified institutions" to confine beggars. From 1960 onward, each state began to bring in its own anti-begging laws. The first legal challenge to the law came in 2018, when the Delhi High Court struck it down as unconstitutional, leading to the decriminalization of begging in the state of Delhi. However, the decriminalization of homelessness has yet to be taken up by other Indian states and Mumbai's anti-begging laws are still in effect. But why has this colonial-era "solution" of criminalizing homelessness and holding them in detention centers persisted for well over seventy years after independence?

A homeless person's mere presence in the public realm ruptures the image of an ordered, well-functioning city or society. At the beginning of the British Raj, the European Vagrancy Act was enacted so as to not pollute the sanitized image of the colonial project perpetuated by the establishment. Perhaps the country's anti-begging laws have endured into the postcolonial period due to similar anxieties among the city's elites and middle classes. Today, the government, for example, routinely rounds up homeless individuals and relocates them to the periphery of the city, out of the public gaze, during important international events or visits from foreign heads of state. Meanwhile, local police forces announce drives to make Mumbai "beggar-free" as the government continues to increase the capacity of its homeless detention centers.[5] And beyond outcry from a few civil society organizations, these actions by the government evoke very little outrage from the general public. Even in the case of the provision of night shelters, the reforms are being pushed by the judiciary branch and not through local legislative bodies.

On the sidewalk: sleepers under their protective nets in Mumbai

Many dimensions of class, caste, and lack of political power account for this apathy for the homeless among most of the city's elites and middle classes. However, as urbanists it is also important to understand how the image of the modern Indian city that is projected by the state and the city's elites impacts how homelessness is perceived and addressed in Mumbai. In 2003, a nonprofit organization called Bombay First, in collaboration with the international consultancy firm McKinsey, developed a report called "Vision Mumbai," which was widely circulated and discussed. The report called for making Mumbai a "World-Class City" by the year 2013 and identified eight programs the city needed to implement in order to achieve this goal. The first order of business was to "Boost economic growth to 8–10 percent per annum by focusing on services, developing hinterland-based manufacturing and making Mumbai a consumption centre."[6]

Today, in the age of digitalization, the "world-class city" has been replaced by the "smart city."[7] While there is still no clear consensus on what exactly a smart city is, by and large the concept evokes a utopian idea where urban India's problems are preempted and solved through technological means like smart traffic and smart surveillance systems. Following the liberalization of the Indian economy in 1991, economic growth became an important imperative of every government, and cities and urbanization were seen as the primary engines to achieve economic growth and attract global investment. The paradigms of the world-class city and the smart city attempt to mold efficient, productive cities in the service of global capital.

But within each specific image of the city also lies an image of its ideal citizen. The citizen of the world-class city is primarily a tax-paying consumer, whereas, in the case of the smart city, they are a digitally savvy individual, someone who is connected to and participates in the internet economy. People experiencing homelessness have very little or no role in either one of these imaginary cityscapes. Following India's independence from colonial rule, the hegemonic image of the city has mostly catered to the middle classes and the elites, framing homeless people as illegitimate or criminals and rendering them invisible. In the case of other vulnerable groups of the city, it took a sustained lockdown in a pandemic for the state to become publicly cognizant of the millions of migrant workers that labor in the city but are not seen as citizens eligible for public services and with a right to access amenities. It is this exclusive and aesthetic image of the city that urbanists must challenge. India is set to more than double its habitable environment over the next two decades, with 70 percent of new construction taking place in urban areas.[8] The image of the city we create today can influence how just and inclusive the cities we build in the future can be.

1 Shruti Ganapatye, "Only 12,000 homeless in city, claims survey," *Mumbai Mirror,* March 5, 2020.

2 *Census of India,* Government of India, New Delhi, 2011.

3 Sahil Joshi, "Cops lathicharge migrants as thousands gather at Bandra Station to leave Mumbai, defy lockdown orders," *India Today,* April 14, 2020.

4 Manas Raturi, "Raj and the begging brawl: The colonial roots of India's anti-beggary laws echo even now," *The Leaflet,* June 27, 2018.

5 Lokmat English Desk, "Beggar Free Mumbai: Mumbai Police launches drive to make city 'begging free,'" *Lokmat English,* February 13, 2021.

6 Bombay First and McKinsey & Company, Inc., *Vision Mumbai,* Mumbai, September 2003, p. 1.

7 Vaibhav Maloo, "Smarter Cities Can Solve Most Problems," *Business World,* March 15, 2021.

8 International Energy Agency, *India Energy Outlook 2021* (Paris: IEA, February 2021).

Shanghai

Population
1990: 13.34 million
2000: 16.73 million
2010: 23.01 million
2021: 24.87 million

Population of People Experiencing Homelessness
1990: 2,668
2000: 3,347
2010: 4,603
2021: 4,974

How many people in the city are considered to be living below the poverty line by local standards?
People who received alms (低保) in 2019: 182,942 people (135,963 families)

Unemployment Rates
1990: 1.50%
2000: 3.50%
2010: 4.35%
2020: 3.67%

Ownership Rate / Rental Rate in the Housing Market
Ownership rate: 63.2%
Renters of housing in Shanghai: over 8,000,000

In 2015, approximately

30,000 individuals were rescued

by **official relief stations.**

Average Buying Price per Square Meter in 2020

75,700 CNY (€9,980) per m^2

Highest: Huangpu District: 131,200 CNY (€17,298) per m^2

Lowest: Chongming District: 20,200 CNY (€2,663) per m^2

Average Salary and Minimum Monthly Salary in 2020

2020 average annual income per individual: 124,056 CNY (€16,380)

2020 average monthly salary per individual: 10,338 CNY (€1,365)

2020 minimum monthly salary: 2,480 CNY (€327)

Sources, see p. 270

Where Are Shanghai's Homeless?
The Gentrification of the Visual

Zairong Xiang and Elena Vogman

The old and the new. Street view at Laoximen, Huangpu District, Shanghai, June 2021, from the *Disappearing* series by He You

In contrast to global metropolises like London, Paris, or New York, where people experiencing homelessness are visible in urban public spaces like train stations or parks, homeless individuals in Shanghai are not able to find even temporary refuge in public, due, in part, to increasing surveillance practices aimed at maintaining a certain aesthetic of the city that depicts it as progressive, civilized, and organized. However, the lack of visibility of homelessness in Shanghai is also the result of government assistance programs that effectively provide aid and shelter to people in need, thus removing homelessness from the streets.

In Shanghai, homelessness is included in the definition of three closely related but different terms, each representing a different lived reality of homelessness in the city. The term 生活无着人员 (shēnghuó wúzhuó rényuán) is used to describe people without a reliable income, who cannot afford to access basic needs, including housing. Meanwhile, 被收容人员 (bèi shoūróng rényuán) refers to people who find temporary accommodations in a state-run relief station, and 流浪人口 (liúlàng rénkǒu) denotes the city's "vagrant" population, who live on the streets but have not sought shelter at a relief station.

Beyond these terms, however, in order to gain a better sense of how homelessness is addressed in Shanghai—and China in general—it is necessary to become familiar with a system that is essential to population management and social structure in China: the hukou. It is a household registration system that identifies an individual as a resident of a certain area, determining whether they are eligible to receive state subsidies in a given location. Different scales of government deal with their own hukou-registered population and distribute subsidies accordingly. As such, hukou plays an essential role in the bureaucracy of state assistance, a process that is both top-down and localized. The system is particularly pertinent to understanding the country's ongoing poverty alleviation campaigns, along with the ways in which the state renders homelessness invisible in the urban landscape.

In addition to surveillance and hukou, a threefold institutional structure addresses homelessness in the state, allowing the condition to be rendered invisible. In 2003, the State Council of China released an administrative code referred to as the Measures for the Administration of Relief for Vagrants and Beggars without Assured Living Resources in Cities, which are implemented by different echelons of government at the provincial, city, and county levels. As part of the measure, relief stations (救助站, jiùzhù zhàn) have been constructed across the country, becoming an essential urban space for understanding the

current state of homelessness (or homeless-lessness) in Shanghai and in China at large. The main purpose of the city's relief stations, which replaced the old Detention and Repatriation Stations (收容遣送站, shoūróng qiǎnsòng zhàn), their aim being to compel people to return to their hukou-defined homes,[1] is to assist homeless people (mainly those without Shanghai hukou), providing them with temporary shelter, mental health support, and other services on a more or less voluntary basis. Relief stations receive direct funding from the state and are rarely backed by nonprofit organizations or are seldom open to cooperation.

Relief stations also continue to provide assistance for people to either return to their home (in the case of a hukou registration) or identify and find their next of kin, especially in the case of victims of human and child trafficking. Relief stations serve people experiencing homelessness, but they also aid other individuals in need of assistance, including tourists who have lost their wallets. People who seek refuge in relief stations can either receive assistance to return home, opting to permanently leave Shanghai, or to stay in Shanghai under the condition that they will not "negatively influence" the image of the city. These alternatives confirm our argument that the aesthetics of the city are integral in perpetuating the self-image of the city as a middle-class urban space.

Beyond the relief stations, the Shanghai Civil Affairs Bureau also runs social assistance centers and help centers, with each institution serving a slightly different function. While relief stations cater to the non-Shanghai domiciled population (without hukou), the latter two are exclusively reserved for Shanghai residents. Social assistance centers provide aid to targeted groups, such as low-income individuals and children with disabilities. They collaborate with nonprofit organizations and other institutions, such as mental health centers, to provide services, like helping with applications and distributing food and oil tickets. They are also in charge of connecting these individuals with their families and extended social networks. Meanwhile, help centers are social welfare organizations directly under the Social Affairs Bureau that work closely with social assistance centers and street committees to address the needs of the city's low-income population. They also provide medical help and medical insurance for populations in need who do not meet the requirements to be eligible for a low-income subsidy. Help centers also provide assistance for the low-income subsidy applications.

Shanghai government's low-income pension increases by 9 or 10 percent each year. While in 2009–10, the pension amounted to 425 yuan (€44.20) per month, by 2020

Quarter prepared for demolition, Laoximen, Huangpu District, Shanghai, June 2021, from the *Disappearing* series by He You

it had risen to 1,240 yuan (€156) per month. In 2020, the Shanghai government also implemented a new policy for low-income single households, which provides aid to individuals who are not eligible for the low-income policy. This includes people who do not have an income at all, or those who live with a disability or suffer from a serious illness.

The invisibility of homelessness in Shanghai is noteworthy for two reasons. On the one hand, it is impacted by the state-sanctioned gentrification of the inner city, which requires the state to protect a sanitized image of the city created and preserved for an idealized middle-class taste and sensibility. On the other hand, the state of homelessness in Shanghai is also the result of successful governance in terms of poverty alleviation and the provision of assistance for people in a state of economic and social need.

Shanghai:
China's Financial Capital without Homelessness

There are no homeless people in Shanghai. Even when we intentionally look for them, they are almost nowhere to be seen. One of China's—and also the world's—most expensive cities, Shanghai has made homelessness disappear from the landscape of its inner city. How is it that a social reality so integral to any developed economy, and one that is almost always glaringly visible, is nowhere to be seen in the forerunner of global financial capitalism of China, East Asia, and the world?

Shanghai is home to numerous state-run shelters across the city, which, according to official reports, do, in fact, attend to homeless people. Each year, the country's National Bureau of Statistics releases a population census on the number of persons without a reliable living income (生活无着人员, *shēnghuó wúzhuó rényuán*), a figure that stands in sharp contrast with what we can see on the streets of Shanghai.[2] Is it possible that China has solved the social problem of homelessness as a result of its economic development or poverty alleviation campaigns?[3]

Homelessness implicitly, and maybe paradoxically, reveals a phenomenological character: defined as lacking a home, this condition tends to manifest in public spaces—in parking lots, constructions sites, subway or train stations, streets, shopping mall entrances, and other places. As

Quarter prepared for demolition, Laoximen, Huangpu District, Shanghai, June 2021, from the *Disappearing* series by He You

such, homelessness is both a social and a visual phenomenon, one that is often associated with poverty. However, while poverty is a cause of homelessness, it is not the only one. And though it may be a significant cause, it is also and most likely the consequence of experiencing homelessness.

China's poverty alleviation campaign has been a primary concern of the country's communist-led central government since 2015. Central to the campaign were the goals to eradicate poverty and transition the country to a "moderately prosperous society" by 2020, which official reports claim have been met,[4] if slightly delayed by the outbreak of the coronavirus pandemic. Another visible success of the state's campaign against poverty can be seen in the orderly landscapes of China's cities. These cities portray an image of prosperity that is almost entirely devoid of people experiencing homelessness, who just some years ago could be regularly seen on the streets of cities large and small, including central Beijing, Shanghai, and Guangzhou. Starting in 2003, homeless individuals were increasingly brought to shelters across the city of Shanghai for temporary residence, after which they were sent back to their places of birth. The Chinese system of

hukou—household registration papers held by every Chinese citizen linking them to their birthplace—is a form of localized population governance. It was instrumental in implementing this strategy to reduce homelessness in China's cities.[5]

Our investigation, emerging from a primarily visual experience of Shanghai's homeless-lessness as its temporal and privileged dwellers, addresses the political implications behind the aesthetically pristine societal image that the Chinese state aims to construct and promote. We argue that the visual homeless-lessness of the city is symptomatic of the state's quest to create a "moderately prosperous" China, a term that is synonymous with "middle class." As such, the gentrification of the city is justified through the gentrification of the visual.

Consequentially, the question of the visual, of the aesthetic, can be understood as an essential concern in current Chinese policies directed toward homelessness, especially following the outbreak of Covid-19. These policies reinforce "traditional" measures of local population governance, achieved by means of increasingly pervasive surveillance and digital monitoring technologies, such as

A building prepared for demolition, Laoximen, Huangpu District, Shanghai, June 2021, from the *Disappearing* series by He You

Health Codes[6] and digital transactions, which go far beyond the *hukou.* They also actively promote an image of the city that is sterile and aseptic, an image that, in the time of the pandemic, addresses a collective rather than an individual perception. The individual becomes part of this new aseptic city landscape and is in advance deprived of any deviant behavior. It is interesting to note that the elimination of the virus and its potential ways of spread coincides with the elimination of cash money, which also affects the possibility of begging.[7]

The increased surveillance of public spaces and surfaces of contact contributes not only structurally but also aesthetically to the sterility of Shanghai, aiding in the deployment of an image exempt of homelessness, reserved for the urban middle class. In this context, the disappearance of homelessness must be approached not only as a symptom of economic prosperity and growth but also as a powerful medium: as an essential gentrification of the visual. This rendering invisible of homelessness can be regarded as a part of another big-scale mediation project: an architectonic utopia of Shanghai emblematically embodied in the famous city skyline or in the Shanghai Tower.[8] It offers an image of the future available in the present. The completion of the 1990 initiated construction of Pudong District is only one part of this glorious architectonic ensemble. Visitors of the historical waterfront area facing Pudong, the Bund, contemplate in the evenings a nearly cinematic mass spectacle of animated light show, projected on Shanghai's skyscrapers. Another notable example is the demolition of the West Gate (Laoximen) District—a historical part of the city where the former French Concession once met the districts of the nineteenth-century opium trade and prostitution—which will soon be replaced by skyscrapers and gated private compounds. This is just another paradigmatic metamorphosis of Shanghai which overcomes homelessness like many other remnants of the past.

1   Before the decree "Measures for the Administration of Relief for Vagrants and Beggars without Assured Living Resources in Cities" was issued, in March 2003 a college student named Sun Zhigang was brutally beaten to death in a Detention and Repatriation Center in Guangzhou, which spurred nationwide protests against the brutality of coercive detention and repatriation laws in general. These laws can be dated back to the 1990s, when Detention and Repatriation Stations were established to coercively send homeless people back to their original home, where one's *hukou* is registered. The city of Shanghai for example, built these stations in rural suburbia and in the neighboring Jiangsu Province to receive homeless people (1) with a record of being repatriated, (2) who have a record of minor law infractions, (3) who lie about their *hukou* identification information, making repatriation difficult, or (4) whose *hukou* were in far-away provinces such as Yunnan, Guizhou, Sichuan, or Xinjiang because it took a long time to send them back.

2   During the second quarter of the year 2021 alone, for example, 2,280 people in "extreme poverty" and 4,322 people "without reliable life support" in the city of Shanghai were offered help, according to the statistics published on the website of the ministry of civil affairs of the PRC. See http://www.mca.gov.cn/article/sj/tjjb/2021/202102fssj.html (all URLs accessed in August 2021).

3   两不愁、三保障 (*Liǎng bù chóu, sān bǎozhàng;* Two no worries and three guarantees), for example, is a governmental campaign that aims to make sure that people living in poverty will no longer need to worry about food and clothing. It also guarantees access to compulsory education, basic medical care, and safe housing. See the explanation of the term "*liǎngbùchóu sānbǎozhàng:* Two no worries

and three guarantees" on *China Daily,* https://www.chinadaily.com.cn/a/201904/23/WS5cbe5248a3104842260b7a39.html.

4   On February 25, 2021, the Chinese president Xi Jingping announced the victory of the poverty alleviation campaign. See the official report "脱贫攻坚战，全面胜利！" (*Tuōpín gōngjiānzhàn, quán shèng!;* The Poverty Alleviation Campaign: A Full Victory!), http://www.gov.cn/xinwen/2021-02/25/content_5588879.htm (in Chinese); and "Census results attest to China's complete victory in eradicating absolute poverty," http://english.www.gov.cn/archive/statistics/202102/26/content_WS603858f0c6d0719374af99ab.html (in English).

5   "Chinese people can only claim benefits, education and health care from their Hukou province, services which are often nonexistent in rural areas, meaning that migrants working in the city have almost no social support." In the case that an individual's *hukou* cannot be determined, establishing a *hukou* affiliation at the shelter's location is possible. See Jenny Hammond, "Homelessness in China," *Wayback Machine,* July 17, 2012, https://web.archive.org/web/20160930015343/http://gbtimes.com/life/homelessness-china.

6   The so-called Alipay Health Code System was widely introduced in China in the spring of 2020. The system uses software in smartphones to dictate quarantines, deciding in real time whether someone poses a contagion risk or is allowed into subways, malls, and other public spaces. For more on the Alipay Health Code System and automated social control, see Paul Mozur, Raymond Zhong, and Aaron Krolik, "In Coronavirus Fight, China Gives Citizens a Color Code, With Red Flags," *The New York Times,* March 1, 2020, https://www.nytimes.com/2020/03/01/business/china-coronavirus-surveillance.html.

7   Twice in a twelve-month period we witnessed people experiencing homelessness carrying with them a QR code to panhandle digitally.

8   上海中心大厦 (*Shànghǎi zhōngxīn dàshà;* Shanghai Tower or literally Shanghai Center Building), situated in Lujiazui, Pudong District, is the highest skyscraper in China (632 meters) and the second highest in the world.

Tokyo

Population
1990: 11.86 million
2000: 11.98 million
2010: 13.08 million
2020: 13.96 million

Population of People Experiencing Homelessness
1990: no data
2000: 5.521
2010: 3.125
2020: 889

How many people in the city are considered to be living below the poverty line by local standards?
1983: 10.4%
1993: 12.3%
2003: 15.2%
2013: 14.8%

Unemployment Rates
1990: no data
2000: 5%
2010: 5.5%
2020: 3.2%

According to the latest
official information from 2015,
15.7% of Japanese households
live below the poverty line,
which is about **$937**
(€799) per month.

Ownership Rate / Rental Rate in the Housing Market
1990: 42.3% / 57.7%
2000: 43.7% / 56.3%
2010: 46.6% / 53.4%
2015: 47.7% / 52.3%
2020: no data yet

Average Buying Price per Square Meter in 2020
Average price for land designated for housing: 378,100 JPY (€2,947) per m²

Average Monthly Salary and Minimum Hourly Wage in 2019/2020
2019 average monthly salary in Tokyo: 414,622 JPY (€3,230)
2020 minimum hourly wage in Tokyo: 1,013 JPY (€7.89)

Sources, see p. 270

Tokyo:
Current Homelessness Biography

Helena Čapková and Erez Golani Solomon

Street in the Shinjuku ward of Tokyo

The distinction of Tokyo's homelessness biography is revealed, first, through scale. The homeless population of Tokyo as a proportion of the general population is extremely low. Estimates remain low even if we take into account that homelessness is defined by the Japanese Ministry of Health, Labour and Welfare only as "people sleeping rough." This narrow definition sees the homeless as people who live their daily life in areas like parks, riverbanks, roadsides, station buildings, or other public spaces. The exclusion of all other definitions (e.g., those living in emergency shelters, accommodations for the homeless, institutions, unconventional dwellings, conventional houses of family or friends, and other places) contributes to Tokyo being one of the cities with the smallest homeless populations in comparison with other major urban centers, and to Japan being the country with the smallest proportion of homeless people in the world.

A peak in the homeless population occurred between the collapse of the Japanese bubble economy in 1991 and the enactment of the Homeless Autonomy Support Law in 2002. The economic collapse brought particular difficulties to the construction and mining industries, with the consequence that people who worked in these industries, often day workers who were already living under precarious conditions, could no longer afford their rent and became homeless. On the other hand, the new law is considered a significant step toward the reduction of the obstacles standing between homeless individuals and government support, and toward a gradual reduction of the homeless population en route to the current state.

The homeless and those at risk of becoming homeless are generally not left to their own devices. People at risk of losing their homes due to financial problems or unemployment are eligible for a protective subsidy under the Housing Security Benefit law, while a person who is already homeless has the right to join a government program that could, if followed, end his or her homelessness. This institutionalized path begins when the homeless are taken off the streets for a short stay in an emergency shelter, where they are given basic care, followed by a sojourn lasting several months in a self-reliance support center where residents are guided back into mainstream society, and ends in a rented apartment where the former homeless person lives independently. Difficulties often arise when an individual is either mentally unable or simply unwilling to commit.

The distinctiveness of Tokyo's homelessness biography is subsequently revealed in the homeless profile. The homeless person in contemporary Tokyo is likely to be an elderly male, financially burdened and/or distressed by debt. Alcohol and drugs play a role, while, compared to most other countries, racial discrimination or the psychological consequences of experiencing war or disaster play no decisive role. According to professor Tom Gill of Meiji Gakuin University, the male predominance of the homeless population of both the city of Tokyo and Japan as a whole could be explained by the "general expectation that, throughout the course of their lives, women will be looked after by their parents, then their husbands and later their children."[1] According to Gill, the conservative idea that men are independent, while women are dependent, has a continuing influence today. The common differentiation in gender perception, both literally and figuratively, shelters women. It is rare that the homeless recruit from disaster evacuees, as is seen in the context of the 2011 earthquake and tsunami in East Japan. This showed that a large "home imbalance" caused by the destruction of buildings and the subsequent evacuation of approximately 470,000 people did not significantly influence the homelessness figures.

A third aspect of Tokyo's homelessness is associated with forms of invisibility and visibility. As a means of evading debt collectors, financially troubled people sometimes choose homelessness and avoid shelters or applying for national subsidies, such as Livelihood Protection, until the statute of limitations on their debts lapses after five years. In such cases, homelessness becomes a form of disappearance and submersion. It also explains why the majority of the homeless in Tokyo live on the streets for a period of five years and longer. The homeless are also drawn to invisibility in terms of their interactions with the non-homeless, since both begging and giving are less common in Japanese society, being generally associated with monks or charities, not individuals. Thus, the homeless are reluctant to ask and take because of shame and pride, and the passersby are reluctant to notice and respond because they are generally less familiar with other religions' traditions of giving to the poor directly, without an intermediary. Lastly, we see how the preparations for the Tokyo 2020 Olympic Games intertwined with the precarious status of the Tokyo homeless. In this case, the homeless position was weakened because of efforts to use the games in order to construct, and later project, the "right" brand image of the city.

The Tokyo homeless are, at the same time, clearly visible. The majority of Tokyo's homeless population can be seen in parks and on riverbanks, and in the streets. They are traditionally concentrated in certain areas of the city. They are usually remote or kept out of sight, but their

Empty house in Saitama, September 2018, from the series *Empty Houses* by Stav Tsur

remoteness is "expected." They are expected to be where they are, and always in the same form: improvised cardboard structures and temporary shack structures, makeshift wooden frames and blue tarp. These structures and their homeless tenants have now become part of the city's architectural landscape. They are well known to the local and global publics, "well photographed" for architecture exhibitions/publications, and, as such, granted a form of protection. But they are at the same time illegal, for the occupation of public space in Japan is illegal, and as such they are vulnerable to inspection, displacement, discrimination, redevelopment projects, administrative subrogation, and occasional harassment by the authorities and neighboring residents.

Tokyo's homelessness, in our eyes, should not be referred to as a "catastrophe." It is not catastrophic within the local, Japanese, context; and it is certainly not so within the global context, as this exhibition shows. This doesn't mean that homelessness in Tokyo is a less complex phenomenon, or that there is a less urgent need to talk about homelessness, but rather that there is a particular problematization in Tokyo's current state of homelessness, as described above, through issues of scale, profile, and in/visibility. In the texts below, we will describe two other "special cases"—both extreme forms of the people-housing imbalance that is unique to contemporary Tokyo.

Too Few Too Many: The Imbalance of People and Housing

Erez Golani Solomon

Contemporary Tokyo presents a dramatic imbalance of people and housing. The case of Tokyo shows us that there is no direct relationship between the availability of housing and the state of homelessness. It shows also, and above all, that there is a larger discrepancy between the availability of and need for housing—that is, what we consider to be availability and what we assume to be people's needs.

In 2018, the total number of households in Tokyo—6.69 million—was approximately 14.6 percent smaller than the total number of houses—7.67 million.[2] The national ratio at that time was even more extreme. There is a housing excess in present-day Tokyo of approximately 810,000 units.[3] Three quarters of a century ago, when the Second World War in Asia ended in August 1945, there was a housing shortage in Tokyo of about 900,000 units.[4] The early extreme was an outcome of warfare destruction, repatriation of soldiers, and growth of the urban population after the war. The current extreme results from demographic tendencies and modes of urbanization and is just as dramatic. The two moments mark a passage from deficiency to excess, and from the post-war to post-growth urban context.

Empty house in the Ota ward of Tokyo, September 2018, from the series *Empty Houses* by Stav Tsur

The recent figures tell a story of a paradoxical mode of urban development during a period of demographic decline. They tell a story of industries and government that promotes economic measures and market logic inconsistent with demographic tendencies. The figures show a tension between two "sides." On the one side, there is a recent wave of urban development fueled by the decision to host the 2020 Olympics, an activation of real-estate investment trusts (J-REITs), low interest rates, and the mobilization of inheritance tax to real-estate investments. The other side is represented by the established prediction that the Japanese population will drop from 126.17 million at present to 88.08 million by 2065. The Japanese housing market is therefore to a certain extent indifferent to context, and one outcome of this dynamic is surplus housing.

A vacant house (*akiya* in Japanese), according to Japan's Ministry of Land, Infrastructure, Transport and Tourism, is any house which has not been used for more than one year. This definition relates to the history of utility—to house use. There are a number of reasons for this large vacancy. The reasons ensue, to begin with, from the discussion above: old houses are left empty because of the demographic consequences of low fertility and an aging population, and because they are losing the "competition" with new developments, entrepreneurial urbanism, investment interests, and fashions and trends—everything that falls in the categoy of people's wants, needs, and desires. This

basic imbalance of people and housing is then further added to by a value-wealth imbalance—the difficulty of maintaining the value of houses relative to the standing wealth of owners—*and* a quality-turnover imbalance—the difficulty of maintaining construction quality relative to the houses' turnover time. Vacant houses are proliferating also due to the relative weakness of sustainability schemes such as reuse, due to the legal obstacles that often stand between heirs of houses and their inheritance, due to the changing demands of one housing typology over another, and even because demolition is expensive. Lastly, a dominating factor in Tokyo's housing vacancy could be associated with the 1981 amendment to the Japanese Building Standard Law, which accelerated the depreciation of houses that had been constructed prior to 1981, or that were not reconstructed to meet new building standards. It encouraged the vacating of houses and contributed to the large vacancy situation in Tokyo.

Vacant houses are mostly thought of as a problem. They are usually criticized for having a bad influence on the surrounding environment, for jeopardizing the housing market's balance of supply and demand, and for burdening the public with superfluous taxation on urban infrastructure development and maintenance, among other factors. But the problem that we should see in such empty houses—within the context of this exhibition—is that they are a surplus to a large, nationwide housing system that fails to meet the actual needs of the domestic population.

Narrow alley with vending machines in the Kamata ward of Tokyo

Hidden Homelessness

Helena Čapková

New research conducted as a part of this project has confirmed yet again that homelessness in Tokyo, in comparison to other large capital cities, is a relatively minor issue. In contrast with the research, the living experience of the city, either in the center or in the suburbs, reveals different images of a Tokyo that seems to be struggling with homelessness. What are the possible shortcomings of the data collection and where, if not on paper, is homelessness manifested?

One of the issues confirmed by the analysis of data is that the official definition of homelessness in Japan is reduced to only a single condition describing a homeless person as someone who lives roughly outdoors. On the other hand, the other three common internationally recognized conditions, including living in shelters, with friends, or in institutions, are not considered valid in Japan.

Aside from the government data, an independent survey conducted in 2019 by Tokyo's Advocacy and Research Centre for Homelessness (ARCH) reported that the actual number of homeless individuals in the city is at least 2.8 times higher than the official report.[5]

One of the characteristics of Japanese hidden homelessness is the stereotypical view of its demographics. Although a middle-aged or older Japanese male is recognized as the most prolific demographic, females and young adults are increasingly pushed to the edge of poverty and further into what is generally, but perhaps not in Japan, defined as homelessness. Especially in the last few years, in relation to economic crises and the pandemic taking place in parallel, homelessness and rising poverty levels have been discussed as a pressing issue.

Although government institutions offer help to the homeless, there is a reported lack of awareness of the existence of support measures. Moreover, when one enters the system, it is regarded as unnecessarily complicated by the applicants/homeless. They have described the process as "a humiliating interrogation, filled with insinuations and prejudicial disapproval."[6] As a result, many homeless people choose to cope individually. Upon closer inspection, it was revealed that the governmental systems also suffer from a lack of staff in the social services, as well as the actual funds needed.[7]

Like other big cities, Tokyo has accommodated the global phenomenon and implemented "defensive architecture" en route to the Olympics.[8] These elements have started filling Tokyo in the past ten years. Large public art projects and public spaces filled with uncomfortable furniture are now a common feature. The distinction in terms of use becomes visible, as "normal" users can enjoy the quirky spots, while for the homeless they make daily survival more challenging.[9] A good example of this is a new retail complex called Miyashita Park in the Shibuya district of Tokyo, which displaced the local homeless populations. Many NPOs are involved in helping the community, such as the volunteer-based organization Nojiren,[10] which launched its soup kitchen operation in 1998.

The last area of possible hidden homelessness in Tokyo discussed in this text is the abundance of empty houses (*akiya*). The weakening demand for housing in combination with the continuing supply of new residential buildings (especially in large cities) has generated an increasing number of abandoned/vacant homes across all regions of Japan.[11] The number of vacant/abandoned units and the related vacancy rate has increased in recent decades, meanwhile reaching historical highs of approximately 8.5 million houses throughout the country, or 13.6 percent (Japan-wide average) in 2018.[12] Although the vacancy rate is lower in prefectures such as Tokyo, it is still present.

The *akiya* provide a living environment for people who otherwise lead a virtually homeless lifestyle. They use public spaces for hygiene and for warming up, before returning to their precarious accommodations. The inhabitants of these ruin-like homes may well be their owners, or family relatives of the owner, for whom, paradoxically, the property burden has become the cause of their de facto homelessness. This common phenomenon is often caused by the severe inheritance and property taxes. These dilapidated houses and their inhabitants can be found in diverse neighborhoods in Tokyo and provide a dark and dramatic element to counter the overall polished impression of the local residential cityscapes. They stand in contrast with the stereotypically recognized and rather romanticized image of homeless people in Tokyo, with their cardboard boxes and blue tarps by the river, "living a pastoral life" with goats and chickens.

1 "Who are Japan's Homeless? (Part 2)" (2017), video by Life Where I'm From, https://www.youtube.com/watch?v=-9RgkZebW1s (all URLs accessed in August 2021).

2 "Trends in population and number of households" (2019), Tokyo Metropolitan Government, https://www.juutakuseisaku.metro.tokyo.lg.jp.

3 "Housing" (2020), Tokyo Metropolitan Government, Statistics Division, Bureau of General Affairs, https://www.toukei.metro.tokyo.lg.jp/kurasi/2020/ku20-03.htm.

4 André Sorensen, *The Making of Urban Japan: Cities and Planning from Edo to the Twenty-First Century* (New York: Routledge, 2004), pp. 158–59.

5 Advocacy and Research Centre for Homelessness (ARCH), https://www.archomelessness.org.

6 David H. Slater and Sara Ikebe, "Social Distancing from the Problem of Japanese Homelessness under Covid-19," *The Asia-Pacific Journal: Japan Focus* 18, no. 18/4 (September 15, 2020), https://apjjf.org/2020/18/Slater-Ikebe.html.

7 Shuji Ozaki, "'1 cup of noodles per day': COVID-19 aggravates poverty among isolated young in Japan," *The Mainichi*, March 22, 2021, https://mainichi.jp/english/articles/20210320/p2a/00m/0na/011000c.

8 Rowland Atkinson and Aidan While, "Defensive Architecture: Designing the Homeless out of Cities," *The Conversation*, December 30, 2015, https://theconversation.com.

9 Igarashi Tarō, "Haijo āto to kabōbitoshi no tanjō: Fukanyō wo meguru āto to dezain, Bijutsutechō," *INSIGHT*, December 12, 2020, https://bijutsutecho.com/magazine/insight/23127.

10 Nojiren Online, http://www.jca.apc.org/nojukusha/nojiren/e-home/.

11 Yuko Hashimoto, Gee Hee Hong, and Xiaoxiao Zhang, "Demographics and the Housing Market: Japan's Disappearing Cities," *International Monetary Fund Working Papers* (September 2020), p. 24.

12 Japan Ministry of Internal Affairs and Communications, 2018 Survey.

The Glowing Homeless, 2011, a neon light sculpture by the artist Fanny Allié, addressing the invisibility of homeless people in New York City

A Cut Above the Streets

Lluís Alexandre Casanovas Blanco in Conversation with Robert M. Hayes

Excluded from housing through cuts to social subsidies, layoffs, and the speculative real-estate policies of the 1970s, New York City's homeless population has ballooned as a result of the city's persistent income inequality and long-term lack of affordable housing. But, despite the steady rise in homelessness, this social crisis has become less and less visible over the course of the last decades.[1] In February 2020, before the outbreak of the coronavirus pandemic, the New York City Department of Homeless Services estimated that 3,857 individuals slept on the streets and subways of the city every night.[2] In comparison, that same year, 37,814 individuals slept in one of the 236 facilities that make up the city's shelter system.[3] These numbers should make us reconsider whether public space is actually the privileged site of contemporary homelessness, and should force us to turn instead toward a different architectural device: that of the shelter.

This shift, from the homelessness of the streets to the homelessness of the shelter, can be traced back to the late 1970s. Alarmed by the degrading conditions of the municipal Men's Shelter in the Bowery, the twenty-seven-year-old lawyer Robert M. Hayes gathered a series of homeless plaintiffs to bring a class-action lawsuit against the city of New York, which would force the NYC Department of Social Services to guarantee shelter to all individuals in need. On December 5, 1979, the New York State Supreme Court pronounced its first decision, requiring the city government to address the shelter shortage. In order to ensure adequate implementation by the city,

Hayes cofounded the advocacy group Coalition for the Homeless, which, in conjunction with the Legal Aid Society, developed in the 1980s a dense fabric of laws encoding the spatial relations of homelessness in New York City. The following conversation with Hayes endeavors to understand the architectural implications of the Coalition's legal activities.

LLUÍS ALEXANDRE CASANOVAS BLANCO: The Coalition for the Homeless has been a key actor ensuring federal, state, and municipal provision of assistance for individuals in need. The organization's legal strategy has been to articulate this provision in the form of a right.[4] Yet during the litigation that took place throughout the 1980s, there was a continuous back-and-forth between the recognition of the conceptual "right to shelter" and the specific material, spatial, and managerial conditions of the actual shelters that were to be provided. On some occasions, judges would recognize the right to shelter while failing to define minimum standards. On other occasions, judges would *not* recognize the right to shelter but would establish that, if provided, shelters would need to meet minimum standards. The concept of shelter thus experienced a twofold disassociation: on the one hand, in severing the political right from its material conditions, the notion of shelter was abstracted, obscuring its wider social and economic implications; on the other hand, in determining the material conditions of shelters without accounting for their political significance, shelter was separated from its ideological underpinnings.[5]

ROBERT M. HAYES: The right to shelter granted under the *Callahan vs. Carey* litigation was initially ordered by the court in 1979 without any specific quality standards.[6] From the start, my abiding principle was for shelter to be, at the very least, meaningful. That might sound ridiculous now, but when the litigation started, there were many people who viewed homelessness as a matter of choice as opposed to a condition caused by a lack of alternatives.[7] The guiding criteria was that shelter had to be preferable to public space—to streets and subways. Our demands were very much influenced by the extremely unpleasant conditions of the first shelters set up under the initial non-quality court order. Thus, we demanded a consent decree—that is, a civil settlement reached by the parties that is approved by the court without a trial— to establish some minimum standards that would be added to the initial right to shelter ruling from the Callahan preliminary injunction, finally approved in 1981. The criteria would be to set up a series of conditions that were, as one judge put it, "not palatial, but a cut above the streets." It was not exactly an architectural or design decision.

LLUÍS ALEXANDRE CASANOVAS BLANCO: This "cut above the streets" standard—the question of what domesticity means in relation to the public sphere, and how the differences between the two realms are articulated— seems to me to be an architectural question, and a very important one at that. In fact, I think that the inefficacy of architects in engaging with topics such as homelessness is caused, in part, because architecture is seen as separate (along with many other fields) from legal discussions.

ROBERT M. HAYES: We could truly have resorted to the opinion of experts such as architects, social workers, psychologists, or psychiatrists to help the court define these conditions. And, at some point, as we could not agree on the maximum number of people that each facility should accommodate, we did have real testimony from architects. But the fact is that the whole principle of law argues that the duty of the court is to enforce policy, not to define it. Thus, we struggled to try to find what you may call in law "justiciable" conditions; that is, standards that could be credible to the judge, and, thus, enforced onto the right to shelter. We finally derived shelter standards from regulations for adult homes run by the New York State Department of Social Services.[8] We convinced the judge that these should be applicable, as they had been determined, following due diligence, by the executive branch of government, not the judicial branch. And this is how we arrived at the very arcane standards that are still in place.

LLUÍS ALEXANDRE CASANOVAS BLANCO: In the decree, the overall definition of shelter is kept architecturally loose, while the material and technical conditions of every single element that makes up the space of the shelter are over-defined. For example, the decree states that a bed should be "substantially constructed, in good repair and equipped with clean springs," furnished "with both a

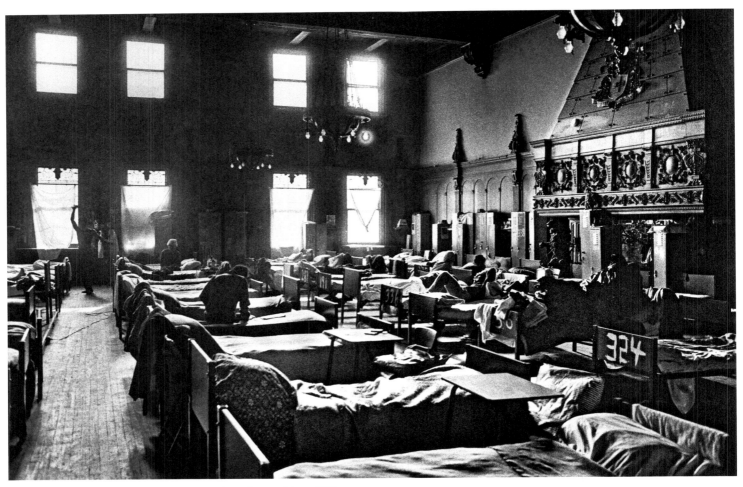

Men's Shelter, Atlantic Avenue Armory (AAA), Brooklyn, 1985

clean, comfortable, well-constructed mattress standard in size ... and a clean, comfortable pillow of average size."[9] The use of terms such as "clean" or "well-constructed" when talking about furniture suggests that common sense might not be sufficient, and, thus, that a consensus must be achieved on what a bed is.

ROBERT M. HAYES: Indeed, and it is embarrassing in retrospect ... The whole negotiation with the judge was like a crazy trench warfare. At some point, we even argued about whether there was one sheet or two sheets—one to cover the mattress and an in-between linen under the blanket. The city wanted one sheet, but I argued, "Well, if you are only going to have one sheet, are you going to wash the blanket for every user?" And that is how we got to two sheets—because the city would not have to wash the blanket every time someone used it.[10]

LLUÍS ALEXANDRE CASANOVAS BLANCO: In the early eighties, the implementation of the *Callahan vs. Carey* resolution forced a record expansion of the shelter system, including the reconversion of armories for sheltering purposes. You were strongly opposed to this decision.

ROBERT M. HAYES: Well, at that point in time, they needed space. But they could have done a lot better. Much of my concern with armories was that they were too damn big. A quote that I was known for using and abusing was "big is bad; very big is very bad." And that is true; it is just a human thing.

LLUÍS ALEXANDRE CASANOVAS BLANCO: So, could we say that your opposition was based, among other reasons, on architectural or spatial conditions? Or, to put it more specifically, on questions of scale?

ROBERT M. HAYES: Only in part. It had more to do with keeping limited the number of beds in any facility. The city was in desperate need of beds, that's for sure. But, for me, the bottom line was to make sure that every bed was secure, and seen as safer and less undignified than living in public space. Thus, being one person in a 1,000-bed armory, as it happened in the shelter at Fort Washington, Maryland, was not acceptable. We ended up using the number 200, although this number is, of course, relative. If we think of a shelter as an open-for-all, ward-like space, then having more than 200 beds would be awful. And even

Photograph by Don Hamerman included in Joe Klein, "The Homeless on Park Avenue," *New York Magazine* (April 16, 1984)

200 is awful; it is still too many. Yet, it would be different if we had a 250-unit Plaza Hotel-like space. The proportion, which established that "there shall be a minimum of one toilet and one lavatory for each six residents and a minimum of one tub or shower for each ten residents,"[11] was used as a tool to keep the overall volume of beds in a shelter as low as possible. This way, you could have a billion square feet of space, but if you only had ten toilets, then you could only shelter a hundred people there.

LLUÍS ALEXANDRE CASANOVAS BLANCO: At the present moment, several groups are putting pressure to shift discussions away from the "right to shelter" toward the "right to housing." In a way, this convergence between housing and shelter erases the notion of emergency ingrained in the provision of shelter, while reasserting the sense of normality inscribed to housing. As such, it illusorily depicts homelessness as a temporary disjuncture of the sociopolitical system to be amended, while I believe it is pretty much part of its logic.[12]

ROBERT M. HAYES: Well, the difference between shelter and housing can indeed be debated—and maybe an architect

can do it better than me. It did not take very long to recognize that the right to shelter was not a good end point. It is always going to be a sort of stopgap, nothing but a way station to a better solution. So, how you depart from it—in which direction you move to truly palliate the problem rather than just responding to a state of emergency—is something that every New York administration has struggled with ever since *Callahan vs. Carey*. Shelter as a minimum, legally enforceable right was eventually used politically to push the agenda for housing. The increase of affordable housing as a consequential achievement from the right to shelter court order may have been more valuable than the right to shelter itself.

LLUÍS ALEXANDRE CASANOVAS BLANCO: Was the irruption of the coronavirus pandemic in 2020 a real stress test to the "cut above the streets" standard that served to legally define shelter?

ROBERT M. HAYES: As more information about the patterns of viral infection of the coronavirus became available, it was clear that the smaller, self-contained spaces of housing units were safer than the large congregation of bodies in shelter facilities. Right now there are so many kinds of shelter—and, fortunately, none of them house a thousand individuals like the armories of the mid-1980s—but all these facilities share a commonality: they all put, to a greater or lesser degree, different individuals in close contact with each other. To some extent, these spaces became a coronavirus petri dish. That is why, in the early days of the pandemic, many users decided to leave the shelters for the streets. The eviction moratorium dictated by the Centers for Disease Control and Prevention in September 2020 prevented the number of individuals in the streets from being even higher.[13] To the extent that people were able to stay in their homes, the order clearly saved lives in a way unseen, at least in my lifetime.

LLUÍS ALEXANDRE CASANOVAS BLANCO: One of the issues that I believe is of extreme significance when dealing with socially sensitive topics and disenfranchised populations is the role that one, as an outsider to those everyday realities, should play, in order to avoid "speaking for others." In the early days of the Coalition for the Homeless, you insisted that the advocacy group's work had to significantly depart from the attitudes and strategies of what you then referred to as the "mainstream charitable industrial complex." And yet, the Coalition has been often criticized for acting as a delegated actor for the actual sufferers of this social crisis, and for insufficiently integrating the voices of the unhoused.

ROBERT M. HAYES: It is not easy. And it is likely that I am still not politically correct on some of these issues. Hopefully then—and hopefully now—it all starts with being respectful of the individual. I always recognized that I was, in a sense, a delegated advocate. I had never been homeless or poor; I never had to put those working boots on and fight that battle. The Coalition—and I, personally—have supported many organizations across the country led by people who were or have been homeless. The trouble with making the experience of homelessness a requirement to credibility, leadership, or ownership of this kind of organization is that, when you are homeless, survival is hard enough without trying to also change the world. At the end of the day, a homeless person does not want to be homeless for long. Their entire energy is focused on getting out of that state. I believe that if you are in a position where, to be a credible voice of homelessness you must be homeless yourself, you are very quickly going to become an outlier as well, and not representative of homeless people any more than I might be. Although I acknowledge the contradictions in this argument, I still believe there is a little bit of truth in it.

1   The journalist Ian Frazier has asserted that the lack of awareness of this crisis is a consequence of the invisibility of contemporary homelessness, which has been internalized within the shelter's architecture: "[Most New Yorkers] say they thought there were fewer homeless people than before, because they see fewer of them." Ian Frazier, "Hidden City," *The New Yorker,* October 28, 2013, p. 39.

2   The Homeless Outreach Population Estimate (HOPE) is a point-in-time, citywide survey conducted annually by volunteers under the supervision of the New York City Department · of Homeless Services (DHS). The survey has received wide criticism from various nonprofit organizations, which accuse the city of intentionally minimizing the problem through the survey's methodology. See NYC Department of Homeless Services, "NYC HOPE 2020 Results," https://www1.nyc.gov/assets/dhs/downloads/pdf/hope-2020-results.pdf (all URLs accessed in August 2021).

3   NYC Department of Homeless Services (DHS), "Daily report 2/28/2020," data from Thursday, February 27, 2020, https://www1.nyc.gov/assets/dhs/downloads/pdf/dailyreport.pdf.

4   For an accurate description of the legal strategies adopted by Robert M. Hayes, see Kim Hopper and L. Stuart Cox, "Litigation in Advocacy for the Homeless: The Case of New York City," *Development: Journal of the Society for International Development* 2 (1982), pp. 57–62.

5   My reading of the "right to shelter" is informed by Michael Ignatieff's account of human rights advocacy. See Michael Ignatieff, "Human Rights," in *Human Rights in Political Transitions: Gettysburg to Bosnia,* ed. Carla Hesse and Robert Post (New York: Zone Books, 1999), pp. 313–24.

6   *Callahan v. Carey,* no. 79-42582 (Sup. Ct. N.Y. County, Cot. 18, 1979), www.coalitionforthehomeless.org/wp-content/uploads/2014/08/CallahanConsentDecree.pdf.

7   The epitome of this attitude is President Ronald Reagan's own comments on the homelessness crisis. In an interview for the television show *Good Morning America* in 1984, Reagan stated, "the homeless . . . are homeless, you might say, by choice." See Sydney H. Schanberg, "Opinion: New York; Reagan's Homeless," *The New York Times,* February 4, 1984.

8   Hayes refers here to eighteen N.Y. Comp. Codes R. & Regs. 491.2: Official Compilation of the Codes, Rules and Regulations of the State of New York. Title 18: Department of Social Services. Chapter II: Regulations of the Department of Social Services. Subchapter D. Adult-care Facilities. Part 491. Shelter for Adults.

9   The *Callahan vs. Carey* Consent Decree, August 1981, www.coalitionforthehomeless.org/wp-content/uploads/2014/06/CallahanConsentDecree.pdf.

10   The administrative staff in charge of implementing the consent decree has described the "Kafkaesque discussions" around the life cycle of objects in the shelter system. The anecdote regarding the "mystery of the short-lived sheets" is particularly telling. Apparently, the city had to resort to the Department of Corrections' municipal facilities at Rikers Island to comply with the required high volume of laundry. When leaving the building, guards punched the packaged sheets with sharp bayonets, tearing the sheets, in order to detect any potential hidden detainees trying to escape. This anecdote can be found in Thomas J. Main's interview with Bonnie Stone, the first assistant deputy at the municipal Human Resources Administration, October 2011. Quoted in Thomas J. Main, *Homelessness in New York City: Policymaking from Koch to de Blasio* (New York: New York University, 2017), p. 42.

11   The *Callahan vs. Carey* Consent Decree, August 1981 (see note 9).

12   For a discussion of homelessness as intrinsic to capitalism and not as a failure within its functioning, see Peter Marcuse, "Neutralizing homelessness," *Socialist Review* 88, no. 1 (1988), pp. 69–97.

13   This declaration, which established that the evictions of tenants would be detrimental to public health control measures to slow the spread of the coronavirus, protected many individuals at risk of becoming unhoused at the height of the pandemic. See "Temporary Halt in Residential Evictions to Prevent the Further Spread of COVID-19," Centers for Disease Control and Prevention (CDC), Department of Health and Human Services (HHS), September 4, 2020.

Editor's note:

A first version of this interview appeared as "A Cut Above the Streets: Robert M. Hayes, Co-Founder of Coalition for the Homeless, in Conversation with Lluís Alexandre Casanovas Blanco," *Ed Journal* 2, *Architecture of Disaster* (Spring 2018), pp. 58–65. I would like to thank the editors Nicholas Korody and Joanna Kloppenburg for their insights on this first version.

The Role of Race in Homelessness

Binyamin Appelbaum in Conversation with Veronica Lewis

A growing number of people are experiencing homelessness in most major cities along the expensive Atlantic and Pacific coasts of the United States. The crisis is particularly visible in Los Angeles, where thousands of people live on sidewalks in the shadows of the city's skyscrapers. Some people without homes sleep in vehicles parked in special guarded lots. Some people without cars sleep on the beaches, after the surfers and sunbathers have returned to their homes.

The contrast between glamorous wealth and abject poverty presents a striking visual indictment of a society that has so much and nonetheless, for some, provides so little.

In recent years, Los Angeles also has commanded the spotlight due to the city's growing commitment to helping those experiencing homelessness. Both the local government and the state of California are pouring money into aid programs, including the construction of temporary shelters and permanent supportive housing. But the homeless population continues to grow, primarily because California simply does not have enough housing stock and the state is not willing to allow a significant increase in housing construction.

Veronica Lewis runs one of the largest homeless aid providers in Los Angeles, HOPICS, which serves people who are experiencing homelessness in the predominantly Black and Hispanic communities to the south of the city's downtown. I opened our conversation by asking her to address the common but outdated perception that people who are homeless are struggling with mental illness or substance abuse—that they are unable or unwilling to live in a home.

VERONICA LEWIS: We've been working hard to change the narrative about people pushing baskets or sleeping on the sidewalk. People are on the street because they can't afford to live inside. These are people going to work every day. People sleeping in their vehicles because that's the last thing they own. Moms and dads and grandparents, who have rented their homes for a long time, losing their homes and falling out.

People say that people experiencing homelessness come to California because our weather is better. That's not really true. What you do see is people that came to pursue a dream. They had arrangements to stay with family or a friend, and something happens and they end up homeless.

Many people are living in poverty and are one paycheck away from a crisis. They have unexpected medical bills or some other emergency and they simply cannot catch up and they fall out of housing.

And it includes a significant number of children. One of the biggest concerns for me is that we know children who have been homeless have a likelihood of being homeless as adults. And we have been doing the work long enough to see that come true—where we see children that we served ten years ago now as adults falling into homelessness.

It's just people. It's not a subset of society. It's people—people who have families, loved ones, careers—people who couldn't afford housing and didn't have a support network, and now they don't have a stable place to live.

BINYAMIN APPELBAUM: In LA, and in most American cities, it's disproportionately Black people . . .

VERONICA LEWIS: We are the most impacted. In South LA, Compton, Lynwood—these are some of the highest-poverty census tracts, and we have a disproportionate number of families falling into homelessness because landlords are increasing rental amounts. Salaries and wages are staying stagnant in comparison to the costs of living, and people just can't afford it.

Even with the increase in wages, it's still significantly lower than we need. There was an article showing that people need to make $33 an hour just to basically make it.

Homelessness is the most extreme manifestation of poverty. And so you have these urban centers where there's a significant number of people living in poverty and most of their family and friends are in the same boat, and that's where you have people falling out. It's not because Black people are the only ones that struggle, but because there's such a lack of resources, because of racist policies that have led us to where we are today.

BINYAMIN APPELBAUM: Let's focus first on the idea that homelessness is on the rise because the cost of housing is on the rise. There just aren't enough homes to house everyone.

VERONICA LEWIS: It's not that people are poorer; it's that rents are rising. You have poor Black people that always have been poor but they've been able to sustain. They never had enough but the difference now is that landlords are literally forcing them out and we do not have sufficient resources to offer a reprieve to prevent housing instability. We have all this development and people moving back into the city and landlords are evicting people in very creative ways. So you have a grandmother showing up with her children and her children's children because the place she called home for the last twenty years has been taken from her.

During the coronavirus pandemic, because of the eviction moratoriums, we've seen somewhat of a slowdown. But those eviction moratoriums are ending and, especially now that California is opening up, I anticipate before the end of the calendar year that we'll be seeing the numbers going up.

BINYAMIN APPELBAUM: And then the second part of what you said, which is very interesting, is that the effect of

A homeless encampment in front of a restaurant in the Venice neighborhood of Los Angeles

racism, of this long history of racism, isn't just that each person is more vulnerable, but also that the surrounding community has less ability to help when the crisis comes.

VERONICA LEWIS: We are dealing with generational poverty, the welfare system that perpetuated single-mother families, the overrepresentation of Black men in the criminal justice system . . . Skid Row is a sea of Black men's faces. Men come out of prison and sometimes there is no family anymore. Or their family says, "Come get a plate," but they can't stay there so they end up on Skid Row.

I could talk to you for hours about all of those types of policies that are directly related to where we find ourselves today. Society created these pockets and places that were under-resourced and folks were forced into that—by redlining and all these other policies. And our communities are still reeling from the war on drugs. You have people constantly going in and out of prison and jail, broken families, health disparities, years of divestment

in communities full of people of color, over-criminalization of young Black men, single-parent homes . . . Welfare policies, sentencing policies, and the generational cycle—the brokenness of families and never being able to get a foot ahead. And in the last year you've seen a recognition of how policies and social norms have disadvantaged people of color.

BINYAMIN APPELBAUM: In 2017, voters in Los Angeles County approved a sales tax increase to provide about $355 million in annual funding for ten years to address homelessness. How much of a difference has that money made?

VERONICA LEWIS: There has been a significant amount of progress: the projects to help some of the most vulnerable people, to remove red tape, to invest in supportive services. There have been 25 percent more people housed in the last two years than normal. But at the same time, you still have a lot of people falling into

A man sitting in front of a homeless encampment on Third Avenue in Venice, selling his handmade bird- and dollhouses

homelessness. We're housing a lot of people, we are removing some of the barriers to services, but at the same time, because the homeless service system is really meant to move people off the street and help them stabilize, we don't have a robust system, really, to address the significant inflow that we have of people experiencing homelessness, and it is largely new people experiencing homelessness.

We've made great progress, but we still have a lot of people falling into housing instability.

BINYAMIN APPELBAUM: Earlier this year, a federal judge ordered Los Angeles to provide shelter for every homeless person. But there's a big difference between shelter and housing. In New York, where a similar court order has been in effect for decades, the city has created a vast system of temporary shelters but has made little progress in helping people move into stable housing. Is this court order helpful or is it just a street-cleaning program?

VERONICA LEWIS: The positive is that it has caused a level of urgency to be creative and innovative and remove the necessary barriers to move resources and shift funding to get people off the street more quickly.

The challenges come because the drive is not necessarily about helping people. I think the judge is well meaning, but this is driven by businesses, and it's about, "Get them off the sidewalk."

The system we have spent the last five years creating is at risk. You have some City Council members who have tried to stop permanent supportive housing projects in process to divert funds to temporary housing. To say that you should forget permanent housing and just get everybody off the street and put them into temporary housing, with no throughput for where they'll go—it's not sustainable. They're not going to stay there. They will be back on the street and the danger is that we go back to an environment of criminalization where the police will say, "We gave you a place to go and you didn't stay there and now we're going to throw away your stuff and arrest you."

We want the options that you offer them to make sense, to be humane, to be accessible, and to offer these individuals a path for them to come from outdoors to indoors and ultimately their own place.

BINYAMIN APPELBAUM: The coronavirus pandemic also injected a sense of urgency ...

VERONICA LEWIS: Have you heard about Project Roomkey? The governor of California, probably in April of last year, issued dollars to the cities and the counties of California to lease motels so the most vulnerable people will be brought inside. So over 4,000 people in LA County—and more than 22,000 statewide—were brought indoors, with their own rooms and supportive services.

We operate two of those sites. And now there's Project Homekey, which is moving from leasing motels to buying them. They will be used temporarily for interim housing and, ultimately, the plan is to convert them in the next two or three years into permanent supportive housing.

BINYAMIN APPELBAUM: The basic problem in Los Angeles is that there aren't enough living spaces. So how do we create more spaces? How can architecture help?

VERONICA LEWIS: We're part of a project that is using shipping containers; that will create forty permanent units (using these containers). And those types of explorations related to more quickly and less expensively creating places for people to live; that's where we need architects to come into play. What are some creative, innovative ways that we can create more spaces, safe spaces, aesthetically pleasing spaces, for people to come inside from outdoors?

You also have something happening with accessory dwelling units, to have homeowners who have space in their backyards to create apartments using modular materials, to build those out and drop them down into people's backyards.

Those kinds of creative things are the direction that we're headed in because there's a finite amount of space and land. We need to figure out how to get more housing onto that land.

BINYAMIN APPELBAUM: Maybe the place to close is with the long view. Are you optimistic that Los Angeles is taking the necessary steps to make homelessness, as the saying goes, rare, brief and non-recurring?

VERONICA LEWIS: Overall yes, we're moving in the right direction. There's a significant amount of resources, and I do think within ten years there will be a difference. I'm hoping within the next two years we will be able to visibly see a difference. Because now you drive the streets of LA and it's pretty ridiculous. I hope we'll be able to see a difference.

What Else It Takes to Make a Home

Giovanna Borasi in Conversation with Michael Maltzan and Alexander Hagner

In this interview, Giovanna Borasi, the director of the Canadian Centre for Architecture (CCA) in Montréal, speaks with the Los Angeles-based architect Michael Maltzan and the Vienna-based architect Alexander Hagner. Two years after sharing their approaches to designing for homelessness for the CCA-commissioned film *What It Takes to Make a Home* (2019), the architects reflect on the challenges the profession now faces, in part but not exclusively due to the coronavirus crisis.

GIOVANNA BORASI: We have seen a lot of images, especially here in North America and in Europe, that show how the coronavirus pandemic has aggravated the situation of unhoused people and homelessness. Has this event brought new considerations to the things you thought before, or led to new understandings of the work you have done, as a kind of path forward?

MICHAEL MALTZAN: Well, in Los Angeles, the homelessness challenge has become an even greater crisis. The number of people who are homeless in the city has grown almost exponentially. Homelessness, which had traditionally been contained mostly to Skid Row, is now everywhere in the city. This comes from a whole range of reasons; some of them existed before and some were exaggerated by the economic downturn. They vary from individuals who have substance-abuse issues, people who have had some kind of a devastating turn in their life—mostly either a physical challenge or losing work—to, increasingly, a number of families with younger children on the street. It is difficult

to be optimistic about it, and, arguably, it has become a great existential crisis for the city. It will continue to have major impacts on almost everything going on here— socially, economically, politically, humanistically.

GIOVANNA BORASI: I did not know about all this. I knew about the increasing numbers we see in Canada . . .

MICHAEL MALTZAN: There have been some fairly significant programs that came out of the pandemic situation. One example is the government funding programs, such as the idea to take over underutilized hotels, because no one was traveling anymore. The city worked out arrangements with some of the hotels for long-term housing. In some ways it has been a positive development because it did help a number of people get off the street. But hotels do not provide all the services that an individual would need to live a more stable life.

If Los Angeles opens up more, there is going to be more pressure on those hotels to go back to being profit-making businesses. The only potentially useful thing— though by no means optimistic—is that people are coming out after the lockdown. More and more people are moving around the city and are having to confront how much the crisis has grown; and again, I cannot say it is a positive thing, but at least it is making the reality more visible. You can hear conversations about how extraordinarily amplified homelessness has become in the city. It is a real crisis on the Westside, in Venice Beach, where homelessness has always existed. People who live there are really being vocal about the problem. The politics there have become supercharged; it is one of the places where homelessness is most visibly contentious.

ALEXANDER HAGNER: I totally agree with what Michael said. It must be horrible in Venice Beach, but it's also horrible in Europe. During the pandemic, homelessness has grown to a completely new dimension. As always, the ones who do not have a lot are the ones who are most affected. Here in Austria, we are lucky, because we have, in general, a social government system. Right now, however, we have a problem: up until May or June, everyone who could not pay their rent did not have to. Now, a lot of people's lives have gone back to normal, so they are being asked for this unpaid rent. Therefore, many people are close to losing their homes. Recently the government put together a package of €20 million trying to support those affected, but they did not look at all of the costs that start accumulating when you lose your home. Earlier, mostly single people were affected. Now, families are close to losing their homes, too.

GIOVANNA BORASI: I really understand the aggravation of the crisis, and the context. I wonder if the work that you have done and are continuously doing is still impactful in the same way . . .

ALEXANDER HAGNER: It is a kind of island work at the moment. I always say that it is not so important to think about how many people we reach. If we reach even one person, and get them housed, then we will flip his or her life right side up. The last time we talked, I was more positive than I am now. We have a new association we are working for with our students. But these are small islands in a big ocean, which is constantly growing. I would give up if I didn't believe that we can change every single person's life when we get them housed.

GIOVANNA BORASI: You said that you might be able to impact a few at an individual level. The growth of the crisis shows us now that these projects only serve a very limited community. When you now rethink your work, are there new strategies that you think should be put in place?

MICHAEL MALTZAN: Well, that touches on something we have been working on. I was thinking about Alex's point about feeling like he is a bit on an island. It is a perfect metaphor. There are two things that have been on my mind: one is time and the other is scale. I am quite convinced that the work we have been doing has made the problem of homelessness more visible because of how other architects, writers, government officials, et cetera, are beginning to work on the problem. The architecture community has started to become very conscious that there is a part that architects can and should be doing. However, there is a mismatch between, on the one hand, what seems like an extraordinary expansion of the architectural role in this housing crisis and, on the other, just how much of a crisis it has actually become.

Alexander Hagner in the film *What It Takes to Make a Home* (documentary by the CCA, 2019)

From the standpoint of time, it is a question of whether there is enough time to catch up, based on how out of control the problem has gotten. That leads to the second problem, which is scale. The RAND Corporation came out with a study saying that in Southern California there is a deficit of about 500,000 units of housing. Many people are being displaced because affordability has become such a problem. And we have been very successful as an architecture office in developing housing of all types; we have completed about 900 units of housing. Still, 900 units of housing against a 500,000-unit deficit makes a very small impact. That has pushed us toward finding ways to scale up housing. We have been trying to work with the for-profit sector, because I am still convinced it is going to be part of the solution; for instance, we have been in conversations with government agencies and politicians around ways of trying to create some kind of business model to allow more housing to be built.

We are working with other developers on the possibility of doing a small demonstration project, way out in the desert, with the goal of taking over an old manufacturing warehouse, to start building housing on the outskirts of the city. One of the challenges is that they are in a fight with Amazon, because Amazon is trying to buy all of the big warehouse spaces for distribution. It is either housing or packages.

GIOVANNA BORASI: The two parameters—scale and time—and their relationship are so evident. But being able to find a solution seems to be a struggle. Maybe prefabrication, as you already explored at Star Apartments,

Michael, can serve as an immediate solution. Alex, what do you think?

ALEXANDER HAGNER: I totally agree with Michael. I see a chance in young people, in architecture students. As Michael already said, our architecture colleagues have started to recognize that working in this field is their job. Still, there remains the question of what we really can do. For me, the government has to ensure that someone is able to keep their living situation. Otherwise, it will cost the government much more money in the long term. The longer someone lives on the streets, the more problems this person attracts. If someone leads a normal life, then his home base is at the same time the space for all that his life entails. So, if he loses that, he will have more problems.

But this is not my job: I am an architect. I always try to determine how far my arm can reach. And I cannot do everything alone. We need to engage young people who are professionally thinking about how a house can be affordable for someone. We do not have any influence on the price of land. This is not in our "arm-reach region." If we bring affordable housing to people who do not have enough money, then we are bringing them homes—not only a shelter and a roof over their heads. They want to have the opportunity to make friends, to have relationships. Their social life is as necessary as being protected from rain and wind.

So, how could we address an architectural project in the worst phase of a personal catastrophe? My students

Michael Maltzan in the film *What It Takes to Make a Home* (documentary by the CCA, 2019)

developed a small house. If we talk about the fact that people do not have money, then we need to think about reducing living spaces—a table, two chairs, a shelf to store your clothing, a place to sleep, and a place to meet someone in your home. Now we have used less than 12 square meters. We do not include bathrooms, because they are very expensive. We create a platform in the middle, where three or four small houses can come together. Connected to the platform there is a bathhouse. If we can offer it to three or four units, then we can invest more money in this bathhouse.

We have also thought about the fact that many people who have lived on the streets for a long time face mental health challenges. If it is a community project, an overnight shelter for 80 people or a social housing project for 120 people, it is always a mass of people you have to get along with. You are not asked: Do you want to step into the community? You are immediately in the community when you enter a social project. And that is what we need to think about if someone has mental health problems. So we tried to offer a second entrance through which they can enter their small home without meeting anyone. But if they take the door through the community space, they have an opportunity to connect. We have discussed at length if the entrance door at the community side should open toward the outside or toward the inside . . . and we decided that if the door opens to the outside, then it would create another outside space which is protected. If someone rings on your door, and you open it, he must step back first, meaning that he cannot come in immediately. So this, again, is about feeling safe. We concentrated

on small spaces, where a bed can be very secure and hidden—this should be a safe place. Then we made a small interior space that we connected on the private side with a large terrace that extends the living space and results in you having the feeling of living on 20 square meters.

I have never worked so many hours on just a single room. We thought about so many details. We try to provide more than just shelter, but there are so many people and there is no time. We need to act as fast as we can, but I still want to design the kind of architecture that we would like to live in ourselves. In this prototype, we managed to produce at an architectural level that I have not seen in micro-houses. We produce it in pieces that we can prefabricate, and once we finish it, we evaluate and then make the next one work even better, if possible.

After this, we want to start contacting prefab-house companies, of which there are many in Austria, and ask them to collaborate, in order to not only provide one person or one family with a small home, but to integrate them into a community. These are the things we are thinking about, and, as I mentioned before, it is an island. I feel a bit ashamed to offer such a small thing, but this is how far my arm reaches right now.

GIOVANNA BORASI: Thank you, Alex. I understand your point. We have seen a lot of sharing and community living. If you want to live alone, it is more expensive. In the end, people maybe need to give up on that idea and share space with others. In the places where you can go to sleep as a homeless person, you are forced to share

Tents in Los Angeles: image from *What It Takes to Make a Home* (documentary by the CCA, 2019)

accommodations. And this is even more evident now, in the time of the coronavirus pandemic, when people have felt they cannot choose where they can go anymore or with whom to share space.

MICHAEL MALTZAN: I was struck by what Alex is making there, because it seems to me there is an emergency aspect to working on the challenge of homelessness as architects: How can you do as much as you can possibly do to try to change the situation? If we only evaluate our success based on how much of an impact we have had on the specific crisis, then it is difficult and we will never feel like we have done enough. I was really struck by Alex's allegory of how far his arm might reach. When you look at what he is doing, trying to not only make things less expensive while getting more housing into the world, but also taking on the larger cultural and social challenges around community, I think that is still a powerful part of what architecture and architects can do. Because many of the challenges around things like loneliness, which you were just touching on, Alex, are not only, of course, present in the homeless community. It is an epidemic at all levels of culture. I think that the things you are doing have resonance and a potential ripple effect well beyond the specifics of homelessness, all the way to culture itself. If there is something that keeps me optimistic, it is that the effects of what architecture touches are probably broader than the acute problem at hand.

GIOVANNA BORASI: The coronavirus crisis has brought more people to the streets; many at the same time have also lost their jobs. The director of the Housing First organization Y-Foundation in Finland stated that, at this point, the idea behind his foundation is no longer about just having a home; it is about offering a combination of a home and a job. So what you get, in the beginning, is a room and some work hours. Even if it is not enough to pay for the room, the job helps to integrate the individual into society.

MICHAEL MALTZAN: One of the things that has been most challenging for the people we work with has been the way that the financing for these projects changes constantly.

It is a problem because they spend so much of their time chasing funding to do the projects, which has an effect on what these projects can be at the end. If you look at the history of, for instance, Skid Row Housing Trust, they never were set up to do one thing. Once they started trying to house homeless individuals, one half of the organization was focused on saving old buildings in Los Angeles and reusing them. It was a perfect place to develop housing in a more social, forward-leaning, progressive way.

When we did Star Apartments, the reason they wanted to keep the ground floor as retail space was partially to make something happen urbanistically. They were trying to start a small business where they were designing and fabricating denim clothes; it was meant to be a way for the people who live there to have a potential job. So they were interested in creating this full economy within the project.

Vienna: image from *What It Takes to Make a Home* (documentary by the CCA, 2019)

Film poster

It seems to me that there is a sensibility in the younger generation, which is willing to be interested in taking on architecture in different ways—to find a way to use architecture not just from a physical design standpoint, but also from a political and advocacy side of things, to try to address the problem by thinking of other possibilities for doing things like building housing. I think that architects are able to see connections across traditional boundaries. If there is something that keeps me optimistic and keeps me trying to work on things, it is exactly that the effects— just because of what architecture touches—are probably broader than the acute problem at hand. That could be very useful right now. I have started to talk to some of the architecture schools about that, but I do not know if that can go anywhere or if it is just a dead end.

GIOVANNA BORASI: We did a show some years ago at the CCA that was called *The Other Architect,* which was pushing the idea that there are other ways of imagining being an architect. As an architect, you work on these projects in order to change also the context of working on these issues. So much is limited by policies, and the legal framework is also a challenge . . .

MICHAEL MALTZAN: Many of the challenges that we see are indeed because of the system—the economic system, the political system. It feels like some of the questions have to be answered within these systems. I am not terribly excited about that world. There is not a lot of pleasure in that. So I am conflicted about it.

ALEXANDER HAGNER: Young architects recognize that they are not only designing the material—they are designing life. Every form has another meaning. Looking beautiful is a given, but with how I turn the door and open it, I decide how someone is living there. At the moment, the students are figuring out these abilities; they really are starting to learn them. I hope that the new generation of architects wants to discuss these abilities with developers. And if we succeed in bringing such abilities back into our profession, I think we will be much more powerful in our work than if we were only designing shapes.

The Importance of Design, or
What Can Architecture Do?

Architecture is both a profession and a discipline, meaning that it describes skills which apply knowledge toward designs for the built environment, and that there is also a history of buildings and ideas which can be studied when solving new design challenges. It is also a system of thought that has developed tools and discourses enabling architects to think about both the spatial and the social conditions of the world. Architects as professionals are experts in designing and providing instructions for how and what to build, but not actually in building, which in the simplest of terms means that they are specialists in measuring and applying these measures. There is also an expanded set of necessary knowledge about materials, climates, structures, ventilation, illumination, acoustics, and so forth. Architectural design alone can and will not solve a social problem like homelessness. However, when called to the fore and held responsible, designers can respond to many of the problems that arise when trying to rehouse those without proper shelter. Whether responses focus on the collective or the individual, on singles, couples, or family groups, on people with special needs, on customized or wholesale housing, we suggest that architects have the responsibility of thinking about these problems, and that the contribution should involve schemes and new design strategies. Moreover, as architecture coordinates other professions during the design and construction process, architects have the additional responsibility of visualizing how and what to change in society through buildings and their programs.

Star Apartments

NAME OF THE PROJECT: Star Apartments

COUNTRY: United States

ADDRESS: 240 E. 6th St., Los Angeles, CA 90014

NEIGHBORHOOD: Skid Row

ARCHITECTURE: Michael Maltzan Architecture

STRUCTURAL ENGINEERING: B.W. Smith Structural Engineers, Nova Structures Inc.

CLIENT: Skid Row Housing Trust

INITIAL BUDGET: €16,600,000

FINAL COST: €17,500,000

FINANCED BY: Los Angeles County Department of Health Services, Genesis LA, Skid Row Housing Trust

PROJECT AND CONSTRUCTION YEARS: 2008–13

PROJECT TYPE: remodeling of an existing one-story building and addition of a new community level and residential levels above

PROGRAM: permanent supportive housing

TARGET GROUP: people experiencing chronic homelessness, suffering from mental/physical illness, with high emergency room use

NUMBER OF UNITS: 102

NUMBER OF BEDS PER UNIT: 1

TOTAL NUMBER OF DWELLERS: 102

RELATED FACILITIES IN THE BUILDING: headquarters of the Housing for Health Division of the LA County Department of Health Services (DHS), retail, social services, laundry rooms, community recreational facilities, Piece by Piece (arts and skill-building affiliate)

Star Apartments is a mixed-use complex in Los Angeles commissioned by the Skid Row Housing Trust, an institution that engages architects, designers, and researchers in the health and social services to design buildings that are not only functional but that also favor safe and stable lives for the dwellers. The building provides both housing and additional help services. Located on the edge of Skid Row, the six-story structure designed by Michael Maltzan Architecture sets a new model for urbanism and increased density close to the city center by remodeling an existing one-story commercial building and adding community space and residential levels above. The building is divided into three zones: a street level zone providing public health services, a more private zone for community activity, and, on top, four residential stories, consisting of 102 apartments. Common spaces for residents include a community kitchen, a lounge, classrooms, laundry rooms on every floor (a decision that has been part of the learning process of the architecture firm while designing dwellings for people who may find it problematic to go to a single laundry area in the basement of a building), social-service offices, a walking track, exercise equipment, and an outdoor recreation area. In addition to the accessible ground floor use, the open design of the complex provides connections to the surrounding city throughout the whole building. Using the aesthetics of the building as a tool, it is intended to highlight the problem of homelessness, and the role of architecture, on a scale visible within the city of Los Angeles. The construction was conducted with the help of prefabricated elements, accounting for a more sustainable result within a shorter construction time frame and limited budget.

Roof terrace in between units as a protected meeting place

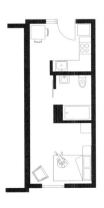

1:200

View of Star Apartments from 6th street, Skid Row, Los Angeles

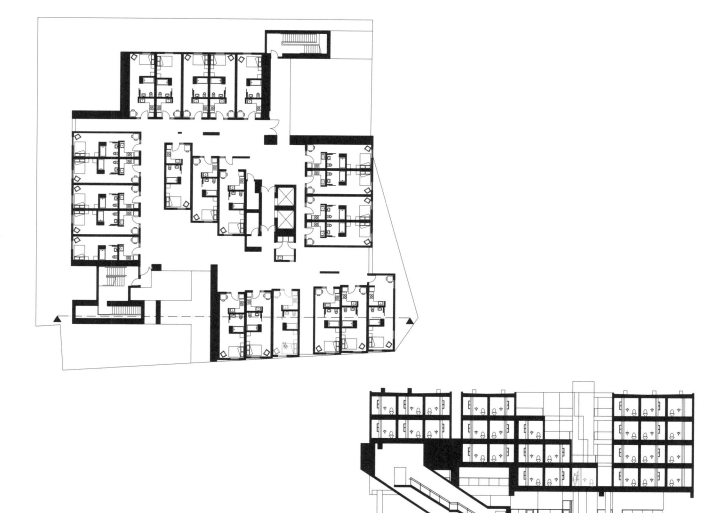

1:500

Wohnungen für obdachlose Menschen

NAME OF THE PROJECT: Wohnungen für obdachlose Menschen

COUNTRY: Germany

ADDRESS: Jahnstraße 14a–c, 86899 Landsberg am Lech

NEIGHBORHOOD: residential area

ARCHITECTURE: eap Architekten.Stadtplaner

CLIENT: city of Landsberg am Lech

INITIAL BUDGET: €3,533,400

FINAL COST: €3,500,000

FINANCED BY: city of Landsberg am Lech

PROJECT AND CONSTRUCTION YEARS: 2016–18

PROJECT TYPE: residential building

PROGRAM: emergency shelter, often permanent

TARGET GROUP: homeless individuals and families

NUMBER OF UNITS: 26; 23 one-room apartments, 3 two-room apartments with a kitchen and bathroom per unit

NUMBER OF BEDS PER UNIT: 1–2

TOTAL NUMBER OF DWELLERS: 29

RELATED FACILITIES IN THE BUILDING: social care, community room with kitchen, laundry

Designed by eap Architekten.Stadtplaner, the facility Wohnungen für obdachlose Menschen (Housing for Homeless People) comprises three buildings grouped around a green inner courtyard, located in a residential area near a lake called Altöttinger Weiher, in order to encourage integration. The two-story buildings with flat pitched roofs and arcaded access provide twenty-six apartments in total: twenty-three single-room units and three double-room units housing two to four residents. The former variant has a living room, hallway, kitchenette, and bathroom. The latter has an additional room. The separate points of accesses via the arcades lead directly to the outside, thus giving the individual apartments a sense of independence and ensuring a certain amount of privacy for the residents. To reinforce the feel of community, all units share a high-quality, communal outdoor area in the inner courtyard. Furthermore, a group room, located directly between the inner courtyard and the main access road, offers residents an opportunity to cook together and organize events, while at the same time creating a connection with the neighborhood. Additionally, the building provides a laundry room, auxiliary rooms for building services, and an office for social workers who are helping the residents integrate back into society.

Resident room

View of the courtyard and exterior access to the units

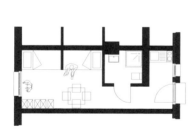

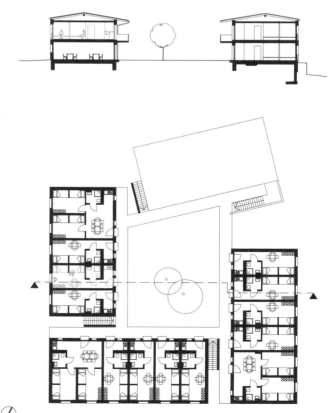

1:200

1:500

Shelter from the Storm

NAME OF THE PROJECT: Shelter from the Storm

COUNTRY: United Kingdom

ADDRESS: London, address unknown to avoid overflow and unscheduled arrangements, guests only allowed to stay with referral

NEIGHBORHOOD: Islington

ARCHITECTURE: Holland Harvey Architects

CLIENT: Shelter from the Storm charity

INITIAL BUDGET: confidential

FINAL COST: confidential

FINANCED BY: donations

PROJECT AND CONSTRUCTION YEARS: 2018–19

PROJECT TYPE: renovation of a vacant supermarket

PROGRAM: temporary shelter helping guests into permanent housing, education, and employment

TARGET GROUP: individuals over 18 who became homeless legally, including refugees

NUMBER OF UNITS: 3

NUMBER OF BEDS PER UNIT: unknown

TOTAL NUMBER OF DWELLERS: 38

RELATED FACILITIES IN THE BUILDING: helpers assisting guests into permanent housing, education and employment, communal areas including dining, lounge, pool area, meeting rooms, and retail unit which sells groceries and has a bike workshop

On a daily basis, homeless people face a storm, be it climatic, social, or emotional. Therefore, the founders of the facility Shelter from the Storm and its architects placed special emphasis on the coziness of the building. Originally, the shelter was an old 450-square-meter supermarket in the borough of Islington in London. Now it offers thirty-eight beds per night in three dorms (two male, one female). Even though the shelter is only to be used as a temporary dwelling with an average stay of two months, the team of Holland Harvey Architects made sure to offer further facilities such as a commercial kitchen, meeting space, counseling room, clothing store, IT facilities, lounge area, and dining room. Helpers assist the guests with obtaining permanent housing, education, and employment. More private and informal spaces are the dorms, which are equipped with warm materials such as cork cladding for the bunk-bed niches and light-efficient wooden flooring. A special emphasis was placed on the quite narrow female dorm with sixteen available beds, each with its own locker and direct access to the shared communal garden. The dual use of a community café at the front of the shelter intends to soften the border between homeless individuals and the general public, therefore giving rise to a more open discourse. The space aims predominantly to make itself accessible to whomever may be homeless at any age or in any situation.

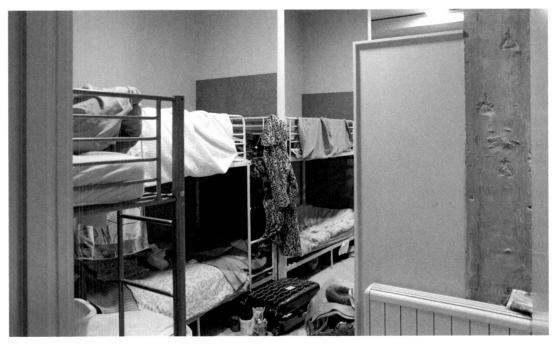

View of a dorm

Common dining area of Shelter from the Storm

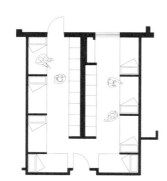

1:200   1:500

PLACE/Ladywell

NAME OF THE PROJECT: PLACE/Ladywell

COUNTRY: United Kingdom

ADDRESS: 261 Lewisham High St., London SE13 6AY

NEIGHBORHOOD: Lewisham

ARCHITECTURE: Rogers Stirk Harbour + Partners: Andrew Partridge (lead), Ivan Harbour (project partner), and team (Jack Baker, Ivan Harbour, Ben Goble, Lennart Grut, Sho Ito, Sandra Kolacz, Ann Miller, Lucie Olivier, Andrew Partridge)

CLIENT: Lewisham Council

FINAL COST (CONSTRUCTION): €5,800,000

FINANCED BY: Lewisham Council

PROJECT AND CONSTRUCTION YEARS: 2014–16

PROJECT TYPE: residential building

PROGRAM: temporary housing in a deployable residential system, both residential and commercial

TARGET GROUP: families with high-priority housing needs, low-income or homeless individuals

NUMBER OF UNITS: 24 residential units and 4 ground-floor community/retail units

NUMBER OF BEDS PER UNIT: two-bedroom apartments with 2 to 4 beds (double-sized beds or bunk beds)

TOTAL NUMBER OF DWELLERS: ca. 96 people

RELATED FACILITIES IN THE BUILDING: community/retail units on the ground floor, residential units with a private kitchen and bathroom, utility room in the cellar

PLACE/Ladywell is a temporary supportive housing project commissioned by the Lewisham Council. The project was built on the site of the former Ladywell Leisure Centre, which was demolished in 2014 and left vacant pending redevelopment. Rogers Stirk Harbour + Partners designed an experimental housing project using stackable housing units, creating two-bedroom apartments, 77 square meters each. By doing so, they exceeded London space standards by 10 percent. The goal of the project was to respond to the high demand for housing in the borough by offering a short-term solution for people in need, while creating community commercial spaces on the ground floor. This aims to regenerate life in the neighborhood and encourage interaction. To find a way back into social life, the cafés and shops additionally provide a chance for reintegration and work for those in need. Utilizing prefabrication and modular design has made for a cost-effective building, in turn providing large and adaptable family housing. The modular approach of the fully demountable structure furthermore provides the opportunity to relocate or even divide the building once requirements shift.

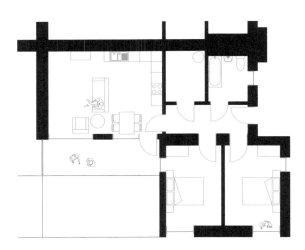

1:200

Outside access to a modular unit at PLACE/Ladywell

View of two rooms

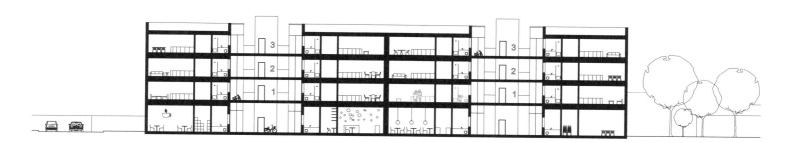

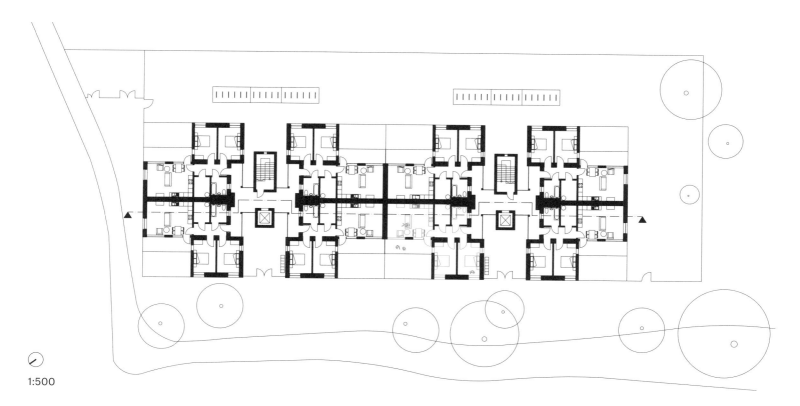

1:500

Notwohnsiedlung Brothuuse

NAME OF THE PROJECT: Notwohnsiedlung Brothuuse

COUNTRY: Switzerland

ADDRESS: Mühlackerstrasse 4, 8046 Zürich-Affoltern

NEIGHBORHOOD: Zurich-Affoltern

ARCHITECTURE: Baubüro in situ AG, Mépp AG

CLIENT: Sozialwerk Pfarrer Sieber

INITIAL BUDGET: €2,300,000

FINAL COST: €2,300,000

FINANCED BY: Stiftung Sozialwerk Pfarrer Sieber

PROJECT AND CONSTRUCTION YEARS: 2010–12

PROJECT TYPE: modular wood construction

PROGRAM: emergency social housing for 10 years

TARGET GROUP: homeless women and men, between 25 and 55 years

NUMBER OF UNITS: 27 rooms, 10 bathrooms, 5 kitchens, 1 common room (including 1 bathroom and 1 kitchen), 4 offices

NUMBER OF BEDS PER UNIT: 1–2

TOTAL NUMBER OF DWELLERS: 50 (in 2020)

RELATED FACILITIES IN THE BUILDING: community center and event space; the foundation regularly organizes religious services and other public nonreligious events to enable an exchange; gardens in front of the individual buildings can be planted by the residents

Designed by Ménard Partner Projekte, the Notwohnsiedlung Brothuuse buildings were erected in 2012 under the leadership of the pastor Ernst Sieber, financed by his social fund called Sozialwerk Pfarrer Sieber. Through this project, the pastor provides a safe harbor and a warm place to stay for people who are not socially integrated. Notwohnsiedlung Brothuuse has been located in the northern district of Zurich for ten years. The complex is based on a modular wooden construction, which can be disassembled, transported, and reassembled at another location, making Notwohnsiedlung Brothuuse resource efficient. It is composed of two residential buildings (one for women, one for men), a community building, a central court, and a garden. The units provide space for three to seven residents who share two bathrooms and a kitchen. Those components are designed and placed in a way to help people learn to integrate themselves into an already existing community. The main goal is to teach dwellers passively how to manage a home of their own and to cultivate a social life within a group, mirroring life outside of the Brothuuse community.

Mounting of the modular wooden construction

View of Notwohnsiedlung Brothuuse right after construction

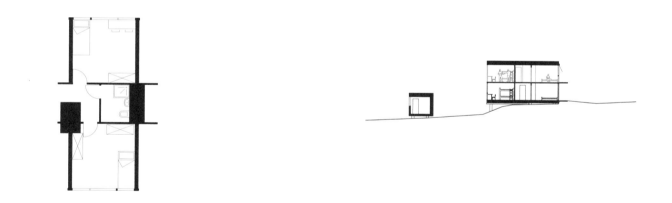

1:200

1:500

VinziRast-mittendrin

NAME OF THE PROJECT: VinziRast-mittendrin

COUNTRY: Austria

ADDRESS: Währinger Strasse 19, 1090 Vienna

NEIGHBORHOOD: Alsergrund

ARCHITECTURE: gaupenraub+/- (Alexander Hagner and Ulrike Schartner)

CLIENT: Vinzenzgemeinschaft St. Stephan

FINAL COST: exact statements about the production costs cannot be made, since much donated material was used

FINANCED BY: Foundation of Hans-Peter Haselsteiner's family

PROJECT AND CONSTRUCTION YEARS: 2010–13

PROJECT TYPE: renovation of a Biedermeier house with a new roof and the addition of new, barrier-free access

PROGRAM: permanent housing for a minimum of 1 year

TARGET GROUP: formerly homeless people and students

NUMBER OF UNITS: 10 apartments with 3 rooms each on 3 floors

NUMBER OF BEDS PER UNIT: 3

TOTAL NUMBER OF DWELLERS: 30

RELATED FACILITIES IN THE BUILDING: communal kitchen with a shared living room on each floor, counseling rooms, 1 office, 1 study room, 1 event room, 1 roof garden with an adjoining roof studio for free use, 3 workshops, 1 public area with a guest garden plus various adjoining rooms

Designed by gaupenraub+/- (Alexander Hagner and Ulrike Schartner), VinziRast-mittendrin is a student-initiated project that aims to provide people who are unstably housed with opportunities for both housing and employment. Ten apartments laid out across three floors house a total of thirty residents. Each floor has three smaller kitchens, located within individual apartments, as well as a larger shared kitchen connected to a shared living space, providing residents with the ability to choose private or less-private dining options. The building also includes consultation rooms, an office, a study, an event room, a publicly accessible roof garden with an attached roof studio, three workshop spaces, and a public restaurant with a guest garden. The most unique feature of this project is the composition of residents: half are people who are unstably housed, while the other half are students. Residents are mixed and spread across the ten three-person apartments. Interested students are chosen via an application process, while the homeless residents are chosen via referral from city institutions. This kind of co-living model is advantageous on many levels. For one, it is immensely beneficial to the re-integration process of the formerly homeless residents. The students are also exposed to a range of diverse life experiences. VinziRast-mittendrin also functions as a social hub for people from all backgrounds, many of whom would normally have either limited or no contact with people experiencing homelessness. The restaurant and guest garden on the ground floor and the roof studio, which provides a space for public events, allow regular contact to take place between marginalized and non-marginalized groups, which ultimately helps in reducing stigmatization.

Resident room in one of the shared apartments

Exterior of VinziRast-mittendrin: renovation of an existing structure and addition of a new roof

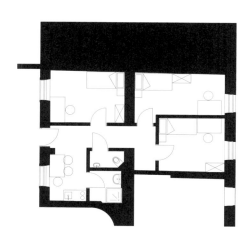

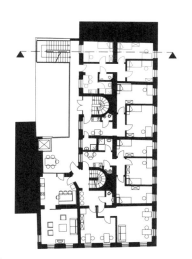

1:200

1:500

Plaza Apartments

NAME OF THE PROJECT: Plaza Apartments

COUNTRY: United States

ADDRESS: 988 Howard St., San Francisco, CA 94103

NEIGHBORHOOD: SOMA District

ARCHITECTURE: Paulett Taggart Architects and Leddy Maytum Stacy Architects

STRUCTURAL ENGINEERING: Nibbi Brothers (general contractors, construction)

CLIENT: Public Initiatives Development Corporation (PIDC)

INITIAL BUDGET: €13,500,000

FINAL COST: €13,700,000

FINANCED BY: Public Initiatives Development Corporation (PIDC), San Francisco Redevelopment Agency, and the Department of Public Health

PROJECT AND CONSTRUCTION YEARS: 2002-06

PROJECT TYPE: new construction, key role in revitalization efforts on 6th Street

PROGRAM: permanent supportive housing for formerly homeless individuals

TARGET GROUP: low-income individuals, chronically homeless people

NUMBER OF UNITS: 106 studio apartments

NUMBER OF BEDS PER UNIT: 1

TOTAL NUMBER OF DWELLERS: 106

RELATED FACILITIES IN THE BUILDING: retail, community theater, roof deck, communal spaces

Plaza Apartments was designed by Paulett Taggart Architects and Leddy Maytum Stacy Architects and inaugurated in March 2006. The aim was to demonstrate how housing can help chronically homeless individuals attain permanent stabilization, while at the same time reducing San Francisco's expenditures for servicing the homeless population. The city pays approximately €8,500 a year for each inhabitant of the Plaza Apartments, which is six to ten times less than for people who are still experiencing homelessness. In the nine-story building, 106 chronically homeless people reside in individual units. Each unit is 30 square meters and provides a platform bed, a bathroom, and a fully equipped kitchenette. Furthermore, there are several communal spaces meant to strengthen the cohesion of the inhabitants. The ground floor is partially public featuring a retail space, a landscaped courtyard, a community theater, and a communal laundry room. In addition to these shared spaces, the hallways of the upper floors are illuminated by natural light, which reaches the center of the building through the pinwheel-shaped floor plan and offers a view outside the building. Due to the sustainable strategies integrated into the building design and the high percentage of recycled materials used in construction, Plaza Apartments is not only socially but also environmentally sustainable.

Resident room

Plaza Apartments in an urban context

1:200

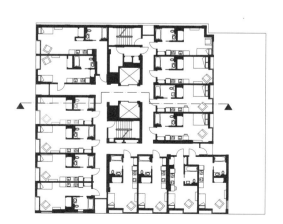

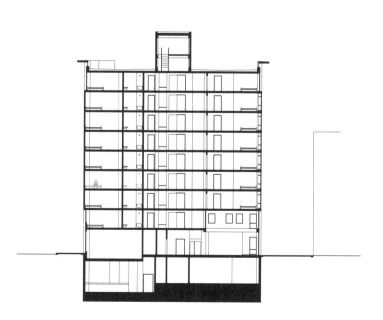

1:500

The Six Disabled Veteran Housing

NAME OF THE PROJECT: The Six Disabled Veteran Housing

COUNTRY: United States

ADDRESS: 811 S. Carondolet St., Los Angeles, CA 90057

NEIGHBORHOOD: MacArthur Park

ARCHITECTURE: Brooks + Scarpa

STRUCTURAL ENGINEERING: IEG Mechanical

CLIENT: Skid Row Housing Trust

INITIAL BUDGET: €8,500,000

FINAL COST: €8,600,000

FINANCED BY: National Equity Fund, the city of Los Angeles, and the state of California through low-income tax credits

PROJECT AND CONSTRUCTION YEARS: 2013–17

PROJECT TYPE: residential building

AREA: 3,740 m²

PROGRAM: permanent supportive housing for disabled veterans

TARGET GROUP: formerly homeless veterans, mentally ill, elderly, disabled, or LGBTQIA

NUMBER OF UNITS: 52 total; 45 studios and 7 apartments, 18 reserved for veterans

NUMBER OF BEDS PER UNIT: 1

TOTAL NUMBER OF DWELLERS: 52

RELATED FACILITIES IN THE BUILDING: offices and support spaces, bike storage, and parking for 19 cars

The Six Disabled Veteran Housing, a permanent supportive housing project for disabled veterans by Brooks + Scarpa, is located in a multifamily neighborhood called MacArthur Park, which has one of the highest population densities in the US with over 98,000 people per square kilometer. Built on a former parking lot, this infill housing project is well connected to the Los Angeles transit system. The ground floor of the building contains offices, support spaces for the veterans, and areas for parking bicycles and cars, while the second floor features a public courtyard with large openings and green roofs that visually connect to the street below, aiming to link residents to the larger community. The courtyard, being the centerpiece of the design, is surrounded by four levels of housing units featuring balconies wrapped with a wood screen made of recycled boards. The planning and design of The Six Disabled Veteran Housing emerged from close consideration and employment of passive design strategies. A big part of the concept involved the use of low-cost and low-maintenance materials, and during construction 75 percent of the related waste was diverted from landfills.

Resident room with kitchen

Inner courtyard of The Six Disabled Veteran Housing

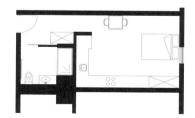

1:200

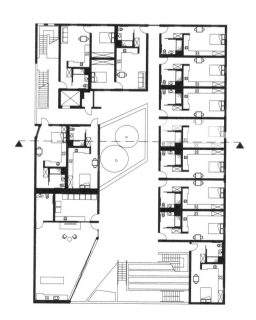

1:500

John and Jill Ker Conway Residence

NAME OF THE PROJECT: John and Jill Ker Conway Residence

COUNTRY: United States

ADDRESS: 1005 North Capitol St. NE, Washington, DC 20002

NEIGHBORHOOD: NoMa

ARCHITECTURE: Sorg Architects

CLIENT: Community Solutions

INITIAL BUDGET: €15,900,000

FINAL COST: €27,800,000

FINANCED BY: nonprofit partnering with a for-profit developer and property management firm

PROJECT AND CONSTRUCTION YEARS: 2005–17

PROJECT TYPE: residential building

PROGRAM: permanent supportive housing

TARGET GROUP: low-income individuals, homeless veterans

NUMBER OF UNITS: 124 studio apartments (100–125 m²); 17 units are low income, 47 units are moderate income, and 60 units are for formerly homeless veterans

NUMBER OF BEDS PER UNIT: 1

TOTAL NUMBER OF DWELLERS: 124

RELATED FACILITIES IN THE BUILDING: ground-floor retail, management offices, community room, recreational facilities, fitness center, laundry room, computer center, and support services like social and psychiatric care, medical services, and job-training spaces

Although veteran homelessness in the Washington, DC, area has decreased in recent years, approximately 500 veterans are among the 6,000 people without a place to sleep in the city. Operating on the principle that homelessness is a preventable circumstance, an unprecedented collaboration between public, private, philanthropic, and nonprofit partners has resulted in the John and Jill Ker Conway Residence designed by Sorg Architects. The architectural design concept aims to create a healthy and inspiring environment for the residents, who are transitioning out of homelessness and back into society. This fourteen-story project has 124 units, with 60 units of permanent supportive housing for formerly homeless veterans, 47 units of affordable housing for tenants at or below 60 percent of the area's median income, and 17 units of affordable housing for tenants at or below 30 percent of the area's median income. The building includes management offices, a lounge, a fitness center, conference space, and ground-floor retail opportunities, as well as on-site support services to address the social, medical, and emotional needs of the residents. The design of the building structure engages its historical context through slim, modulated massing that takes advantage of views to the north and south, including the US Capitol Building and the city's monuments, while also providing outdoor terraces and increased daylight for the units. The extensive use of glazing throughout the building maximizes natural light in common corridors, enlivening interior spaces and connecting residents to the larger urban context.

"God Bless Our Home": resident room

Exterior of John and Jill Ker Conway Residence

1:200

1:500

neunerhaus

NAME OF THE PROJECT: neunerhaus

COUNTRY: Austria

ADDRESS: Hagenmüllergasse 34, 1030 Vienna

NEIGHBORHOOD: 3rd District of Vienna

ARCHITECTURE: pool Architektur

CLIENT: WBV-GPA Wohnbauvereinigung für Privatangestellte, neunerhaus – Hilfe für Obdachlose Menschen

INITIAL BUDGET: €4,995,000

FINAL COST: €5,103,000

FINANCED BY: WBV-GPA, neunerhaus

PROJECT AND CONSTRUCTION YEARS: 2012–15

PROJECT TYPE: residential building

PROGRAM: temporary housing without a time limit, supportive housing

TARGET GROUP: homeless individuals and couples

NUMBER OF UNITS: 73; 67 single apartments and 6 apartments for couples, including 57 units for temporary housing and 22 units for permanent supportive housing

NUMBER OF BEDS PER UNIT: 1–2

TOTAL NUMBER OF DWELLERS: 79

RELATED FACILITIES IN THE BUILDING: medical center, social support, and event area

The residential building called neunerhaus, designed by pool Architekten, opened in 2015 to house homeless people in Vienna's 3rd District near the city center. For the developers, the provision of housing is understood as a central element of integration. The architects divided the basic concept of the building into three fundamental blocks: first, an open circulation zone that runs through the entire building; second, a variety of different apartment types with optimized sanitary units; third, a largely standardized modular and basic furniture design. The functional arrangement follows the sequence from public areas on the ground level (medical and office center) and basement (communal rooms and storage) to the private living areas with communal zones on the upper levels. Communication among all residents is given utmost importance in this straightforward form of housing. A large public space leads from the basement to the attic. This also serves to improve communication in the building and favors a coherent and connected design of all interior spaces. The neunerhaus Gesundheitszentrum carries an immense importance also for the homeless people of Vienna, being the main medical center for a chain of medical services only dedicated to homeless people.

Resident room on the top floor

Exterior of neunerhaus

1:200

1:500

Lebensraum o16

NAME OF THE PROJECT: Lebensraum o16

COUNTRY: Germany

ADDRESS: Ostparkstraße 16, 60385 Frankfurt am Main

NEIGHBORHOOD: Ostend

ARCHITECTURE: Michel Müller, Heiner Blum, Jan Lotter, and HKS Architekten

STRUCTURAL ENGINEERING: Wagner Zeitter Bauingenieure

CLIENT: Frankfurter Verein für soziale Heimstätten

INITIAL BUDGET: €1,300,000

FINANCED BY: local social-work providers in Frankfurt am Main

PROJECT AND CONSTRUCTION YEARS: 2009–ongoing

PROJECT TYPE: residential building

PROGRAM: emergency shelter, in exceptional cases also long-term housing

TARGET GROUP: homeless or low-income individuals and families, individuals suffering from alcohol or drug abuse and mental illness

NUMBER OF UNITS: 78

NUMBER OF BEDS PER UNIT: 1–4

TOTAL NUMBER OF DWELLERS: 150

RELATED FACILITIES IN THE BUILDING: reception, consultation rooms, administration, printing room, medical office, common kitchen, laundry rooms, bathrooms, green outdoor spaces with seating

The Lebensraum o16 shelter for homeless people is situated at the edge of Ostpark in Frankfurt. From the very beginning, the project was in the public eye. What used to be a temporary shelter made of tents for nearby homeless people was heavily criticized after a journalistic investigation. The inadequate conditions of the temporary shelter led the Frankfurter Verein für soziale Heimstätten (Frankfurt Association for Social Housing) to propose permanent units. The shelter was created through a participatory process involving the Frankfurter Verein für soziale Heimstätten, the Grünflächenamt (Parks Department) of the city of Frankfurt, an advisory board of homeless and non-homeless citizens, the architect Michel Müller, and the artists Heiner Blum and Jan Lotter. The purple-gleaming façade of stainless-steel shingles encloses the shelter on the outside toward the park and therefore toward public space. Nonetheless, its sculptural character, which is reinforced through the placement of the window openings, forms a striking image for park visitors. The shelter was originally built for emergency cases, but it also provides room for long-term living. Entrance doors are unconstrained and lead to an anteroom that usually contains two units of just 10 square meters to accommodate two people and one shared toilet. Inside, the units offer minimal furniture with one bunk bed, a locker, and a refrigerator. Even though the admission rules enable long-term stays, the small size of the unit is very limiting in terms of the spatial comfort it gives its residents.

Shared resident room with bunk beds

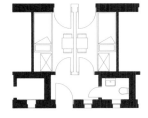

1:200

View of the wood-clad courtyard at Lebensraum o16

1:500

The Brook

NAME OF THE PROJECT: The Brook

COUNTRY: United States

ADDRESS: 457–459 E. 148th St. / 519–529 Brook Ave.,
New York, NY 10455

NEIGHBORHOOD: Bronx

ARCHITECTURE: Alexander Gorlin Architects

STRUCTURAL ENGINEERING: Ysrael A. Seinuk Engineers

CLIENT: Common Ground Community

INITIAL BUDGET: €22,300,000

FINAL COST: €23,000,000

FINANCED BY: Breaking Ground, a nonprofit developer
and social-service provider

PROJECT AND CONSTRUCTION YEARS: 2005–10

PROJECT TYPE: residential building

PROGRAM: permanent supportive housing

TARGET GROUP: low-income, formerly homeless people,
people living with HIV

NUMBER OF UNITS: 190 studios

NUMBER OF BEDS PER UNIT: 1

TOTAL NUMBER OF DWELLERS: 190

RELATED FACILITIES IN THE BUILDING: services from the
Bronx Works and some facilities such as retail,
maintenance, community space, and workshops

The Brook is a social housing project designed by Alexander Gorlin Architects in the Bronx borough of New York City. Addressing individuals with a low income, people experiencing homelessness, and those living with HIV or mental illnesses, the facility is intended to function as a permanent housing opportunity while transitioning into stable employment as well as housing. The 190 housing units, each consisting of a one-bedroom apartment with an individual bathroom and kitchen, are complimented by communal spaces designed for multipurpose use, with individual rooms for fitness, laundry, and computers, that are meant to function as shared living spaces. On the ground floor, social services offer support. The building, located on a formerly empty site at the intersection of 148th Street and Brook Avenue, seeks to be a cornerstone within the city fabric and also a general service provider on the ground floor. The façade is made of bricks and metal panels. Along the corner edge of the six-story building, bright-red-clad terraces are situated on the rooftop and along the façade, creating an interruption in the building's volume that emphasizes the depth variations of its surface. The architects designed an environmentally responsible building by incorporating green spaces on the roof and in the courtyard, and by using as much recycled and regional material as possible, as well as prefabricated elements, during construction.

Inner courtyard with seating area

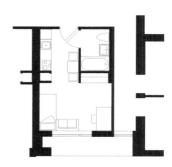

1:200

The Brook at the corner of 148th Street and Brook Avenue, Bronx

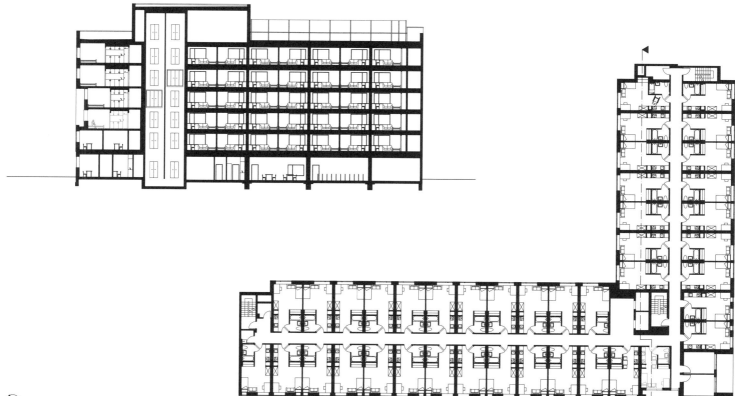

1:500

meinzuhaus.at

NAME OF THE PROJECT: meinzuhaus.at

COUNTRY: Austria

ADDRESS: Hübnergasse 8, 5020 Salzburg

NEIGHBORHOOD: Riedenburg

ARCHITECT: Melanie Karbasch

CLIENT: Caritas Erzdiözese Salzburg, Salzburger Studentenwerk

INITIAL BUDGET: €2,400,000

FINAL COST: €2,700,000

FINANCED BY: urban and rural social departments, RC Salzburg Altstadt, RC St. Rupert, RC Stiftland (partner club of RC Salzburg), Inner Wheel Salzburg, Rotaract Club Salzburg, and Lions Clubs of Salzburg

PROJECT AND CONSTRUCTION YEARS: 2017–18

PROJECT TYPE: residential building

PROGRAM: temporary form of living for homeless residents of Salzburg (maximum of 3 years)

TARGET GROUP: adults or women with children (separate women's living area) who are affected by various forms of housing shortage

NUMBER OF UNITS: 55 (separate women's living area)

NUMBER OF BEDS PER UNIT: 1 (optional 3 two-room units for women with children)

TOTAL NUMBER OF DWELLERS: 55

RELATED FACILITIES IN THE BUILDING: social care and counseling, community garden, room for washing machines and dryers

The number of homeless people in Salzburg has risen sharply in recent years. Designed by the architect Melanie Karbasch, the meinzuhaus.at project is located in the southwestern part of the city and offers temporary housing for people experiencing homelessness. It consists of fifty-five residential units. Residents can find accommodation for a certain period at reasonable prices; and they are looked after by social workers with the aim of being able to return to "normal" life. The project is innovative thanks to its modular housing approach. Each unit is prefabricated to a high degree, which in turn results in short construction times and low building costs. The use of modular elements also enables flexibility. If the building is required for other purposes, it can be dismantled without any difficulty and rebuilt elsewhere. meinzuhaus.at is a joint project by the Sisters of Mercy who are the landowners, Heimat Austria who are the developers and building owners, Salzburger Studentenwerk who manage the facilities, and Caritas Salzburg who provide social support. Due to the cooperation between these organizations, high quality has been achieved in the conception and construction of this residential facility.

Exterior of meinzuhaus.at

Resident room

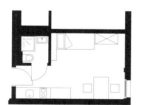

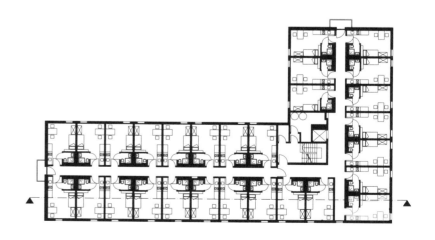

1:200   1:500

VinziDorf Wien

NAME OF THE PROJECT: VinziDorf Wien

COUNTRY: Austria

ADDRESS: Boërgasse 7, 1120 Vienna

NEIGHBORHOOD: Hetzendorf

ARCHITECTURE: gaupenraub+/- (Alexander Hagner and Ulrike Schartner)

CLIENT: Vinzenzgemeinschaft Eggenberg – VinziWerke

FINAL COST: €1,500,000

FINANCED BY: Fond Soziales Wien, Lazaristen, 20 years of land use rights, donations, volunteers, students of HTL Mödling

PROJECT AND CONSTRUCTION YEARS: 2010–18

PROJECT TYPE: construction of new prefabricated living modules and renovation of preexisting structures

PROGRAM: permanent supportive housing

TARGET GROUP: chronically homeless alcoholic men who could no longer accept other existing facilities because of their personal condition or who were rejected by them

NUMBER OF UNITS: 24

NUMBER OF BEDS PER UNIT: 1

TOTAL NUMBER OF DWELLERS: 24

RELATED FACILITIES IN THE BUILDING: social services and support, community garden, guest house with TV and table soccer

The architectural firm gaupenraub+/- has been committed to the realization of the VinziDorf in Vienna since Alexander Hagner met the pastor Wolfgang Pucher, who brought the idea from Graz to Vienna in 2002. The project, however, came to fruition only fifteen years later, in 2018, after immense clashes with the neighboring population. Eventually sixteen prefabricated residential modules, each with their own sanitary facilities, were built. The existing building, a former service building of the Lazarist retreat house property, was completely renovated. The attic of the existing building was converted and accommodates eight additional living spaces with bathrooms. Since the private living areas are very small, they are compensated for by large communal areas. Those who wish to join the community can first visit the "guesthouse" in the completely renovated former service building. The large fruit garden is available to all and offers another way to get into contact with other residents. The project is a prototype of alternative housing that offers long-term homeless alcoholic men a chance for a dignified abode. It has already been studied by other cities, such as Marburg and Klagenfurt, which would like to have a VinziDorf in their domain.

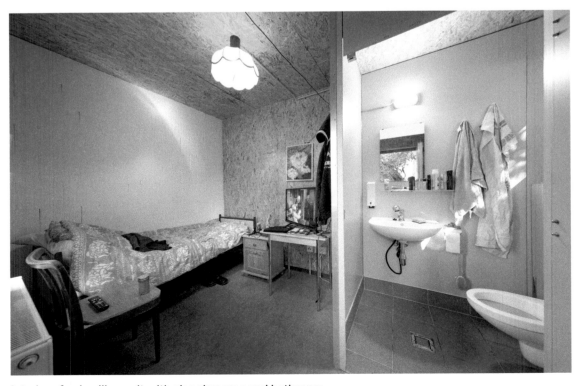

Interior of a dwelling unit with sleeping area and bathroom

Dwelling units at VinizDorf

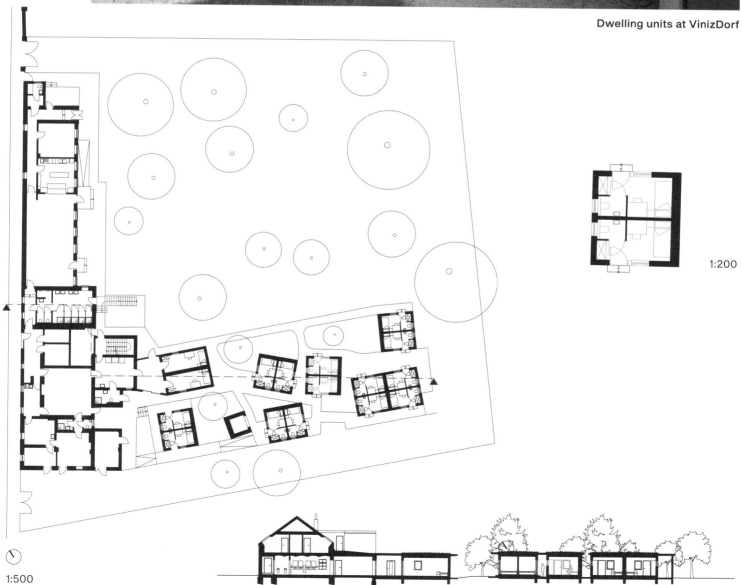

1:200

1:500

New Carver Apartments

NAME OF THE PROJECT: New Carver Apartments

COUNTRY: United States

ADDRESS: 1624 S. Hope St., Los Angeles, CA 90015

NEIGHBORHOOD: Skid Row

ARCHITECTURE: Michael Maltzan Architecture

STRUCTURAL ENGINEERING: B.W. Smith Structural Engineers

CLIENT: Skid Row Housing Trust

INITIAL BUDGET: €15,700,000

FINAL COST: €16,600,000

FINANCED BY: Skid Row Housing Trust

PROJECT AND CONSTRUCTION YEARS: 2006–09

PROJECT TYPE: residential building

PROGRAM: permanent supportive housing

TARGET GROUP: homeless older adults and homeless adults with chronic disease/disability (highly vulnerable people), elderly and those in need of health-care services (due to the building's proximity to a hospital)

NUMBER OF UNITS: 97 (28 m²)

NUMBER OF BEDS PER UNIT: 1

TOTAL NUMBER OF DWELLERS: 97

RELATED FACILITIES IN THE BUILDING: communal spaces like kitchens, dining areas, gathering spaces, roof garden, laundry rooms on every floor, and support facilities for medical and social services

New Carver Apartments by Michael Maltzan Architecture is located in the Skid Row neighborhood of Los Angeles, which is well known for its high population of homeless people. It is the third project that MMA completed with the Skid Row Housing Trust, an institution focused on creating permanent supportive housing; it has been engaging cutting-edge architecture firms to design buildings that are innovative in their internal layout and offer programs that engage the neighborhoods where they are located. The design process is built on existing relationships and the knowledge gained from earlier permanent supportive housing projects. With ninety-seven very similar apartment layouts generating equality among the residents, it creates a base for a community. The studio apartments are small but offer high-quality furnished accommodations, including a kitchen with cooktop. The complex consists of several communal spaces which are distributed throughout the building, such as a community kitchen, dining area, central courtyard, indoor lounge, laundry room, observation platform, and community garden. Also, support facilities for medical and social services are located on the ground floor. The circular form of the building's upper levels is intentionally broken to create visual connections to the city beyond. Rather than blend in, the building's distinctive architecture intends to highlight permanent supportive housing in the city, boosted by the proximity to the freeway.

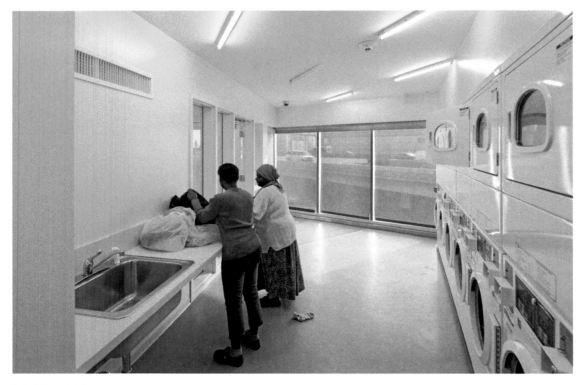

Laundry room

New Carver Apartments next to the Santa Monica Freeway

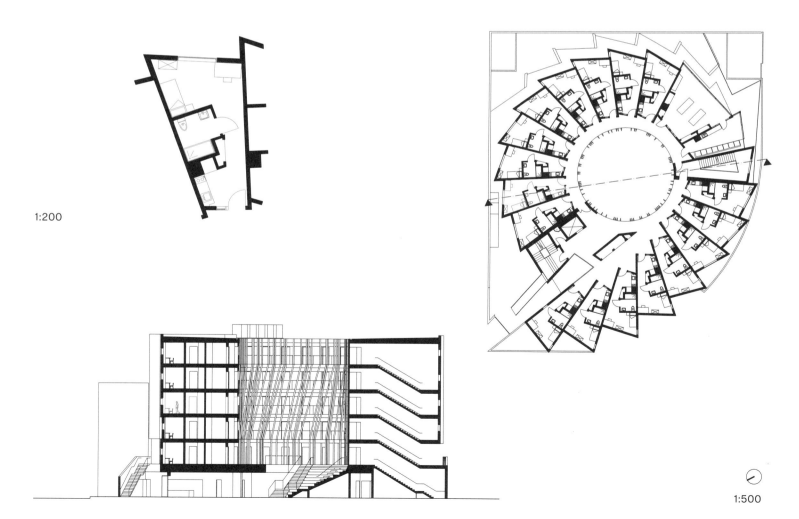

1:200

1:500

Holmes Road Studios

NAME OF THE PROJECT: Holmes Road Studios

COUNTRY: United Kingdom

ADDRESS: 41–43 Holmes Road, Camden, London

NEIGHBORHOOD: Kentish Town

ARCHITECTURE: Peter Barber Architects

CLIENT: LB Camden and GLA Funding

COST: unknown

FINANCED BY: Community Investment Program of the Council of Camden

PROJECT AND CONSTRUCTION YEARS: 2012–16

PROJECT TYPE: refurbishment and new buildings, apartment complex with cottages

PROGRAM: collective and supportive housing

TARGET GROUP: homeless individuals, former abusers of drugs and alcohol; furthermore, there is a high incidence of mental illness

NUMBER OF UNITS: 52 single en suite rooms; 24 are arranged as small houses, only 14 m²; the others are arranged as clusters with typically 3–4 en suite bedrooms with a shared kitchen, living, dining space

NUMBER OF BEDS PER UNIT: 1

TOTAL NUMBER OF DWELLERS: 52

RELATED FACILITIES IN THE BUILDING: training, counseling, and meeting rooms, central communal garden, small medical room

Designed by Peter Barber Architects, Holmes Road Studios is a homeless facility completed in 2016 that provides high-quality residential accommodations. The housing program is combined with training and counseling facilities focused on residents who have a history of drug and alcohol abuse. Furthermore, there is a high incidence of mental illness, and the majority are unemployed. Most of the accommodations are single apartments with their own bathroom and kitchen, which provide secure and private space. Residents have the option of withdrawing from the public and being independent, but they are also given a chance to socialize. The rooms are lit by circular windows, a roof light, and a partially glazed door, so as to encourage interaction with other neighbors. This provides a sufficient amount of light, which supports mental well-being. The central element of the complex is a garden where residents can work together with a gardener to grow their own fruit and vegetables. In this building, the choice of materials, the inclusion of colors in such elements like doors, the spatial qualities of the units, the greenery of the yard, and the combination of all design decisions at large are aimed at creating a sense of belonging for the residents. The idea of the architects is that if residents identify and are proud of the place where they live, it will add to their sense of self and can turn out to be empowering.

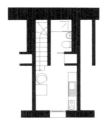

1:200

Entrance area and kitchen of one of the units

Exterior view of Holmes Road Studios

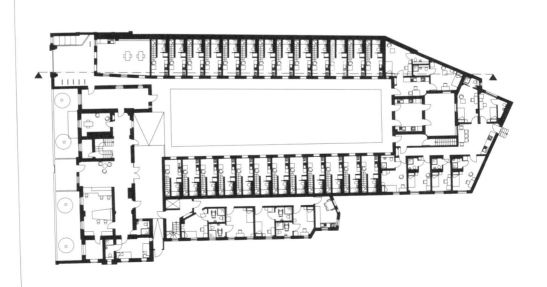

1:500

MLK1101 Supportive Housing

NAME OF THE PROJECT: MLK1101 Supportive Housing

COUNTRY: United States

ADDRESS: 1101 Martin Luther King Jr. Blvd., Los Angeles, CA 90037

NEIGHBORHOOD: Exposition Park, California Science Center, Natural History Museum, parks and gardens

ARCHITECTURE: Lorcan O'Herlihy Architects (LOHA)

STRUCTURAL ENGINEERING: John Labib & Associates

CLIENT: Clifford Beers Housing, Inc.

INITIAL BUDGET: €7,900,000 (original construction bid)

FINAL COST: €13,800,000

FINANCED BY: Wells Fargo Bank, National Equity Fund, LA Housing and Community Investment Department, among others

PROJECT AND CONSTRUCTION YEARS: 2018–19

PROJECT TYPE: residential building

PROGRAM: permanent supportive housing

TARGET GROUP: low-income families, veterans, and chronically homeless individuals

NUMBER OF UNITS: 26 total; 1 manager's unit, 15 units for chronically homeless households and large families with special needs, 10 units for homeless veteran households

NUMBER OF BEDS PER UNIT: 1–3

TOTAL NUMBER OF DWELLERS: ca. 26–60

RELATED FACILITIES IN THE BUILDING: retail, street-level community space, supportive services, and community garden

MLK1101 Supportive Housing by Lorcan O'Herlihy Architects (LOHA) was created to provide a permanent housing solution for vulnerable members of society. Located at the heart of Los Angeles, it gives the residents proximity to unique amenities, as well as excellent access to public transit. MLK1101 consists of a four-story building featuring forty-two apartments of various sizes for low-income families, veterans, and individuals experiencing chronic homelessness. The architect's objective was to create an environment that encourages health and community. Therefore, social spaces arise from a variety of planned and organic strategies, such as an elevated community garden above the building's parking garage. LOHA integrates the building into the community by establishing a street presence through a storefront space and a widened staircase that connects the street to the community spaces. All of the units are accessed through exterior walkways. While the unit layouts are almost identical on each floor, the walkways vary in width for a more dynamic, staggered elevation so as to create informal gathering spaces and opportunities for residents to socialize.

Resident unit with kitchen

Kids playing in the courtyard of MLK1101

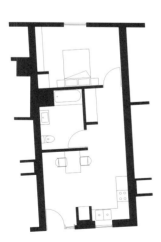

1:200

1:500

Notunterkünfte Liebrechtstraße

NAME OF THE PROJECT: Notunterkünfte Liebrechtstraße

COUNTRY: Germany

ADDRESS: Liebrechtstraße 3, 45277 Essen

NEIGHBORHOOD: Überruhr-Hinsel

ARCHITECTURE: RKW Architektur +

STRUCTURAL ENGINEERING: R&P RUFFERT
Ingenieurgesellschaft mbH

CLIENT: city of Essen

FINAL COST: €8,300,000

FINANCED BY: city of Essen

PROJECT AND CONSTRUCTION YEARS: 2013–18 (partly built)

PROJECT TYPE: shelter

PROGRAM: temporary shelter for homeless individuals

TARGET GROUP: homeless individuals

NUMBER OF UNITS: 101

NUMBER OF BEDS PER UNIT: 1–2

TOTAL NUMBER OF DWELLERS: 120

RELATED FACILITIES IN THE BUILDING: offices for
2 social workers and 2 facility managers

After having commissioned calculations on the feasibility of a dated shelter structure in the Überruhr-Hinsel district of Essen, the city acted on the poor outcome, including high renovation costs, and decided to plan a new shelter building on the same premises. The new building, Notunterkunft Liebrechtstraße, was commissioned to RKW Architektur + and consists of three similar buildings, each with two levels and a rectangular outline. The outer appearance of the building is dominated by three materials, namely, blue tiles for the walls, concrete for the balconies and ceilings, and wood for the doors and window frames. The apartments can be reached via the balconies extending around the building, which also function as circulation areas for the inhabitants. The apartments are entered through a door-window element that leads to the main room of the apartment, which is equipped with a small kitchen. Each apartment has a small separate bathroom, including a toilet, sink, and shower. The concept of the building is carried out in a minimalistic way. Repetition is in the rooms, balconies, and even the buildings.

Empty unit with outdoor access

Exterior elevation of Notunterkünfte Liebrechtstraße, Essen

1:200

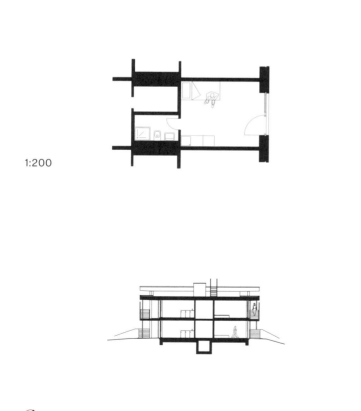

1:500

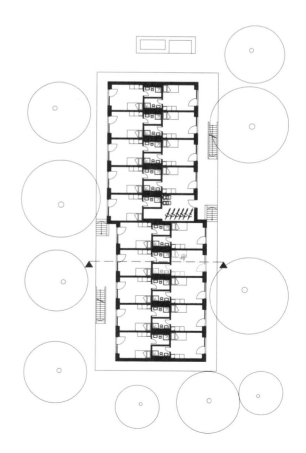

Hope on Alvarado

NAME OF THE PROJECT: Hope on Alvarado

COUNTRY: United States

ADDRESS: 166 South Alvarado St., Los Angeles, CA 90057

NEIGHBORHOOD: Westlake North

ARCHITECTURE: KTGY Architecture + Planning

STRUCTURAL ENGINEERING: R&S Tavares Associates Structural (factory built), PBA (site built)

CLIENT: 166 Alvarado, LLC

INITIAL BUDGET: unknown

FINAL COST: unknown

FINANCED BY: Measure HHH, a private development group that used city bond money

PROJECT AND CONSTRUCTION YEARS: 2018–20

PROJECT TYPE: residential building

PROGRAM: permanent supportive housing

TARGET GROUP: homeless individuals

NUMBER OF UNITS: 84, consisting of one-bedroom units (45 m²) and studio units (30 m²)

NUMBER OF BEDS PER UNIT: 1

TOTAL NUMBER OF DWELLERS: 84

RELATED FACILITIES IN THE BUILDING: parking spaces are provided for social-service staff, while each resident has a bike-storage space

Alvarado Street is not one of Los Angeles's major arteries, so the communities living here offer authentic vibrancy and diversity. It is also easy to see that many people affected by homelessness are camping on the outskirts of the neighborhoods around this street. Hope on Alvarado is the first in a series of supportive homes by KTGY Architecture + Planning and a private developer, aiming to house homeless people by creating both a home and a strong community. Permanent supportive housing in Los Angeles is not a new idea, but the goal of this development was to see if there was a way to build such structures faster and better than traditional methods, which led the design team to consider modular construction as a solution. While the site was being cleared, the foundations poured, and the podium erected on site, the modular units were built off site to speed up the construction process. Once the units arrived, it took about a month to lift them into place, enabling the complex to be completed in just fourteen months. The building was erected around a central courtyard that offers privacy, security, and an immersive sense of community. A partially underground parking garage uses the slope of the site uniquely so that the garage is not visible. Parking spaces are provided for the social-service employees, while every resident has a bicycle parking space. Floor-to-ceiling glazing along the common areas is intended to encourage interaction among the residents and bring movement to the street, thus maximizing the transparency of the spaces.

Resident unit with kitchen

View of Hope on Alvarado

1:200

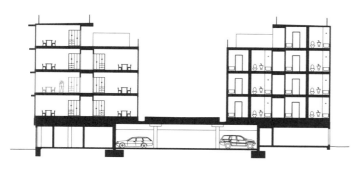

1:500

La Ferme du Rail

NAME OF THE PROJECT: La Ferme du Rail

COUNTRY: France

ADDRESS: 2A Rue de l'Ourcq, 75019 Paris

NEIGHBORHOOD: 19th arrondissement

ARCHITECTURE: Grand Huit (Clara Simay, Julia Turpin)

STRUCTURAL ENGINEERING: Scoping

CLIENT: Rehabail

FINAL COST: €3,500,000

FINANCED BY: funding from several associations and NGOs, partnership with many associations, city of Paris

PROJECT AND CONSTRUCTION YEARS: 2014–19 (contest winner of Réinventer Paris)

PROJECT TYPE: new construction, straw infill in braced load-bearing structure

AREA: 880 m²

PROGRAM: reintegration of disadvantaged people in a sustainable way

TARGET GROUP: socially excluded persons and horticulture students

NUMBER OF UNITS: 15 studios in Centre d'Herbergement and 5 studios in students' social residence

NUMBER OF BEDS PER UNIT: 1

TOTAL NUMBER OF DWELLERS: 20

RELATED FACILITIES IN THE BUILDING: a combination of (urban) environmental and social sustainability, a social reintegration center, a farm with workshops and a production greenhouse, a mushroom farm and outdoor spaces cultivated using permaculture, aquaponics, bag farming and agroforestry, a restaurant open to the neighborhood, and community spaces

In 2014, the architectural firm Gran Huit won the call for innovative urban projects in the Réinventer Paris (Reinvent Paris) program, launched by the Paris City Council, to design La Ferme du Rail. It was developed to meet the need of local residents and associations to create a place that combines urban agriculture and social sustainability. The farm aims to integrate people into a short-circuit, agri-urban space open to all, by simultaneously offering a sustainable building solution constructed with more than 90 percent bio-sourced dry or recycled materials, thus minimizing the need for energy, food, and financial resources by implementing a circular economy. The complex consists of farming land and two buildings: one provides a restaurant with farm-to-table, high-quality affordable cuisine, and the other provides a home to fifteen formerly homeless individuals or former convicts and five horticulture students who are working on the farm. Through housing as well as integration into an existing social network, the farm aims to offer a way back into society, by having access to professional training focused on sustainable agriculture, gardening, and gastronomy, leading to a high standard of qualification. Active interaction between the residents and the neighborhood is encouraged by the restaurant, along with workshops, lectures, and other events. By creating added value for the neighborhood, the project La Ferme du Rail fosters acceptance and sensitizes society to the issue of homelessness. It thus makes a future-proof contribution to counteracting the stigmatization of socially disadvantaged people, in order to promote a resilient, inclusive society.

View into the greenhouse

Harvesting at La Ferme du Rail

The Swift Factory

NAME OF THE PROJECT: The Swift Factory

COUNTRY: United States

ADDRESS: 10 Love Lane, Hartford, Connecticut 06120

NEIGHBORHOOD: North End

ARCHITECTURE: ICON Architecture, Bruner Cott Architects

CLIENT: Community Solutions

FINAL COST: €30,000,000

PROJECT AND CONSTRUCTION YEARS: 2014
(from design to the end of construction)

PROJECT TYPE: redevelopment

PROGRAM (FACILITIES IN THE BUILDING): common spaces: coworking space, future library; working spaces (restaurant or workshops): 465 m² of commercial prep kitchens; retail and/or service rental spaces: 930 m² of shared office/coworking space

NUMBER OF UNITS: 10 commercial kitchens, 12 offices plus coworking space

TARGET GROUP: the Hartford North End community at large, especially individuals with a low income, people in need

Originally opened in 1887 in Hartford, Connecticut, the Swift Goldleafing factory and two adjacent historical homes were donated to the nonprofit group Community Solutions in 2010 to reactivate the space and once again make it a community anchor after the complex had been sitting vacant and deteriorating for five years. Refurbished by ICON Architecture and Bruner Cott Architects, the factory is a pilot site for testing scalable solutions to improve the conditions of poverty. By developing prevention strategies through targeted real-estate investment, the project aims to strengthen high-poverty neighborhoods where the experience of homelessness is most prevalent and also a key indicator of many other system failures, including in health, education, housing, and criminal justice. Community Solutions met with hundreds of residents and conducted extensive research into the most appropriate and impactful use of the space. They then developed a site concept centered around local food entrepreneurship, job creation, and community assets, which was implemented by creating commercial prep kitchens, community spaces, health-care resources, a future library, offices, and coworking spaces. Much of the existing building fabric was restored, as required by state and federal historic tax credit financing. The campus of the factory is a collection of five buildings and two homes taking up an entire block of the neighborhood. Besides developing an adaptive reuse project, other sustainable building practices were implemented throughout the facility, including the installation of native trees and landscaping, while measures were taken to also reduce the building's operating costs.

Exterior of The Swift Factory

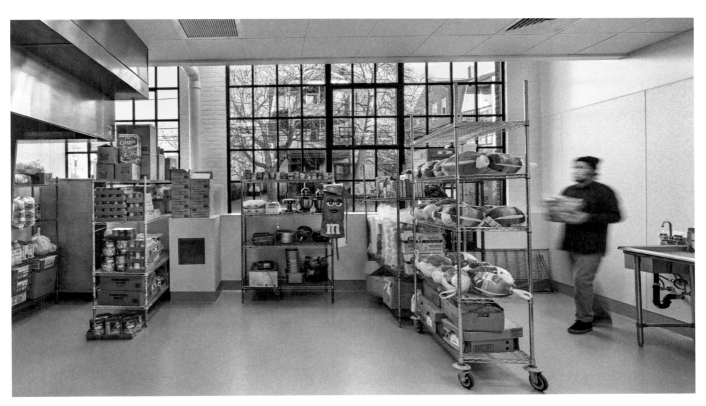

Kitchen area with historical windows

Seattle Public Library

NAME OF THE PROJECT: Seattle Public Library

COUNTRY: United States

ADDRESS: 1000 4th Ave., Seattle, Washington 98104

NEIGHBORHOOD: Downtown Seattle

ARCHITECTURE: OMA (Rem Koolhaas), LMN Architects

STRUCTURAL ENGINEERING: Magnusson Klemencic Associates, Arup

CLIENT: The Seattle Public Library

INITIAL BUDGET: unknown

FINAL COST: €133,000,000

PROJECT AND CONSTRUCTION YEARS: 1999–2004

PROJECT TYPE: new construction, glass and steel

AREA: 34,000 m²

PROGRAM: library

TARGET GROUP: people in need, kids, students, homeless individuals

RELATED FACILITIES IN THE BUILDING: social services and help for those in need; free information about how to get housing, help finding a job and more, offer of free classes and other resources to assist people who want to become US citizens or learn English; kids café with free meals and snacks available after school during the school year and all summer long

As the home to several giant companies like Amazon and Microsoft, Seattle's economy is growing. However, at the same time the city has one of the largest homeless populations in the United States with around 13,000 people sleeping in the streets. In cities around the world, libraries and other public buildings that were not designed specifically for those who are homeless take a leading role in bettering the life conditions of these vulnerable citizens. A prime example of this is the Seattle Public Library, designed by OMA and LMN Architects and finished in 2004, an eleven-story building of 38,000 square meters. As a building conceived to address inclusivity in particular, it has a critical role in catering to the city's homeless population through its generous spaces that integrate reading and lounging areas, yet without being subdivided into smaller programmed rooms. The bookshelves expand throughout the building, and spaces are flexible and can be enlivened by multiple activities. The accessible bathrooms, the seasonal provision of heating and air conditioning, the free Wi-Fi and computers, and the collections of books count among the features that attract people to this building. In particular, the unprejudiced attitude of the institution toward its homeless readers, along with the role of the staff providing professional support, is in symbiosis with the facilities and makes the library one of the most impactful institutions dealing with urban homelessness. With the help of public and private funds, the library has even extended its services to include psychological counseling, medical help, violence support, legal assistance, job training, food aid, and assistance in securing housing. Moreover, the library has a program that installs routers in homeless encampments, thus extending one of the services provided by the library, free Wi-Fi, to the place of residence of some of their readers.

View of the Seattle Public Library from the corner of 4th Avenue and Spring Street

One of the library's common areas

Mausoleo Dignidad

NAME OF THE PROJECT: Mausoleo Dignidad

COUNTRY: Chile

ADDRESS: General Cemetery of Santiago, Prof. Zañartu 951, Recoleta, Santiago

NEIGHBORHOOD: Recoleta

ARCHITECTURE: Grass+Batz+Arquitectos – Arquitectura UC

CLIENT: Fundación Gente de la Calle

PROJECT AND CONSTRUCTION YEARS: 2018–ongoing

PROJECT TYPE: new construction

PROGRAM: cemetery for homeless individuals, public space for reflection

NUMBER OF BURIAL UNITS: 500

TARGET GROUP: individuals experiencing homelessness

In 2018, the School of Architecture at the Pontificia Universidad Católica de Chile signed a collaboration agreement with the Fundación Gente de la Calle, a nonprofit institution dedicated to seeking solutions to the problem of street homelessness. Among the various lines of collaboration requested by the foundation was the development of a mausoleum project to provide decorous burial for people who were experiencing homelessness at the time of their death. The mausoleum was to be located in Santiago's main cemetery. Under the title Mausoleo Dignidad (Dignity Mausoleum), the structure seeks to honor the memory of people who did not live under the best conditions, providing a permanent home for them after their passing. The fundamental theme of this mausoleum is the idea that architecture can contribute, with its specific knowledge, to delivering a gracious burial to people who experienced maximum vulnerability, and this is done through the design of an architectural project. Moreover, it responds to a pending demand for the permanent burial of people who often do not have their own place of memory. In 2019, the proposal received an award in the UC Pastoral Fund Contest to finance the development of the architectural project: a funerary device with a maximum capacity of 500 burial units in a space for public use, encouraging reflection on life and death in the city. The new construction is lightweight and reversible, with readily available, low-cost materials.

Rendering of Mausoleo Dignidad's roofed corridor

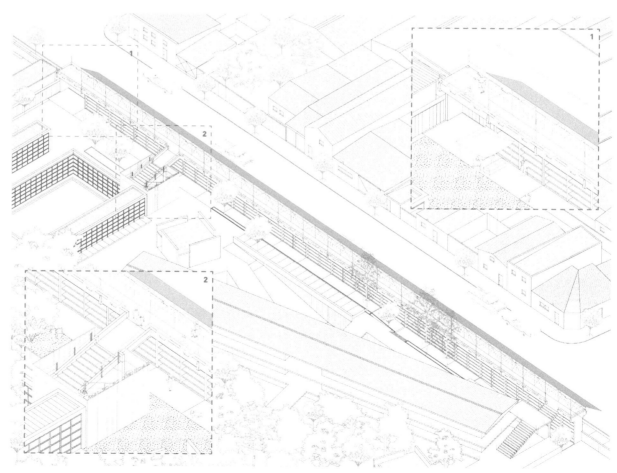

Detailed drawing of the mausoleum project

Acknowledgments

First of all, we would like to thank Thomas Hofmann, president of the Technische Universität München (TUM), the Faculty of Architecture, our former dean Andreas Hild, and our current department head Regine Keller for their generous support of the Architekturmuseum over many years.

Our gratitude is extended to State Minister Carolina Trautner from the Staatsministerium für Familie, Arbeit und Soziales and State Minister Kerstin Schreyer from the Staatsministerium für Wohnen, Bau und Verkehr for their encouragement and words at the exhibition opening.

We would like to thank PIN: Freunde der Pinakothek der Moderne and their chairwoman Dorothée Wahl for their interest in our exhibitions and for backing our institution. We are also grateful to the Stiftung Pinakothek der Moderne, and the chairman of the Foundation Board Markus Michalke, and the Architekturkultur Stiftung for their generous contributions to this exhibition. Many thanks to the Förderverein des Architekturmuseums (Friends of the Architecture Museum) for their constant assistance and encouragement, especially to the member Bernhard Schäpertöns for helping to produce the films for this exhibition and to the company Büschl Gruppe for supporting the exhibition at large. We thank the Stiftung Obdachlosenhilfe Bayern and the manager Verena Zillig for their generous support of this exhibition.

At the Pinakothek der Moderne we would like to thank Katarina Jelic and Katja Doblaski for their help in coordinating the project. At Pavilion 333 of the TUM we thank Enrica Ferrucci for her bighearted help. Our deep gratitude is extended to the whole team at the Architekturmuseum of the TUM for their continuous support and advice: in particular to the administrative staff members Martina Heinemann, Marlies Blasl, and Rike Menacher; the photographer Ester Vletsos; Thomas Lohmaier, Andreas Bohmann, and Anton Heine for the local organization and execution of the exhibition architecture; Vera Simone Bader and the student assistant Clara Frey respectively for their work on press and social media; and also to Dietlind Bachmeier for her outstanding help and active support. We are indebted to our exceptional student assistants: Anna-Maria Mayerhofer and Ann-Kathrin Gügel who helped with content and administration, to Theresa Thanner who was in charge of coordinating the case studies section and other material, and to Ilyas Kerem Yilmaz who co-taught with us in the architectural models class, drew plans for this publication, and revised texts, among many other tasks. The incisiveness, diligence, and skills of all of these students made this exhibition possible.

At the church of St. Bonifaz in Munich we thank Frater Prior Emmanuel Rotter OSB and Pater Dr. Korbinian Linsenmann for their trust and support; and the photographers Ulli Myrzik and Manfred Jarisch for agreeing to exhibit their outstanding Tokyo photographs in our satellite exhibition at St. Bonifaz. At the NS-Dokumentationszentrum (Munich Documentation Centre for the History of National Socialism) we thank the director Mirjam Zadoff and the curators Anke Hoffsten and Juliane Bischoff for engaging with our exhibition and collaborating with us on a temporary installation at their premises. The architect Fanny Allié, based in New York, took an interest in our exhibition project from the early stages, and we are grateful for her interest and delighted that she agreed to design a neon sculpture for Pavilion 333.

There have been several essential collaborators during the whole exhibition process to whom we are grateful for their help and engagement. The exhibition architect Carmen Wolf and the exhibition graphic designer Kathryn Gillmore have been critical in developing this exhibition. We want to thank Christian Bock from Bracher Bock Ingenieure, Munich, for his help with the Litfaßsäule (advertising column) presented in the exhibition. We are also indebted to Kathleen König, Katharina Gruszczynski, and Barbara Heinze for their help in producing and displaying textiles in the context of the exhibition scenography; to Guido Joost from Escher for assisting us with the printing of all exhibition materials; and to the Deutsche Meisterschule für Mode | Designschule München (German Fashion and Design School) for their involvement in textile design using the recycled material from the exhibition scenography.

We are grateful to the collaborating architects who shared their own design projects created as university students, which we are now showing in the exhibition: Jocelyn Froimovich with her Sleepingtory project in Mumbai and Lluís Alexandre Casanovas Blanco with his analysis of the shelter system in New York, both done when they studied at Columbia University; Matthew Ho's documentary on a Kurdish refugee who sleeps rough in London created at the Architectural Association in London; and Moritz Neumann, Paul Haas, and Felix Röttger's manifesto-like set of urban interventions in Munich done while attending our home institution. All of these projects expand the imaginary around the topic and represent approaches to design and research.

For contributing films to our exhibition we are grateful to Giovanna Borasi, director of the Canadian Centre for Architecture in Montreal, such as the outstanding film *What It Takes to Make a Home* (Daniel Schwartz, 2019); Lee Grant for allowing us to show part of her timeless documentary *Down and Out in America* (1986) and all the crew at Hope Runs High Films; and Matthew Ho for permitting us to show his *Urban Nomadism: The City as a Space of Exclusion*, which was part of his diploma project at the Architectural Association in 2019. We commissioned three original documentary films for this exhibition and, again, are thankful to Matthew Ho and his team in Hong Kong, to Nicole Huminski and Nikolai Huber in Munich, and to Fraya Frehse and her team in São Paulo for their outstanding films.

On October 29, 2020, we invited several specialists to a meeting in order to share our ideas and brainstorm together. We are indebted to the following individuals: the sociologist Luisa Schneider from the Vrije Universiteit Amsterdam and Max Planck Institut für ethnologische Forschung, Lydia Stazen as director of the Institute of Global Homelessness, Lien Heidenreich-Seleme as director of the Goethe-Institut in Los Angeles, the sociologist Martina Loew from the Technische Universität Berlin, the urban planner Alejandro Gutierrez from Arup London, and the architectural historian Anna-Maria Meister from the Technische Universität Darmstadt.

We extend our gratitude to all of the city researchers and authors who contributed to this publication and exhibition. Additional thanks go to Shiting Wang and Yutong Shi of Duke Kunshan University in Shanghai who helped the Shanghai team, Lisa Eidt who helped the Tokyo team, and the Architecture Foundation India which supported the Mumbai team. We are grateful to all of the architects and architectural offices that agreed to have their work exhibited and that helped us along the way with information, and to all of the photographers who allowed us to show their documentation of the exhibited projects.

In the winter semester of 2020–21, at the TUM, the Chair of History of Architecture and Curatorial Practice offered a graduate seminar and studio entitled "Who's Next? We Need to Talk about Homelessness" in order to understand the current state of homelessness in Germany, Austria, and Switzerland. This effort, which included relevant architectural projects, exceptional situations in each city, in-depth analyses of land prices, housing values, and rent costs, among other topics, ended in a student-designed exhibition at the Künstlerhaus Palais Thurn und Taxis Bregenz that ran from March 19 to May 2, 2021. We are grateful to the PhD candidates Clara Teresa Pollak and Marcelo Della Giustina for their assistance, and to the students Ann-Katrin Gügel, Ella Neumaier, Theresa Thanner, Ilyas Kerem Yilmaz, Antonia Cruel, Piet Kretschmer, Lavinia Krick, Lisa Luksch, Georg Meck, Ann Sophie Megerle, Ginnya Pryscilla, Ellen Scheer, Christopher Schmollinger, and Leonie van Kempen. Additionally, Michelle Hagenauer joined in some of the collective work and also made her graduate thesis on homelessness in Munich available to us. A fraction of these students attended a second class the following semester and were joined by Sofia Avdeeva, Francesco De Marchi, Matteo Lorenzi, and Sabrina Witzlau. The second group organized a week of panel discussions following the exhibition opening and an installation between December 13, 2021, and January 6, 2022, in the Pavilion 333 outside the museum.

The architectural models in the exhibition were constructed by students from one of our seminars; we are thankful to Mudar Alsaid, Marco Bär, Helena Leonie Bauer, Louise Bernsdorf Steffensen, Monica-Mariana Ciobotar, Chiara De Vuono, Luisa Decker, Aurélien Emberger, Amélie Giraud, Konstantin Maria Gutsch, Kilien-Robinson Heiland, Jonathan Sangmin Hoff, Christoph Hultsch, Judith Lea Hümer, Simon Christopher Arne Jensen, Feng Jiao, Rodion Kosmin, Mathilde Eva Andrée Marest, Adham Nagib, Ramona Overhoff, Nathanael Raharimanana, Hans Richter, Michele Scarlata, Melina Schechinger, Márton Sibelka, Anna Elisabeth Stevenson, Silvia Stitzinger, Tao Sun, Alexandra Tischkina, Jiayin Xu, Chaeeun Yoon, Johanna Zehntner, and Davida Zimmermann.

This publication was made possible because of the diligence of the English copyeditors Camila Schaulsohn and Dawn Michelle d'Atri and the German copyeditors Sonja Altmeppen, Ilka Backmeister-Collacott, Michael Bröderdörp, Arne Steingräber, and Julika Zimmermann, as well as the translators Amy Klement, Alexandra Titze-Grabec, and, coordinated by VerlagsService Mihr, Martin Bayer, Sabine Reinhardus, Cornelia Stoll, and Hans Freundl. Last but certainly not least, we are thankful for the commitment of Cristina Steingräber and Sonja Bröderdörp at ArchiTangle Publishers, the fantastic work of the graphic designer Julia Wagner, and the work of our outstanding and relentless editorial assistant Ella Neumaier, all of whom made this publication happen.

Biographies

BINYAMIN APPELBAUM is the lead writer on business and economics for the editorial board of *The New York Times*. Before joining the board in 2019, he was a longtime economic policy correspondent for the *Times*, based in Washington, DC. He writes regularly about housing issues, including the critical shortage of affordable housing in the United States and the growing number of Americans who are experiencing homelessness as a consequence. He is the author of *The Economists' Hour: False Prophets, Free Markets, and the Fracture of Society*, published in German translation in 2020 by S. Fischer Verlage as *Die Stunde der Ökonomen*.

JULIANE BISCHOFF works as a curator at the NS Dokumentationszentrum München at the interface between exhibition and digital mediation. Together with Nicolaus Schafhausen and Mirjam Zadoff, she co-curated the exhibition *Tell me about yesterday tomorrow* (2019–20). From 2016 to 2019, she worked at Kunsthalle Wien, where she curated, among others, the exhibition *Kate Newby: I can't nail the days down* (2018) and also co-curated and organized group exhibitions and discursive programs. Previously, she has worked at institutions like Kunsthalle Basel (2012) and Ludlow 38 at Goethe-Institut New York (2015). She is the editor of the publications *Kate Newby: I can't nail the days down* (Sternberg Press, 2019) and *Ineke Hans: Was ist Loos?* (Sternberg Press, 2017) and is a regular contributor to publications in the fields of art, culture, and society.

JOÃO BITTAR FIAMMENGHI is an architect and urban planner based in São Paulo with a degree from the Faculdade de Arquitetura e Urbanismo da Universidade de São Paulo (FAU-USP) in 2020, where he is conducting research for his master's degree in the field of architectural history (advisor: professor José Lira). As a researcher, Bittar Fiammenghi is affiliated with a joint Brazil/UK project called "Translating Ferro / Transforming Knowledges of Architecture, Design and Labour for the New Field of Production Studies," funded by the AHRC and FAPESP, informed by the work of the Brazilian architect and theorist Sérgio Ferro. In this context, he is also a technical trainee with the FAPESP scholarship program.

GIOVANNA BORASI is an architect, editor, and curator. She joined the Canadian Centre for Architecture (CCA) in 2005 and has been the director of the CCA since January 2020. Borasi's work explores alternative ways of practicing and evaluating architecture, considering the impact of contemporary environmental, political, and social issues on urbanism and the built environment. She studied architecture at the Politecnico di Milano, worked as an editor of *Lotus International* (1998–2005) and *Lotus Navigator* (2000–04), and was the deputy editor in chief of *Abitare* (2011–13). One of Borasi's latest curatorial projects is a three-part documentary film series that reconsiders architecture's relationship to and understanding of home and homelessness, living alone, and the elderly. The first film *What It Takes to Make a Home* (2019) screened at film festivals and institutions worldwide.

HELENA ČAPKOVÁ is a researcher, curator, and associate professor of the history of art at Ritsumeikan University, Kyoto. She has written extensively on transnational visual culture and architecture in Japan and Europe. In 2017–19, she worked as a curatorial researcher for the bauhaus imaginista project and published an article called "Framing Renshichirō Kawakita's Transcultural Legacy and His Pedagogy" in the 2019 exhibition catalogue *bauhaus imaginista: A School in the World*, edited by Marion von Osten and Grant Watson. In 2021, she curated a project to mark a hundred years of diplomatic relations between Japan and the Czech Republic, investigating architectural parallels: "1920–2020 PRAGUE–TOKYO / EXCHANGES, PARALLELS, COMMON VISIONS."

JAMES CARSE is a cofounder of ALAO with extensive experience leading award-winning projects around the world. Carse is a registered architect, certified urban planner, and accredited LEED Professional. He has served as an adviser for the American Planning Association's International Outreach Program and collaborated with public and private entities to reimagine the way we live, work, and create. James holds a Master of Architecture in Urban Design with Distinction from Harvard's Graduate School of Design and a Bachelor of Architecture from Tulane University. He has taught courses in urban design, architecture, and interior design at Columbia University, Cornell University, Parsons, and Tulane University.

LLUÍS ALEXANDRE CASANOVAS BLANCO, born 1985 in Barcelona, is an architect, curator, and scholar based in New York and Madrid. He is a doctoral student at Princeton Universty and serves as a scientific advisor for the new architecture collection at Museo Nacional Centro de Arte Reina Sofía, Madrid, where he also works as a curator. He was the chief curator of the Oslo Architecture Triennale 2016 together with the After Belonging Agency.

His design work has been recognized by several prizes, including the Simon Architecture Prize 2018 and the Bauwelt Prize 2019.

ALEJANDRA CELEDÓN is an architect who graduated from the Universidad de Chile in 2003. She earned her MSc Advanced Architectural Studies from The Bartlett, University College London, in 2007 and her PhD from the Architectural Association, London, in 2014. She was the curator of the Stadium, Chilean Pavilion, at the 16th Venice Architecture Biennale (2018) and the co-curator of *The Plot: Miracle and Mirage* at the 3rd Chicago Architecture Biennial (2019). Her recent publications include the book *Stadium: A Building That Renders the Image of a City* (Park Books, 2018) and the essays "The Chilean School: A Room for Upbringing and Uprising" (*AA Files*, 2020) and "The Plot: Miracle and Mirage" (*Revista 180*, 2021). She is the headmaster of the architecture program at the School of Architecture, Pontificia Universidad Católica de Chile.

CLARA CHAHIN WERNECK is an architect and urban planner with a degree from the Faculdade de Arquitetura e Urbanismo da Universidade de São Paulo (FAU-USP) in 2020, having done an exchange program at Accademia di Architettura di Mendrisio, Switzerland. During her studies, she received a scholarship to conduct under-graduate research on the topics of spatial perception and phenomenology in architecture. Chahin Werneck has worked in architectural firms in São Paulo such as Studio MK27 and Nitsche Arquitetos. She is interested in exploring the combination of practice and theoretical knowledge by engaging in projects on different scales and contexts, with a respectful consideration for the use of resources and materiality.

TATIANA EFRUSSI is an artist and art historian currently based in Paris. In 2011, she graduated from Lomonosov Moscow State University with a paper on Soviet connections to the Bauhaus. On the basis of this research, in 2012 she curated the exhibition *Bauhaus in Moscow* at Moscow's VKhUTEMAS gallery and graduated with a PhD from Kassel Universiät with a dissertation entitled "Hannes Meyer: A Soviet Architect." Her artistic work combines archival research and research into the archaeology of spaces with images and fiction. Recent exhibitions include *Escapism: Training Program* (Fabrika CCA, Moscow) and *Eccentric Values after Eisenstein* (with Elena Vogman, Diaphanes space, Berlin, 2018). An interest in the contemporary conditions of cultural labor inspired her to cofound the collective Flying Cooperation in 2015.

MARÍA ESNAOLA CANO is an architectural designer and educator based in Los Angeles. She is a registered architect in Spain and a Fulbright Scholar holding a Master's of Science in Advanced Architectural Design and a Master's of Science in Advanced Architectural Research from the Columbia Graduate School of Architecture, Planning and Preservation (GSAPP) in New York. Through her diverse affiliations with Los Angeles city institutions and as a member of the board of directors of the Los Angeles Forum for Architecture and Urban Design, she seeks to engage in current debates over the future of urban landscapes by studying the city as a physical phenomenon and as a cultural artifact. Esnaola Cano is a professor at the USC School of Architecture and is currently a visiting professor at ETH Zurich.

LEILANI FARHA is the former UN Special Rapporteur on the Right to Housing and the Global Director of The Shift. Her work is animated by the principle that housing is a social good, not a commodity. Leilani has helped develop global human rights standards on the right to housing, including through her topical reports on homelessness, financialization of housing, informal settlements, rights-based housing strategies, and the first UN Guidelines for the implementation of the right to housing. She is the central character in the documentary PUSH regarding the financialization of housing, which has been screening around the world. Leilani launched The Shift in 2017 with the UN Office of the High Commissioner for Human Rights and the organization United Cities and Local Governments.

FRAYA FREHSE is a professor of sociology at the Universidade de São Paulo, where she coordinates the Center for Studies and Research on the Sociology of Space and Time (NEPSESTE) and acts as a lead partner of the Global Center of Spatial Methods for Urban Sustainability (GCSMUS, Technische Universität Berlin). She is an alumna of the Alexander von Humboldt Foundation, a research fellow of the Brazilian National Council for Scientific and Technological Development, and a life member of Clare Hall College (University of Cambridge). Her research focuses mainly on urban theory; space, everyday life, and history; space and time in sociology; body, public space, and urbanization (in Brazil); urban mobility; urban inequality/poverty; cultural heritage; urban visual culture; and sociology of everyday knowledge.

JOCELYN FROIMOVICH is an architect in Chile and New York State. Her work ranges in focus and scale, from collaborative residential projects in New York State to installations such as MoMA's Young Architects Program exhibition *COSMO* held in 2015 at MoMA PS1. Current collaborative projects include the new Biblioteca Lorenteggio in Milan to be built by 2022. She has taught at

Columbia University, Pontificia Universidad Católica de Chile, Technische Universität Darmstadt, and the University of Liverpool. Froimovich's approach has a strong collaborative emphasis, believing that successful designs depend upon the close integration of multiple disciplines and a thorough understanding of the various aspects that constitute the built environment.

EREZ GOLANI SOLOMON earned his PhD in Architecture from the University of Tokyo. He is currently a senior lecturer in architectural design and theory in the Architecture Department at Bezalel Academy of Arts and Design, Jerusalem, and he also teaches in the Graduate School of Media and Governance at Keio University, Tokyo. His research work encompasses a range of issues concerning the contemporary city, and the ramifications of architectural developments under contemporary cultures and politics. Golani Solomon practices architecture as a partner at the Tokyo-based firm Front-Office. In 2021, he took over a senior fellow position at the Azrieli Architecture Archive of Tel Aviv Museum of Art.

SAMIA HENNI is a theorist and a historian of the built, destroyed, and imagined environments, and an assistant professor at Cornell University. She is the author of the multi-award-winning *Architecture of Counterrevolution: The French Army in Northern Algeria* (gta Verlag, 2017, EN; Editions B42, 2019, FR), the editor of the *War Zones: gta papers no. 2* (gta Verlag, 2018), the convener of the 2020 Preston Thomas Memorial Lectures *Into the Desert: Questions of Coloniality and Toxicity*, and the maker of exhibitions such as *Housing Pharmacology* (Manifesta 13, Marseille, 2020) and *Discreet Violence: Architecture and the French War in Algeria* (Zurich, Rotterdam, Berlin, Johannesburg, Paris, Prague, Ithaca, and Philadelphia, 2017–19).

ANDRES LEPIK is the director of the Architekturmuseum at the Technische Universität München (TUM), and a professor of history of architecture and curatorial practice at the TUM. He studied art history, graduating with a PhD on Architectural Models in the Renaissance. From 1994 he worked as a curator at the Neue Nationalgalerie, Berlin, where he presented the exhibitions *Renzo Piano* (2000) and *Content: Rem Koolhaas and AMO/OMA* (2003). From 2007 to 2011 he was a curator in the Architecture and Design Department at The Museum of Modern Art, New York, presenting the exhibition *Small Scale, Big Change: New Architectures of Social Engagement* (2010). In 2011–12, Lepik was a Loeb Fellow in the Graduate School of Design at Harvard University.

AYA MACEDA, a Filipino-Australian architect and professor at Parsons School of Design in New York, cofounded ALAO, a practice that bridges design, research, and social advocacy. A registered architect in Connecticut and Australia, she has worked with prestigious practices in Australia, Singapore, and the Philippines on the design of award-winning residential and institutional projects that enhance the public domain. Maceda received her M.S. Advanced Architectural Design and has taught at Columbia University's Graduate School of Architecture, Planning and Preservation (GSAPP). A board member of Westbeth Artists Housing and the Gowanus Canal Conservancy, she is dedicated to her advocacies. She has published her work in publications globally.

DAVID MADDEN is an associate professor of sociology and the director of the Cities Programme at the London School of Economics. Madden holds a PhD from Columbia University. He researches housing, urban theory, and urban politics, with a particular focus on New York City and London. He is the author, with Peter Marcuse, of *In Defense of Housing: The Politics of Crisis*, which has been translated into six languages. His writing has also appeared in *The Washington Post, The Guardian,* and *Jacobin*. He can be found on Twitter as @davidjmadden.

DON MITCHELL is a professor of human geography in the Department of Social and Economic Geography at Uppsala Universitet and Distinguished Professor of Geography Emeritus at Syracuse University. His work focuses on historical and contemporary struggles over the urban public, homelessness, the relationship between capital and labor in making the geographical landscape, and historical-geographical materialist theories of culture. His most recent book is *Mean Streets: Homelessness, Public Space, and the Limits of Capital* (UGA Press, 2020).

STEPHEN PRZYBYLINSKI is a postdoctoral researcher in the Department of Social and Economic Geography at Uppsala Universitet. His current research concerns justice theorizing in geography. His ongoing research focuses on property, political rights, houselessness, and the justification for liberal democracy.

TRUDE RENWICK is a scholar of architecture and urbanism whose research examines the intersection of the built environment, globalization, and spirituality. Her dissertation is an ethnographic study of the intersection of commercial and spiritual space in Bangkok. She graduated from the University of California, Berkeley, with a PhD in Architecture and currently holds a fellow position at Hong Kong University in the Society of Fellows in the Humanities.

VALENTINA ROZAS-KRAUSE is a postdoctoral LSA Collegiate Fellow in the History of Art Department at the University of Michigan. She is both a professional architect and a historian of the built environment with a focus on global cultural practices across the Americas and Europe. Rozas-Krause holds a PhD in Architectural History from the University of California, Berkeley, a Master's Degree in Urban Planning, and a B.Arch, both from the Pontificia Universidad Católica de Chile. She has published two books: *Ni Tan Elefante, Ni Tan Blanco* (Ril, 2014) and the coedited volume *Disputar la Ciudad* (Bifurcaciones, 2018).

ADITYA SAWANT is an architect and urban designer and practices as a researcher and academic in Mumbai. He is particularly interested in issues related to housing for low-income groups in urban India and was the research director for the *State of Housing India* exhibition held in Mumbai in 2018. He completed his Bachelor's in Architecture from the Kamla Raheja Vidyanidhi Institute of Architecture (KRVIA), Mumbai University, and his Master's in Architecture and Urban Design from the Graduate School of Design, Harvard University. He currently works on research projects about housing with the Architecture Foundation India and is an assistant professor of urban design at KRVIA.

LUISA SCHNEIDER is an assistant professor in anthropology at Vrije Universiteit and a research partner at the Max Planck Institute for Social Anthropology in the Law & Anthropology Department. She holds a DPhil in Anthropology from Oxford University and is working on the anthropology of violence, intimacy, and law. Since 2018 she has been conducting research with rough sleepers on how they can live privacy and intimacy if these rights and protections are tacitly tied to housing.

NICOLÁS STUTZIN is an architect who graduated from the Universidad de Chile in 2006. He holds an MSc in Advanced Architectural Design and a Diploma in Advanced Architectural Research from the Graduate School of Architecture, Planning and Preservation (GSAPP) at Columbia University (2011). He was the co-curator of *The Plot: Miracle and Mirage* at the 3rd Chicago Architecture Biennial (2019). His publications include *More Permanent than Snow: The Photographing of Aldo van Eyck's Playgrounds* (AA Files, 2014), *Cerro Sombrero: Mirages of Modernity* (Andinas, 2017), *Ahead of Their Time* (ARQ, 2018), and *The Plot: Miracle and Mirage* (Revista 180, 2021). Stutzin is an associate professor in the School of Architecture, Universidad Diego Portales, and an assistant professor in the School of Architecture, Pontificia Universidad Católica de Chile.

DANIEL TALESNIK is a curator at the Architekturmuseum of the Technische Universität München (TU Munich), where in 2019 he curated *Access for All: São Paulo's Architectural Infrastructures*, which was later shown in 2020 at the Center for Architecture in New York City and in 2021 at the Schweizerisches Architekturmuseum (S AM) in Basel. He is an architect who studied at the Pontificia Universidad Católica de Chile (2006) and earned a PhD from Columbia University (2016) with the dissertation "The Itinerant Red Bauhaus, or the Third Emigration." He teaches at the TUM and has also taught at the Pontificia Universidad Católica of Chile, Columbia University, and the Illinois Institute of Technology.

ELENA VOGMAN is a scholar of comparative literature and media. She is the principal investigator of the research project "Madness, Media, Milieus: Reconfiguring the Humanities in Postwar Europe" at the Bauhaus Universität Weimar. She is the author of *Sinnliches Denken: Eisensteins exzentrische Methode* (diaphanes, 2018) and *Dance of Values: Sergei Eisenstein's Capital Project* (diaphanes, 2019). Vogman was a visiting assistant professor of history at New York University Shanghai and held postdoctoral research positions in the Deutsche Forschungsgemeinschaft (DFG) project "Rhythm and Projection" at the Freie Universität Berlin and at the Internationales Kolleg für Kulturtechnikforschung und Medienphilosophie, Weimar. Together with Marie Rebecchi and Till Gathmann she curated the exhibitions *Sergei Eisenstein: The Anthropology of Rhythm* at Nomas Foundation, Rome (2017) and *Eccentric Values after Eisenstein* at espace diaphanes, Berlin (2018).

ZAIRONG XIANG is an assistant professor of comparative literature and the associate director of art at Duke Kunshan University in Suzhou, China. He is the author of *Queer Ancient Ways: A Decolonial Exploration* (punctum books, 2018). He was the chief curator of the "minor cosmopolitan weekend" at the HKW Haus der Kulturen der Welt (2018), and the editor of its catalogue *minor cosmopolitan: Thinking Art, Politics, and the Universe Together Otherwise* (Diaphanes, 2020). As a member of the Hyperimage Group, he has co-curated the 2021 Guangzhou Image Triennial. He is working on two projects, both dealing with the concepts of "transdualism" and "counterfeit" in the Global South, especially Latin America and China. He was a fellow at the ICI Berlin Institute for Cultural Inquiry (2014–16) and a postdoc of the Deutsche Forschungsgemeinschaft (DFG) Research Training Group called "Minor Cosmopolitanisms" at the Universität Potsdam (2016–20).

Bibliography

All URLs accessed and verified in September 2021 unless otherwise noted.

WRITTEN SOURCES

Advocates for Children of New York. "New Data Show Number of NYC Students who are Homeless Topped 100,000 for Fourth Consecutive Year." October 28, 2019. https://www.advocatesforchildren.org/node/1403.

Akademischer Sportverband Zürich (ASVZ). "Entspannen: Mit Erholung Energie tanken." https://asvz.ch/sport/245229-entspannen.

Akaishi, Ana Gabriela. "O 'problema' do centro de São Paulo não está nas ocupações de prédios vazios, mas nos prédios vazios em si." *Cidades para que(m)?* (blog). May 24, 2019. https://cidadesparaquem.org/blog/2019/5/24/o-problema-do-centro-de-so-paulo-no-est-nas-ocupaes-de-prdios-vazios-mas-nos-prdios-vazios-em-si.

Amadeu Antonio Stiftung. "Norbert Plath." July 24, 2000. https://www.amadeu-antonio-stiftung.de/todesopfer-rechter-gewalt/norbert-plath-staatlich-anerkannt/.

Apple. "Apple Allocates More than $400 Million to Combat California Housing Crisis." Apple Newsroom. July 13, 2020. https://www.apple.com/newsroom/2020/07/apple-allocates-more-than-400-million-to-combat-california-housing-crisis/.

Apuktina, Yulia, in collaboration Maria Abakulova. "Zolotaia moia: Reiting glavnykh benefitsiarov pokhoroshevshei Moskvy." The Project. October 22, 2020. https://www.proekt.media/guide/moskva-sobyanina/.

ARCH Advocacy and Research Centre for Homelessness. https://www.archomelessness.org.

Atkinson, Rowland, and Aidan While. "Defensive architecture: designing the homeless out of cities." *The Conversation.* December 30, 2015. https://theconversation.com/defensive-architecture-designing-the-homeless-out-of-cities-52399.

Augé, Marc. *No Fixed Abode: Ethnofiction.* Translated by Chris Turner. 2013. Reprint, London: Seagull Books, 2019.

——. *Tagebuch eines Obdachlosen.* Translated by Michael Bischoff. Munich: C. H. Beck, 2012.

Avvakumov, Yuri. *Bumazhnaya Arkhitektura: Antologiya.* Moscow: Garage, 2019.

——. *Paper Architecture: An Anthology.* Moscow: Artguide Editions, 2021.

Ayaß, Wolfgang. "'Asoziale': Die verachteten Verfolgten." In *Dachauer Hefte: Studien und Dokumente zur Geschichte der National Socialist Konzentrationslager*, edited by Wolfgang Benz and Barbara Distel. Vol. 14, no. 14, pp. 50–66. Munich: Dtv, 1998.

——. "'Demnach ist z.B. asocial ...': Zur Sprache sozialer Ausgrenzung im Nationalsozialismus." In *Ungleichheiten im Dritten Reich: Semantiken, Praktiken, Erfahrungen*, edited by Nicole Kramer and Armin Nolzen. Vol. 28 of *Beiträge zur Geschichte des Nationalsozialismus*, pp. 69–89. Göttingen: Wallstein, 2012.

——. "'Wohnungslose im Nationalsozialismus': Eine Wanderausstellung der BAG Wohnungslosenhilfe." In *Integration statt Ausgrenzung: Gerechtigkeit statt Almosen*, edited by Werena Rosenke, pp. 170–87. Bielefeld: Bundesarbeitsgemeinschaft Wohnungslosenhilfe, 2006.

Barros, Joana da Silva. "Moradores de rua, pobreza e trabalho: interrogações sobre a exceção e a experiência política brasileira." PhD diss., FFLCH-USP, São Paulo, 2004.

Batko, Samantha, Alyse D. Oneto, and Aaron Shroye. "Unsheltered Homelessness: Trends, Characteristics, and Homeless Histories." Urban Institute. December 3, 2020. https://www.urban.org/sites/default/files/publication/103301/unsheltered-homelessness.pdf.

Bay Area Regional Health Inequities Initiative. "Housing Insecurity and Displacement in the Bay Area." Metropolitan Transportation Commission, San Francisco, CA, February 20, 2016.

Bell v. City of Boise. "Eighth Amendment – Criminalization of Homelessness – Ninth Circuit Refuses to Reconsider Invalidation of Ordinances Completely Banning Sleeping and Campingin Public. – Martin v. City of Boise, 920 F.3d 584 (9th Cir. 2019)." *Harvard Law Review* 133 (December 10, 2019), p. 699.

Berger, Peter, and Brigitte Berger. *Sociology: A Biographical Approach.* New York: Basic Books, 1972.

Bezuglov, Dmitrii, Artem Beresnev, Maria Makarova, Nikita Malolkin, and Julia Senina. "Putting a figure on the cost of homelessness in Russia, and discussing ways to collect reliable data in the future." Oxford Russia Scholarship student project, March 15, 2021.

Bischoff, Alexander. "Die Tote von den Bahngleisen: Frau (25) wurde in Leipzig im Streit erschlagen." *Tag 24.* March 18, 2020. https://www.tag24.de/leipzig/leipzig-die-tote-von-den-bahngleisen-frau-wurde-im-streit-erschlagen-1462512.

Blasi, Gary. "UD Day: Impending Evictions and Homelessness in Los Angeles." UCLA Luskin Institute on Inequality and Democracy. May 28, 2020. https://challengeinequality.luskin.ucla.edu/2020/05/28/ud-day-report/.

Bloch, Sam. "Shade: It's a civic resource, an index of inequality, and a requirement for public health. Shade should be a mandate for urban designers." *Places Journal.* April 2019. https://architexturez.net/pst/az-cf-191549-1556163802.

Bloh, Dominik. *Unter Palmen aus Stahl: Die Geschichte eines Straßenjungen.* Weinheim: Gulliver von Beltz & Gelberg, 2021.

Bohn, Sarah, Dean Bonner, Julien Lafortune, and Tess Thorman. "Income Inequality and Economic Opportunity in California." Public Policy Institute of California. December 2020. https://www.ppic.org/publication/income-inequality-and-economic-opportunity-in-california/.

Boie, Kirsten, and Jutta Bauer. *Ein mittelschönes Leben: Ein Kinderbuch über Obdachlosigkeit.* Hamburg: Carlsen Verlag, 2011.

Bombay First and McKinsey & Company, Inc. *Vision Mumbai.* Mumbai, September 2003.

Borges, Sofia, and R. Scott Mitchell, eds. *Give Me Shelter: Architecture Takes on the Homeless Crisis.* San Francisco: Oro Editions, 2017.

The Bowery Mission. https://www.bowery.org/homelessness/.

Brand, David. "NYC Has a Family Homelessness Crisis: Who are the Families?" *CITYLIMITS.* December 10, 2019. https://citylimits.org/2019/12/10/nyc-has-a-family-homelessness-crisis-who-are-the-families/.

Brecht, Bertolt. "Über die Wiederherstellung der Wahrheit." In *Gesammelte Werke*, edited by Bertolt Brecht. Vol. 20, pp. 191–98. Frankfurt am Main: Suhrkamp, 1967.

Bude, Heinz. *Gesellschaft der Angst.* Hamburg: Hamburger Edition, 2014.

Buhayar, Noah, and Christopher Cannon. "How California Became America's Housing Market Nightmare." Bloomberg. November 6, 2019. https://www.bloomberg.com/graphics/2019-california-housing-crisis/.

Bushukhin, Ignat. "Rieltory nazvali srednuu stoimost' arendy zhil'ia v Moskve." *RBK. Nedvizhimost.* January 20, 2020. https://realty.rbc.ru/news/5e25537a9a794760c311cc49.

——. "'Stol'ko v Moskve ne stroili nikogda': itogi Stroikompleksa 2019 goda." *RBK. Nedvizhimost.* December 27, 2019. https://realty.rbc.ru/news/5e05bf029a7947d58ee47d1b.

Butler, Patrick. "London rough sleeping hits record high with 18% rise in 2018–19." *The Guardian.* June 19, 2019. https://www.theguardian.com/society/2019/jun/19/london-rough-sleeping-hits-record-high-with-18-rise-in-2018-19.

Caldeira, Teresa Pires do Rio Caldeira. *Cidade de muros: Crime, segregação e cidadania em São Paulo*. São Paulo: Edusp, 2000.

California Department of Education. "Average Salaries & Expenditure Percentage – CalEdFacts." 2019–20. https://www.cde.ca.gov/fg/fr/sa/cefavgsalaries.asp.

California Energy Commission. "California's Changing Climate 2018." In *California's Fourth Climate Change Assessment*. 2018. https://www.energy.ca.gov/sites/default/files/2019-11/20180827_Summary_Brochure_ADA.pdf.

California State Auditor. "Homelessness in California: State Government and the Los Angeles Homeless Services Authority Need to Strengthen Their Efforts to Address Homelessness." Report Number: 2017–112. April 2018. https://www.auditor.ca.gov/reports/2017-112/chapters.html#chapter1.

Catholic Charities. "Kenton Women's Village." https://www.catholiccharitiesoregon.org/services/housing-services/kenton-womens-village/.

Centers for Disease Control and Prevention (CDC). "Temporary Halt in Residential Evictions to Prevent the Further Spread of COVID-19." Department of Health and Human Services (HHS). September 4, 2020.

Chamard, Sharon. "The Problem of Homeless Encampments." In *Homeless Encampments Guide* 56 (2010). Arizona State University Center for Problem-Oriented Policing. https://popcenter.asu.edu/content/homeless-encampments-0.

Chuchalina, Katerina, Stefan Kalmár, and Alya Sebti (curators). "Traits d'union.s." At *Manifesta 13 Marseille: The European Nomadic Biennial*. Marseille, August 8 to November 29, 2020. https://manifesta13.org.

City of Los Angeles. "REVISED LAMC-SECTION 85.02 Los Angeles City Municipal Code Regarding Vehicle Dwelling." Empower LA. https://empowerla.org/wp-content/uploads/2017/01/REVISED-LAMC-SECTION-85.02-Los-Angeles-City Municipal-Code-regarding-Vehicle-Dwelling-2.pdf.

City of New York. "Turning the Tide on Homelessness in New York City." 2017. https://www1.nyc.gov/assets/dhs/downloads/pdf/turning-the-tide-on-homelessness.pdf.

Coalition for the Homeless. https://www.coalitionforthehomeless.org.

——. "The Callahan Legacy: Callahan v. Carey and the Legal Right to Shelter." www.coalitionforthehomeless.org/our-programs/advocacy/legal-victories/the-callahan-legacy-callahan-v-carey-and-the-legal-right-to-shelter/.

——. "State of the Homeless 2020: Governor and Mayor to Blame as New York Enters Fifth Decade of Homelessness Crisis." March 2020. https://www.coalitionforthehomeless.org/wp-content/uploads/2020/03/StateofTheHomeless2020.pdf.

——. "Why Are so Many People Homeless? – Pre-Callahan." www.coalitionforthehomeless.org/the-catastrophe-of-homelessness/why-are-so-many-people-homeless/.

Coletivo Desentorpecendo a Razão. *O Crack*. Filosofia de Biqueira, March 17, 2021. Podcast, episode 9, 92 min. https://open.spotify.com/episode/0zmskY9naeTekrUfuDcV0a?si=Cg2TayZVTlyAXQFRliYgAw.

Connor, Liz. "A London architect is building spacious pods for London's homeless to bed down in." *Evening Standard*. July 23, 2015.

Co-op City. "Real Estate Advertisement Co-op City." https://coopcitynyc.com/img/apply/apartments_residential_sales_ad.pdf.

Corcoran, Kieran. "California Economy Ranks 5th in the World, Beating the UK." *INSIDER*. May 5, 2018. https://www.businessinsider.com/california-economy-ranks-5th-in-the-world-beating-the-uk-2018-5.

County of Los Angeles Public Health. "Stay Healthy in the Heat." http://publichealth.lacounty.gov/eh/climatechange/ExtremeHeat.htm#:~:text=Heat%20causes%20more%20deaths%20in,health%20impacts%20from%20extreme%20heat.

Crary, Jonathan. *24/7: Late Capitalism and the Ends of Sleep*. New York: Verso, 2014.

Crawford, Margaret. *Building the Working-man's Paradise: The Design of American Company Towns*. Haymarket Series. London and New York: Verso, 1995.

"Crisis paraliza emblemático proyecto Costanera Center." *Mercurio de Valparaíso*. January 29, 2009. https://www.mercuriovalpo.cl/prontus4_noticias/site/artic/20090129/pags/20090129145954.html.

Cunha, Júnia Valéria Quiroga da, and Monica Rodrigues (orgs.). "Rua aprendendo a contar: pesquisa nacional sobre a população em situação de rua." Brasília: Ministério do Desenvolvimento Social e Combate à Fome, 2009. http://www.mds.gov.br/webarquivos/publicacao/assistencia_social/Livros/Rua_aprendendo_a_contar.pdf.

Daniels, Jessie, and Amy J. Schultz. "Constructing Whiteness in Health Disparities Research." In *Health and Illness at the Intersections of Gender, Race and Class*, edited by Amy J. Schulz and Leith Mullings. San Francisco: Jossey-Bass Publishing, 2006.

Davis, Mike. *City of Quartz: Excavating the Future in Los Angeles*. 1990. Reprint, London and New York: Verso, 2018.

De Lucca, Daniel. "A Rua em Movimento: experiências urbanas e jogos sociais em torno da população de rua." PhD diss., FFLCH-USP, São Paulo, 2007.

Desmond, Matthew. *Evicted: Poverty and Profit in the American City*. London: Penguin Books, 2016.

——. *Zwangsgeräumt: Armut und Profit in der Stadt*. Translated by Volker Zimmermann with Isabelle Brandstetter. Berlin: Ullstein Buchverlage, 2018.

Deutsche, Rosalyn. *Evictions: Art and Spatial Politics*. Cambridge, MA: The MIT Press, 1996.

Dillon, Liam. "How Northern California's destructive wildfires could exacerbate the state's housing crisis." *Los Angeles Times*. December 5, 2018. https://www.latimes.com/politics/la-pol-ca-housing-problems-wildfires-20181205-story.html.

Dinkelspiel, Frances. "Court Rules an Apartment Complex Can Go up on West Berkeley Shellmound." *Berkeleyside*. April 21, 2021. https://www.berkeleyside.org/2021/04/21/court-rules-a-260-unit-apartment-complex-can-go-up-at-1900-fourth-st-a-site-the-ohlone-consider-sacred.

Dogma. *Loveless: The Minimum Dwelling and Its Discontents*. Milan: Black Square, 2019.

D'Ottaviano, Camila. "Política habitacional no Brasil e Programa de Locação Social paulistano." *Cad. CRH* 27, no. 71 (2014), pp. 255–66.

Dougherty, Conor. *Golden Gates: Fighting for Housing in America*. New York: Penguin Press, 2020.

——. "Why $4.5 Billion From Big Tech Won't End California Housing Crisis." *The New York Times*. November 6, 2019. https://www.nytimes.com/2019/11/06/business/economy/california-housing-apple.html.

Dougherty, Conor, and Thomas Fuller. "California Today: Lawmakers Shelve a Potential Remedy to the Housing Crisis." *The New York Times*. May 17, 2019. https://www.nytimes.com/2019/05/17/us/california-today-housing-crisis-sb50.html.

Dremann, Sue. "Fires Point to Risky Conditions in Ravenswood Triangle." *Palo Alto Weekly*. July 10, 2020. https://www.paloaltoonline.com/news/2020/07/10/fires-point-to-risky-conditions-in-ravenswood-triangle.

Duneier, Mitchell. *Sidewalk*. New York: Farrar, Straus and Giroux, 1999.

Efrussi, Tatiana. Conversation with Daria Baibakova. Moscow. March 19, 2021.

——. Conversation with Emelian Sosinskyi (founder, Noah Labor Commune). March 25, 2021.

Eilperin, Juliet, Brady Dennis, and Josh Dawsey. "EPA tells California it is 'failing to meet its obligations' to protect the environment." *Washington Post*. September 26, 2019. https://www.washingtonpost.com/climate-environment/epa-tells-california-it-is-failing-to-meet-its-obligations-to-stem-water-pollution/2019/09/26/b3ffca1e-dfac-11e9-8dc8-498eabc129a0_story.html.

Equipo de Estudios Poblacionales, CIDU. "Reivindicación urbana y lucha política: los campamentos de pobladores en Santiago de Chile." At the seminar *Política y Urbanización*, organized by EURE. Buenos Aires, October 1971.

Erlbaum, Janice. *Girlbomb: A Halfway Homeless Memoir*. New York: Villard, 2007.

European Parliament. "How Parliament wants to end homelessness in the EU." November 24, 2020. https://www.europarl.europa.eu/news/en/headlines/society/20201119STO92006/how-parliament-wants-to-end-homelessnessin-the-eu.

Evans, Dain. "Amazon, Apple, Facebook and Google Are Spending Money to Address the Affordable Housing Crisis They Helped Create." CNBC. December 1, 2019. https://www.cnbc.com/2019/12/01/amazon-google-apple-seek-fix-for-housing-crisis-they-helped-create.html.

Evers, Lothar. "'Asoziale': NS-Verfolgte in der deutschen Wiedergutmachung." In *"minderwertig" und "asocial": Stationen der Verfolgung gesellschaftlicher Aussenseiter*, edited by Dietmar Sedlaczek, Thomas Lutz, Ulrike Puvogel, and Ingrid Tomkowiak, pp. 179–83. Zurich: Chronos Verlag, 2005.

Fachstelle Gender, GMF und Rechtsextremismus. "Feindschaft gegen Obdachlose." *Bell Tower News*. February 6, 2019. https://www.belltower.news/was-ist-das-feindschaft-gegen-obdachlose-80951/.

Family Homelessness Coalition. "Facts about Homelessness." https://fhcnyc.org/the-facts/.

Ferré-Sadurní, Luis. "The Rise and Fall of New York Public Housing: An Oral History." *The New York Times*. July 9, 2018. https://www.nytimes.com/interactive/2018/06/25/nyregion/new-york-city-public-housing-history.html.

Ferro, Sérgio. *Arquitetura e trabalho livre*. São Paulo: Cosac Naify, 2006.

Fessenden, Ford. "Homeless Epidemic in New York? Thousands Hit the Cold Streets to Find Out." *The New York Times*. October 21, 2015. https://www.nytimes.com/interactive/2015/10/21/nyregion/new-york-homeless-people.html.

Figueroa, Juan Pablo. "El Costo humano que deja la paralización del Costanera Center." CIPER Chile. January 30, 2009. https://www.ciperchile.cl/2009/01/30/el-costo-humano-que-deja-la-paralizacion-de-costanera-center/.

Folkers, Andreas, and Nadine Marquardt. "Tents." In *Making Things International 2: Catalysts and Reactions*, edited by Mark B. Salter, p. 68. Minneapolis: University of Minnesota Press, 2016.

Fox, Liana. "The Supplemental Poverty Measure: 2019." United States Census Bureau. Published September 15, 2020.

Frazier, Ian. "Hidden City." *The New Yorker*. October 28, 2013. https://www.newyorker.com/magazine/2013/10/28/hidden-city.

Frehse, Fraya. "For Difference 'in and through' São Paulo: The Regressive-Progressive Method." In *Urban Revolution Now*, edited by Lukasz Stanek, Christian Schmid, and Ákos Moravánsky, pp. 243–62. Farnham Surrey and Burlington, VT: Ashgate, 2014.

——. "The Historicity of the Re-Figuration of Spaces under the Scrutiny of the Pre-Covid São Paulo Homeless Pedestrians." In *Spatial Transformations*, edited by Angela Million, Christian Haid, Ignacio Castillo Ulloa, and Nina Baur. Oxford: Routledge, [forthcoming in 2021].

——. "On the Everyday History of Pedestrians' Bodies in São Paulo's Downtown amid Metropolization (1950–2000)." In *Urban Latin America*, edited by Bianca Freire-Medeiros and Julia O'Donnell, pp. 15–35. London: Routledge, 2018.

——. *A Rua de Máscara (São Paulo, 5 de novembro de 2020)*. São Paulo, 2020. Video documentary. https://www.youtube.com/watch?v=DDhrEFczyko&feature=emb_title.

——. "A rua no Brasil em questão (etnográfica)." In *Pluralidade urbana em São Paulo: vulnerabilidade, marginalidade, ativismos*, edited by Lúcio Kowarick and Heitor Frúgoli Jr., pp. 197–224. São Paulo: Editora 34, 2016.

Frúgoli Jr., Heitor. *Centralidade em São Paulo: trajetórias, conflitos e negociações na metrópole*. São Paulo: Cortez; Edusp, 2000.

——. "Territorialidades e redes na região da Luz." In *Pluralidade urbana em São Paulo: vulnerabilidade, marginalidade, ativismos*, edited by Lúcio Kowarick and Heitor Frúgoli Jr., pp. 249–71. São Paulo: Editora 34, 2016.

Frúgoli Jr., Heitor, and Jessica Sklair. "O bairro da Luz em São Paulo: questões antropológicas sobre o fenômeno da gentrification." *Cuadernos de Antropología Social* 30 (2009), pp. 119–36.

Ganapatye, Shruti. "Only 12,000 homeless in city, claims survey." *Mumbai Mirror*. March 5, 2020. https://mumbaimirror.indiatimes.com/mumbai/civic/only-12k-homeless-in-city-claims-survey/articleshow/74484851.cms.

Garcetti, Eric. "Vision 2018: Why We Must Succeed." April 20, 2018. Panel 1 at the 2018 USC Homelessness Initiative Research Summit, Los Angeles. 46:00. https://www.youtube.com/watch?v=wY-DcqGLDNI.

Gerull, Susanne. "'Unangenehm,' 'arbeitsscheu,' 'asocial': Zur Ausgrenzung von wohnungslosen Menschen." In *Aus Politik und Zeitgeschichte: Wohnungslosigkeit*, edited by Bundeszentrale für politische Bildung, pp. 30–36 (APuZ 25-26/2018). 2018.

Gorman, Steve. "Los Angeles Homelessness Rises Sharply as Housing Crisis Deepens." Reuters.com. June 4, 2019. https://www.reuters.com/article/us-homeless-losangeles-idUSKCN1T609L.

Government of China. "Census of the Ministry of Civil Affairs for Feburary 2021." Ministry of Civil Affairs. August 3, 2021. http://www.mca.gov.cn/article/sj/tjjb/2021/202102fssj.html.

——. "Census results attest to China's complete victory in eradicating absolute poverty." English.GOV.CN. February 26, 2021. http://english.www.gov.cn/archive/statistics/202102/26/content_WS603858f0c6d0719374af99ab.html.

——. "Measures for the Administration of Relief for Vagrants and Beggars without Assured Living Resources in Cities." Ministry of Civil Affairs. June 16, 2003. http://www.mca.gov.cn/article/gk/fg/shsw/201507/20150715849135.shtml.

——. "The Poverty Alleviation Campaign: A Full Victory! (*Tuōpín gōngjiānzhàn, quán shèng!*)." GOV.CN. February 25, 2021. http://www.gov.cn/xinwen/2021-02/25/content_5588879.html.

Government of India. *Census of India*. New Delhi, 2011.

Gowan, Teresa. *Hobos, Hustlers, and Backsliders: Homeless in San Francisco*. Minneapolis: University of Minnesota Press, 2010.

Grau, Urtzi, and Cristina Goberna. "They don't represent us." *Materia Arquitectur* 10 (2014).

Guzman, Edith de, Laurence S. Kalkstein, David Sailor, David Eisenman, Scott Sheridan, Kimberly Kirner, Reagan Maas, Kurt Shickman, David Fink, Jonathan Parfrey, and Yujuan Chen. *Rx for Hot Cities: Climate Resilience Through Urban Greening and Cooling in Los Angeles*. TreePeople, Los Angeles Urban Cooling Collaborative. 2020.

Haag, Matthew. "25 Million Applications: The Scramble for N.Y.C. Affordable Housing." *The New York Times*. June 15, 2020. https://www.nytimes.com/2020/06/15/nyregion/nyc-affordable-housing-lottery.html.

Haas, Gilda, and Allan David Heskin. "Community Struggles in Los Angeles." *International Journal of Urban and Regional Research* 5, no. 4 (1981), pp. 546–63.

Hagenauer, Michelle. "Räume der Wohnungslosigkeit: Urbane Strukturen Münchens zwischen Wohnung und Straße." Master's thesis, Technische Universität München, Munich, 2020–21.

Hallerstein, Erica. "It's Official: Bay Area Has Highest Income Inequality in California." KQED. January 31, 2020. https://www.kqed.org/news/11799308/bay-area-has-highest-income-inequality-in-california.

Hammond, Jenny. "Homelessness in China." The Wayback Machine, Internet Archive. July 17, 2012. https://web.archive.org/web/20160930015343/http://gbtimes.com/life/homelessness-china.

Hans Böckler Stiftung. "Studie zeigt Auswirkungen auf Armut und soziale Ungleichheit: Fast 13 Prozent der Mieterhaushalte in deutschen Großstädten haben nach Abzug der Miete weniger als das Existenzminimum zur Verfügung." August 4, 2021. https://www.boeckler.de/de/pressemitteilungen-2675-13-prozent-haushalte-stadten-miete-existenzminimum-34612.htm.

Hashimoto, Yuko, Gee Hee Hong, and Xiaoxiao Zhang. "Demographics and the Housing Market: Japan's Disappearing Cities." International Monetary Fund Working Papers. September 25, 2020. https://www.imf.org/en/Publications/WP/Issues/2020/09/25/Demographics-and-the-Housing-Market-Japans-Disappearing-Cities-49737.

Haskell, Josh. "Los Angeles experiencing alarming jump in fires at homeless encampments." KABC 7. May 13, 2021. https://abc7.com/los-angeles-homelessness-encampment-fires-fire-department-la/10622381/.

Heitmeyer, Wilhelm. "Gesellschaftliche Entwicklung und Gruppenbezogene Menschenfeindlichkeit: Unübersichtliche Perspektiven." In *Deutsche Zustände*. Vol. 6. Berlin: Suhrkamp, 2008.

Heitmeyer, Wilhelm, Manuela Freiheit, and Peter Sitzer. *Rechte Bedrohungsallianzen: Signaturen der Bedrohung II*. Berlin: Suhrkamp, 2020.

Helene, Diane. "A guerra dos lugares nas ocupações de edifícios abandonados no centro de São Paulo." PhD diss., FAU-USP, São Paulo, 2009.

Henley, Jon. "'It's a miracle': Helsinki's radical solution to homelessness." *The Guardian*. June 3, 2019. https://www.theguardian.com/cities/2019/jun/03/its-a-miracle-helsinkis-radical-solution-to-homelessness.

Henni, Samia. "Housing Pharmacology." Commissioned by Manifesta 13 Marseille. 2020. https://samiahenni.com/IMG/Pharmacologie_Samia_Henni.pdf.

Henry, Meghan, Anna Mahathey, Tyler Morrill, Anna Robinson, Azim Shivji, and Rian Watt. "The 2018 Annual Homeless Assessment Report (AHAR) to Congress." U.S. Department of Housing and Urban Development, Office of Community Planning and Development. December 2018.

Höjdestrand, Tova. *Needed by Nobody: Homelessness and Humanness in Post-Socialist Russia*. Ithaca, NY: Cornell University Press, 2009.

Hörath, Julia. *"Asoziale" und "Berufsverbrecher" in den Konzentrationslagern 1933 bis 1938*. Vol. 222 of *Kritische Studien zur Geschichtswissenschaft*. Göttingen: Vandenhoeck & Ruprecht, 2017.

Ho, Vivan. "'It's barely a Band-Aid': Life inside San Francisco's first sanctioned tent camp." *The Guardian*. May 22, 2020. https://www.theguardian.com/us-news/2020/may/22/san-francisco-sanctioned-tent-camp-homeless-covid-19.

Holland, Gale. "L.A. has greater weather, yet more homeless die of the cold here than in New York." *Los Angeles Times*. February 17, 2019. https://www.latimes.com/local/lanow/la-me-homeless-hypothermia-20190217-story.html.

HOME_EU. "The Project." Homelessness as unfairness. http://www.home-eu.org/the-project/.

Homeless Hub. "NIMBY (Not in My Backyard)." Canadian Observatory of Homelessness. https://www.homelesshub.ca/solutions/affordable-housing/nimby-not-my-backyard.

Hopper, Kim, and L. Stuart Cox. "Litigation in Advocacy for the Homeless: The Case of New York City." *Development: Journal of the Society for International Development* 2 (1982), pp. 57–62.

"Hostely dlja vsekh bezdomnykh v Moskve na vremja karantina oplachivajut blagotvoriteli." Miloserdie.ru. April 25, 2020. https://www.miloserdie.ru/news/blagotvoriteli-oplachivayut-hostely-dlya-vseh-bezdomnyh-v-moskve-na-vremya-karantina/.

Ignatieff, Michael. "Human Rights." In *Human Rights in Political Transitions: Gettysburg to Bosnia*, edited by Carla Hesse and Robert Post, pp. 313–24. New York: Zone Books, 1999.

International Energy Agency (IEA). *Indian Energy Outlook 2021*. Paris: IEA, February 2021. https://iea.blob.core.windows.net/assets/1de6d91e-e23f-4e02-b1fb-51fdd6283b22/India_Energy_Outlook_2021.pdf.

Japan Ministry of Internal Affairs and Communications. 2018 Survey.

Jesdale, Bill M., Rachel Morello-Frosch, and Lara Cushing. "African-Americans were 52% more likely, Asians 32% more likely, and Hispanics 21% more likely than Whites to live in areas where impervious surfaces covered more than half the ground, and more than half the population lacked tree canopy." *Environmental Health Perspectives* 121, no. 7 (July 2013), pp. 811–17.

Jones, Katy, Anya Ahmed, Iolo Madoc-Jones, Andrea Gibbons, Michaela Rogers, and Mark Wilding. "Working and Homeless: Exploring the interaction of housing and labour market insecurity." *Social Policy and Society* 19, no. 1 (2020), pp. 121–32.

Joshi, Sahil. "Cops lathicharge migrants as thousands gather at Bandra Station to leave Mumbai, defy lockdown orders." *India Today*. April 14, 2020.

Kendall, Marisa. "Bay Area Housing Gets $500 Million Boost." *The Mercury News*. January 24, 2019. https://www.mercurynews.com/2019/01/24/bay-area-housing-gets-500-million-boost-from-local-tech-foundations/.

———. "The Bay Area Is Fed up with Homelessness, but Interest in Housing Is Flagging." *The Mercury News*. May 4, 2021. https://www.mercurynews.com/2021/05/04/bay-area-residents-are-fed-up-with-the-homelessness-crisis.

———. "Berkeley Rejects Controversial Project That Sought Fast-Track under New State Law." *The Mercury News*. September 5, 2018. https://www.mercurynews.com/2018/09/04/berkeley-rejects-controversial-project-that-sought-fast-track-under-new-state-law/.

Klein, Ezra. "Opinion: California Is Making Liberals Squirm." *The New York Times*. February 11, 2021. https://www.nytimes.com/2021/02/11/opinion/california-san-francisco-schools.html.

Klemperer, Victor. *The Language of the Third Reich: LTI – Lingua Tertii Imperii; A Philologist's Notebook*. Translated by Martin Brady. London and New York: Bloomsbury Academic, 2013.

———. *LTI: Notizbuch eines Philologen*. 1947. Reprint, Stuttgart: Reclam, 2010.

Klinenberg, Eric. *Palaces for the people: How social infrastructures can help fight inequality; Polarization, and the decline of civic life*. New York: Crown, 2018.

Klueva, Nadezhda. "Housing First v Moskve: Sociologicheskoe issledovanie nuzhd, zhelanij i idej bezdomnykh lyudej." Presentation at the Annual International Conference on Homelessness organized by the NGO called Nochlezhka. Moscow, October 28–29, 2019. https://www.youtube.com/watch?v=7BLUcTkddek.

Kohara, Luiz. "A moradia é a base estruturante para a vida e a inclusão social da população em situação de rua." Postdoctoral report, UFABC, Brazil, 2018.

Kohara, Luiz (founder and researcher at the Gaspar Garcia Center for Human Rights, São Paulo). Conversation with Clara Chahin Werneck and João Bittar Fiammenghi, March 18, 2021.

Kohara, Luiz, Maria Teresa Duarte, and Marina Moreto. "É possível Housing First no Brasil? Experiências de moradia para população em situação de rua na Europa e no Brasil." Ministério da Mulher, da Família e dos Direitos Humanos, Brasília, 2019. https://biblioteca digital.mdh.gov.br/jspui/handle/192/1701.

Kovalenko, E., and E. Strokova. Bezdomnost: Est li Vyhod?. Moscow: Institut Ekonomiki Goroda, 2013.

Kozol, Jonathan. Rachel and Her Children: Homeless Families in America. 1987. Reprint, New York: Three Rivers Press, 2006.

Kromer, Tom. Waiting for Nothing and Other Writings. Edited by Arthur D. Casciato and James L. W. West III. Athens, GA: University of Georgia Press, 1986.

Lefebvre, Henri. Critique de la vie quotidienne. Vol. 2. Paris: L'Arche Éditeur, 1961.

———. La présence et l'absence. Paris: Casterman, 1980.

———. La production de l'espace. Paris: Anthropos, 2000.

———. Das Recht auf Stadt. Hamburg: Edition Nautilus, 2016.

———. The Urban Revolution. 1970. Reprint, Minneapolis: University of Minnesota Press, 2003.

Leibowitz, Ed. "Reinventing Skid Row." Los Angeles Times. December 14, 2017.

Leitão Karina (professor of urban planning at FAU-USP, São Paulo). Conversation with Clara Chahin Werneck and João Bittar Fiammenghi, March 11, 2021.

Liebow, Elliot. Tell Them Who I Am: The Lives of Homeless Women. London: Penguin Books, 1995.

Life Where I'm From. Homeless in Japan. Part 2: "Who are Japan's Homeless?" https://www.youtube.com/watch?v=-9RgkZebW1s.

Litvinova, Daria, and Anna Romshchenko. "Ia – bezdomny: kak v Moskve ustroena zhizn' tekh, komu nekuda poitii." Coda.ru. January 29, 2019. http://codaru.com/war-on-reason/bezdomny/.

Löw, Martina. Raumsoziologie. Frankfurt am Main: Suhrkamp, 2001.

Löwy, Michael. O que é cristianismo de libertação: religião e política na América Latina. São Paulo: Fundação Perseu Abramo / Expressão Popular, 2016.

Lokmat English Desk. "Beggar Free Mumbai: Mumbai Police launches drive to make city 'begging free.'" Lokmat. February 13, 2021.

Lopez, Steve. "Column: Black people make up 8% of L.A. population and 34% of its homeless. That's unacceptable." Los Angeles Times. June 13, 2020.

Los Angeles County Department of Mental Health. "Homeless Task Force Draft Report: Planning and Recommendations for the Homeless Mentally Ill." USC Archives. June 1985.

Los Angeles Homeless Services Authority. "2020 Greater Los Angeles Homeless Count Presentation." June 12, 2020. https://www.lahsa.org/documents?id=4558-2020-greater-los-angeles-homeless-count-presentation.

———. "2020 Greater Los Angeles Homeless Count Results." June 12, 2020. https://www.lahsa.org/news?article=726-2020-greater-los-angeles-homeless-count-results.

———. "Homelessness Statistics by City." March 2021. https://www.lahsa.org/documents?id=5201-homelessness-statistics-by-city.pdf.

Los Angeles Housing Department. "City of Los Angeles: Prop HHH Progress Report." June 2021. https://hcidla2.lacity.org/housing/hhh-progress.

Lowrey, Sassafras, and Jennifer Clare Burke, eds. Kicked Out. Foreword by Judy Shepard. Ypsilanti, MI: Homofactus Press, 2010.

Lynn, Peter. "Examining the Homeless Crisis in Los Angeles." Field Hearing before the Committee on Financial Services, U.S. House of Representatives, 116th Congress, First Session, Serial No. 116-44. August 14, 2019. https://www.govinfo.gov/content/pkg/CHRG-116hhrg40162/pdf/CHRG-116hhrg40162.pdf.

Madden, David, and Peter Marcuse. In Defense of Housing: The Politics of Crisis. London and New York: Verso, 2016.

Main, Thomas J. Homelessness in New York City: Policymaking from Koch to de Blasio. New York: New York University, 2017.

Maloo, Vaibhav. "Smarter Cities Can Solve Most Problems." Business World. March 15, 2021.

Marcuse, Peter. "Neutralizing Homelessness." Socialist Review 88, no. 1 (1988), pp. 69–97.

Marks, Mara A. "Shifting Ground: The Rise and Fall of the Los Angeles Community Redevelopment Agency." Southern California Quarterly 86, no. 3 (2004), pp. 241–90.

Maslow, Abraham. "A Theory of Human Motivation." Psychological Review 50, no. 4 (1943), pp. 370–96. http://psychclassics.yorku.ca/Maslow/motivation.htm.

Matsunaga, Michael. "Concentrated Poverty Neighborhoods in Los Angeles." Economic Roundtable. February 2008.

McPherson, E. Gregory. "Monitoring Million Trees LA: Tree Performance During the Early Years and Future Benefits." Arboriculture & Urban Forestry 40, no. 5 (2014).

Mitchell, Don. Mean Streets: Homelessness, Public Space, and the Limits of Capital. Vol. 47 of Geographies of Justice and Social Transformation. Athens, GA: University of Georgia Press, 2020.

Morello-Frosch, Rachel, Manuel Pastor, James Sadd, and Seth B. Shonkoff. "The Climate Gap: Inequalities in How Climate Change Hurts Americans & How to Close the Gap." University of Southern California, May 2009. https://dornsife.usc.edu/assets/sites/242/docs/The_Climate_Gap_Full_Report_FINAL.pdf

Mozur, Paul, Raymond Zhong, and Aaron Krolik. "In Coronavirus Fight, China Gives Citizens a Color Code, With Red Flags." The New York Times. March 1, 2020. https://www.nytimes.com/2020/03/01/business/china-coronavirus-surveillance.html.

Mühle, Bárbara. "Ocupações de Moradia no Centro: possibilidades do morar." Master's thesis, FAU-USP, São Paulo, 2020.

Mullings, Simon. "Enacting 'intentional homelessness.'" Socialist Lawyer 84 (2020), pp. 40–43.

NASA Earth Observatory. "California Heatwave Fits a Trend." September 6, 2020. https://earthobservatory.nasa.gov/images/147256/california-heatwave-fits-a-trend.

National Alliance to END HOMELESSNESS. "Racial Inequalities in Homelessness, by the Numbers." June 1, 2020. https://endhomelessness.org/resource/racial-inequalities-homelessness-numbers/.

Nerdinger, Winfried, ed. München und der Nationalsozialismus. Exh. cat. NS-Dokumentationszentrum München. Munich: C. H. Beck, 2015.

Neumann, Moritz, Paul Haas, and Felix Röttger. "Solidarische Infrastrukturen im öffentlichen Raum." Project thesis, Technische Universität München, Munich.

Newsom, Gavin. "The California Dream Starts at Home." *Medium*. October 21, 2017. https://medium.com/@GavinNewsom/the-california-dream-starts-at-home-9dbb38c51cae.

Noah Labor Commune. "Dom Trudolubiya Noi." https://dom-noi.ru.

Nojiren Online. http://www.jca.apc.org/nojukusha/nojiren/e-home/.

NYC Department of Homeless Services. "Daily report 2/28/2020." Data from Thursday, February 27, 2020. https://www1.nyc.gov/assets/dhs/downloads/pdf/dailyreport.pdf.

———. "NYC HOPE 2020 Results." https://www1.nyc.gov/assets/dhs/downloads/pdf/hope-2020-results.pdf.

———. "Turning the Tide on Homelessness in New York City." https://www1.nyc.gov/site/dhs/about/tide.page.

NYC Department of Housing. "Our Current Affordable Housing Crisis." City of New York. www1.nyc.gov/site/housing/problem/problem.page.

Oliveira, Francisco de. *Crítica à razão dualista: O ornitorrinco*. São Paulo: Boitempo, 2018.

Oliveira, Luciano. "Circulação e fixação: o dispositivo de gerenciamento dos moradores de rua em São Carlos e a emergência de uma população." PhD diss., UFSCar-PPGS, São Carlos, 2013.

Oosterman, Arjen. *Volume #46: Shelter*. Amsterdam: Archis, 2015. http://archis.org/publications/volume-46-shelter/.

Oreskes, Benjamin, and Doug Smith. "Homelessness Jumps 12% in the County and 16% in the City; Officials Stunned." *Los Angeles Times*. June 4, 2019. https://www.latimes.com/local/lanow/la-me-ln-homeless-count-encampment-affordable-housing-2019-results-20190604-story.html.

Orwell, George. *Down and Out in Paris and London*. London: Collins Classics, 2001.

———. *Erledigt in Paris und London*. Zurich: Diogenes Verlag, 1978.

Ostermair, Markus. *Der Sandler*. Hamburg: Osburg Verlag, 2020.

Ozaki, Shuji. "1 cup of noodles per day: COVID-19 aggravates poverty among isolated young in Japan." *The Mainichi*. March 22, 2021. https://mainichi.jp/english/articles/20210320/p2a/00m/0na/011000c.

Patitucci, Giulia (coordinator of public policy for the homeless at the Municipal Secretariat of Human Rights and Citizenship). Conversation with Clara Chahin Werneck and João Bittar Fiammenghi, March 13, 2021.

Paynter, Sarah. "Here's where NYC's real estate market stands right now." *New York Post*. July 20, 2021. https://nypost.com/article/nyc-real-estate-market-housing-prices/.

Pentiukhov, Andrei. "Smertnost' bezdomnykh ot kholoda sokratilas' v Moskve v 10 raz za 8 let." *RIA Novosti*. February 21, 2011. https://ria.ru/20110221/336987369.html.

Perera, Loreta Marie. "A Moscow Homeless Shelter Moved to Accommodate the World Cup: One Year Later It Has Not Returned." *Moscow Times*. June 27, 2019. https://www.themoscowtimes.com/2019/06/27/a-moscow-homeless-shelter-moved-to-accommodate-the-world-cup-a-year-later-it-has-not-returned-a66191.

Pichai, Sundar. "$1 Billion for 20,000 Bay Area Homes." Google. Company Announcements. June 18, 2019. https://blog.google/inside-google/company-announcements/1-billion-investment-bay-area-housing/.

Piispanen, Jussi. "Our Story." GoSleep. https://gosleep.fi/about-us/.

Pompéia, Anna Ayumy, Beatriz Martinez, Camila Sawaia, and Camila Audrey (Coletivo Co-Criança). Conversation with Clara Chahin Werneck and João Bittar Fiammenghi, March 18, 2021.

Portillo, Lourdes Johanna Avelar, Yao-Yi Chiang, Robert O. Vos, Jose Jesus Rico, Yanyi Qian, Xiaozhe Yin, and Kate Vavra-Musser. "Los Angeles Homelessness and the Access to Water, Sanitation, and Hygiene (WASH)." University of Southern California, 2019.

Prefeitura do Município de São Paulo. *Pesquisa Amostral do Perfil Socioeconômico da População em Situação de Rua*. São Paulo: Secretaria de Assistência e Desenvolvimento Social, 2019.

———. *Pesquisa Censitária da População em Situação de Rua*. São Paulo: Secretaria de Assistência e Desenvolvimento Social, 2019.

———. *Relatório II. Acompanhamento da Fase III do Projeto Piloto de Locação Social para População em Situação de Rua: Trabalho social de acompanhamento da população, pós-ocupação das unidades e gestão do Conjunto Habitacional Asdrúbal do Nascimento II, fevereiro/2019 a julho/2020*. São Paulo: Secretaria de Direitos Humanos e Cidadania, 2020. https://www.prefeitura.sp.gov.br/cidade/secretarias/upload/direitos_humanos/Relatoio%20Asdrubal%20um%20ano.pdf.

Prescott, Katie. "'Having an address got me a job when I was homeless.'" *BBC News*. April 2, 2021. https://www.bbc.com/news/business-56402018.

Przybylinski, Stephen. "Securing Legal Rights to Place: Mobilizing around Moral Claims for a Houseless Rest Space in Portland, Oregon." *Urban Geography* 42, no. 4 (2021).

Ramón, Armando de. "Estudio de una periferia urbana: Santiago de Chile 1850–1900." Instituto de Historia de la Pontificia Universidad Católica de Chile, Santiago, 1985.

Raturi, Manas. "Raj and the begging brawl: The colonial roots of India's anti-beggary laws echo even now." *The Leaflet*. June 27, 2018.

Recktenwald, Nadine. "Der 'Makel' als Protest: Geschlechtsidentitäten unter westdeutschen Gammlern." In *Männer mit Makel: Männlichkeiten und gesellschaftlicher Wandel in der Bundesrepublik Deutschland*, edited by Bernhard Gotto and Elke Seefried, pp. 75–87. Munich: De Gruyter Oldenbourg, 2017.

———. "Räume der Obdachlosen: Obdachlosigkeit und Stadt, 1924–1974." PhD diss., Institut für Zeitgeschichte München–Berlin, 2019.

———. "Räume der Obdachlosen: Städtische Asyle im Nationalsozialismus." In *Städte im Nationalsozialismus: Urbane Räume und soziale Ordnungen*, edited by Winfrid Süß and Malte Thießen, pp. 67–88. Göttingen: Wallstein Verlag, 2017.

———. "Die Topologie der Obdachlosen: Zwischen Öffentlichkeit, Institutionalisierung und Isolierung, München 1918–1933." Master's thesis, Ludwig-Maximilians-Universität München, Munich, 2014.

———. "Vom Kunden zum Vagabund: Der Versuch der Adressierung der Landstraße durch die Bruderschaft der Vagabunden." In *Freunde der Monacensia e.V. Jahrbuch 2015*, edited by Waldemar Fromm, Wolfram Göbel, and Kristina Kargl, pp. 247–63. Munich: Allitera Verlag, 2018.

Reft, Ryan. "Segregation in The City of Angels: A 1939 Map of Housing Inequality in L.A." KCET. November 14, 2017.

Rey, Daniel. "How Seattle's public library is stepping up to deal with the city's homelessness crisis." *The New Stateman*. December 10, 2018.

Robaina, Igor Martins Medeiros. "Entre mobilidade e permanências: uma análise das espacialidades cotidianas da população em situação de rua na área central da cidade do Rio de Janeiro." PhD diss., Dep. de Geografia, UFRJ, Rio de Janeiro, 2015.

Rocheva, A. L., E. A. Varshaver, and N. S. Ivanova. "Vulnerable Groups in Disasters: Solidarity and Trust in Government as the Basis for Migrant Strategies in Russia During the COVID-19 Pandemic." *Monitoring of Public Opinion: Economic and Social Changes* 6 (2020), pp. 488–511.

Ronald, Richard. *The Ideology of Home Ownership: Homeowner Societies and the Role of Housing*. London: Palgrave Macmillan, 2008.

Rosler, Martha. *If You Lived Here: The City in Art, Theory, and Social Activism*. Edited by Brian Wallis. Vol. 6 of *Discussions in Contemporary Culture*. New York: The New Press, 1998.

Rossi, Peter H. *Down and Out in America: The Origins of Homelessness*. Chicago: University of Chicago Press, 1991.

Rothstein, Richard. *The Color of Law: A Forgotten History of How Our Government Segregated America*. New York: Liveright Publishing Corporation, 2017.

——. "Opinion: The Black Lives Next Door." *The New York Times*. August 14, 2020. https://www.nytimes.com/2020/08/14/opinion/sunday/blm-residential-segregation.html.

Rousseau, Bryant. "Napping in Public? In Japan, That's a Sign of Diligence." *The New York Times*. December 16, 2016. https://www.nytimes.com/2016/12/16/world/what-in-the-world/japan-inemuri-public-sleeping.html.

Rui, Taniele. "Fluxos de uma territorialidade: duas décadas de 'cracolândia' (1995–2014)." In *Pluralidade urbana em São Paulo: vulnerabilidade, marginalidade, ativismos*, edited by Lúcio Kowarick and Heitor Frúgoli Jr., pp. 225–48. São Paulo: Editora 34, 2016.

Rust, Susanne. "Near Facebook Headquarters, a Fire-Prone Homeless Camp Is Dismantled, and Springs Back." *Los Angeles Times*. March 4, 2021. https://www.latimes.com/california/story/2021-03-04/silicon-valley-homeless-camp-near-facebook-returns.

Sanyal, Tithi. "The Chawls and Slums of Mumbai: Story of Urban Sprawl." *Agora Journal of Urban Planning and Design* 12 (2018).

Sassen, Saskia. *The Global City: New York, London, Tokyo*. Princeton, NJ: Princeton University Press, 1991.

Saxony Police. "Leblose Person." *Sachsen.de*. March 16, 2020. https://www.polizei.sachsen.de/de/MI_2020_71356.htm.

Schanberg, Sydney H. "Opinion: New York; Reagan's Homeless." *The New York Times*, February 4, 1984. https://www.nytimes.com/1984/02/04/opinion/new-york-reagan-s-homeless.html.

Schenk, Britta-Marie. "Eine Geschichte der Obdachlosigkeit im 19. und 20. Jahrhundert." In *Aus Politik und Zeitgeschichte: Wohnungslosigkeit*, 68, nos. 25–26, edited by Bundeszentrale für politische Bildung, pp. 23–39. 2018.

Schneider, Luisa T. "'My home is my people': Homemaking among Rough Sleepers in Leipzig, Germany." *Housing Studies* (2020), pp. 1–18.

Scott, Anna. "LA's heat wave is deadly for the county's unhoused population." *KCRW*. September 16, 2020. https://www.kcrw.com/news/shows/greater-la/wildfires-air-quality-deaths/heat-wave-la-unhoused.

Sgaier, Sema K., and Aaron Dibner-Dunlap. "How Many People Are at Risk of Losing Their Homes in Your Neighborhood?." *The New York Times*. July 28, 2021. https://www.nytimes.com/2021/07/28/opinion/covid-eviction-moratorium.html?action=click&module=Opinion&pgtype=Homepage.

Sheeley, Kirsten Moore, Alisa Belinkoff Katz, Andrew Klein, Jessica Richards, Fernanda Jahn Verri, Marques Vestal, and Zev Yaroslavsky. "The Making of a Crisis: A History of Homelessness in Los Angeles." UCLA Luskin Center for History and Policy. January 2021. https://luskincenter.history.ucla.edu/wp-content/uploads/sites/66/2021/01/LCHP-The-Making-of-A-Crisis-Report.pdf.

Siqueira, Marina Toneli. "Between the fundamental and the contingent: Dimensions of contemporary gentrification in urban operations in São Paulo." *Cadernos Metrópole* 16, no. 32 (November 2014), pp. 391–415.

Slater, H. David, and Sara Ikebe. "Social Distancing from the Problem of Japanese Homelessness under Covid-19." *The Asia-Pacific Journal: Japan Focus* 18, no. 18/4 (September 15, 2020). https://apjjf.org/2020/18/Slater-Ikebe.html.

Sleeping in Airports. "Airport Sleeping Pods." December 15, 2015. https://www.sleepinginairports.net/blog/airport-sleeping-pods.htm.

Sorensen, André. *The Making of Urban Japan: Cities and Planning from Edo to the Twenty First Century*. London and New York: Routledge, 2004.

Speer, Jessie. "The rise of the tent ward: Homeless camps in the era of mass incarceration." *Political Geography* 62 (2018), pp. 160–69.

Steets, Silke. *Der sinnhafte Aufbau der gebauten Welt: Eine Architektursoziologie*. Frankfurt am Main: Suhrkamp, 2015.

Steinke, Ronen. *Antisemitismus in der Sprache: Warum es auf die Wortwahl ankommt*. Berlin: Dudenverlag, 2020.

Stephenson, Svetlana. *Bezdomnye v sotsial'noi strukture bol'shogo goroda*. Moscow: INION RAN, 1997.

Sudakova, Yuliya. "Skol'ko stoyat uslugi ZhKH v raznykh stranakh?" *CIAN*. July 16, 2019. https://www.cian.ru/stati-skolko-stojat-uslugi-zhkh-v-raznyh-stranah-294566/.

Supreme Court of the State of New York. "The Callahan Consent Decree: Establishing a Legal Right to Shelter for Homeless Individual in New York City (No. 79-42582 [Sup. Ct. N.Y. County, Cot. 18, 1979])." Coalition for the Homeless. www.coalitionforthehomeless.org/wp-content/uploads/2014/06/CallahanConsentDecree.pdf.

Tarō, Igarashi. "Haijo āto to kabōbitoshi no tanjō: Fukanyō wo meguru āto to dezain, Bijutsutechō." *INSIGHT*. December 12, 2020. https://bijutsutecho.com/magazine/insight/23127.

Teidelbaum, Lucius. "Zwischen 'Geh' arbeiten, Du Penner' und 'Penner klatschen': Wohnungs- und Obdachlose als Opfer von Ausgrenzung und rechter Gewalt." In *All Inclusive? Inklusion als Herausforderung in der politischen Bildung*, edited by Bundesarbeitskreis Arbeit und Leben, p. 20. Wuppertal: Bundesarbeitskreis, 2013.

Teixeira, Alessandra, and Fernanda Matsuda. "Sujos, feios e malvados." *Le Monde Diplomatique Brasil*. March 7, 2012. https://diplomatique.org.br/feios-sujos-e-malvados/.

Teuwsen, Peer. "Zwanghaft sportlich." *Neue Zürcher Zeitung*. December 14, 2016. https://www.nzz.ch/karriere/studentenleben/akademischer-sportverband-zuerich-zwanghaft-sportlich-ld.134346.

Tokyo Metropolitan Government. "Housing." Statistics Division, Bureau of General Affairs. https://www.toukei.metro.tokyo.lg.jp/kurasi/2020/ku20-03.htm.

——. "Trends in population and number of households (2019)." https://www.juutakuseisaku.metro.tokyo.lg.jp.

Toro, Paul A., Carolyn J. Tompsett, Sylvie Lombardo, Pierre Philippot, Hilde Nachtergael, Benoit Galand, Natascha Schlienz, et al. "Homelessness in Europe and the United States: A Comparison of Prevalence and Public Opinion." *Journal of Social Issues* 63, no. 3 (2007), pp. 505–24.

Torrey, E. Fuller. "Ronald Reagan's Shameful Legacy: Violence, the Homeless, Mental Illness." *Salon*. September 29, 2013. https://www.salon.com/2013/09/29/ronald_reagans_shameful_legacy_violence_the_homeless_mental_illness/.

Toth, Jennifer. *The Mole People: Life in the Tunnels beneath New York City*. Chicago: Chicago Review Press, 1993.

Townsend, Mark. "UK hotels to become homeless shelters under coronavirus plan." *The Guardian*. March 21, 2020. https://www.theguardian.com/world/2020/mar/21/uk-hotels-homeless-shelters-coronavirus.

Tree People. "Los Angeles Urban Cooling Collaborative." 2020. https://www.treepeople.org/rx-for-hot-cities-climate-resilience-through-urban-greening-and-cooling-in-los-angeles/.

"Two no worries and three guarantees (*liǎngbùchóu sānbǎozhàng*)." *China Daily*. April 23, 2019. https://www.chinadaily.com.cn/a/201904/23/WS5cbe5248a3104842260b7a39.html.

Ulmer Nest. "Goals." https://ulmernest.de/ziele.

——. "How it all started ..." https://ulmernest.de/ursprung.

United Nations. "First Ever United Nations Resolution on Homelessness." UN Department of Economic and Social Affairs. March 9, 2020. https://www.un.org/development/desa/dspd/2020/03/resolution-homelessness/.

United Nations Economic Commission for Europe. "Country Profiles on the Housing Sector: Russian Federation." United Nations. 2004.

United States Environmental Protection Agency. "Heat Island Community Actions Database." January 8, 2020. https://www.epa.gov/heatislands/heat-island-community-actions-database.

USC Libraries Special Collections. "Welfare Planning Council, Los Angeles Region." Collection no. 0434. April 1964.

U.S. Department of Housing and Urban Development. "2019 Point in Time Estimates of Homelessness in the U.S." https://www.hud.gov/2019-point-in-time-estimates-of-homelessness-in-US.

——. "The 2020 Annual Homeless Assessment Report (AHAR) to Congress. Part I: Point-in-Time Estimates of Homelessness." January 2021. https://www.huduser.gov/portal/sites/default/files/pdf/2020-AHAR-Part-1.pdf.

Varshaver, Evgeni. Email communication with Tatiana Efrussi. April 8, 2021.

Verisk. "Verisk Wildfire Risk Analysis." 2020. https://www.verisk.com/insurance/campaigns/location-fireline-state-risk-report/.

Vieira, Maria Antonieta da Costa, Eneida Maria Ramos Bezerra, and Cleisa Moreno Maffei Rosa. *População de rua: quem é, como vive, como é vista*. São Paulo: Hucitec, 1994.

Villaça, Flávio. "São Paulo: urban segregation and inequality." In *Dossiê São Paulo, hoje: Instituto de Estudos Avançados da Universidade de São Paulo* 25, no. 71 (2011), pp. 37–58.

Vink, Jan, and Robin Blakely-Armitage. "Income Inequality in New York State." *New York Minute* 72 (March 2016).

Walker, Peter. "Government pledges £236 m to tackle rough sleeping." *The Guardian*. February 26, 2020. https://www.theguardian.com/society/2020/feb/26/government-pledges-236m-to-tackle-rough-sleeping.

Walker, Richard. "Boom and Bombshell: New Economy Bubble and the Bay Area." *FoundSF*. https://www.foundsf.org/index.php?title=Boom_and_Bombshell:_New_Economy_Bubble_and_the_Bay_Area.

Wallen, Joe. "Migrant workers rush to leave Mumbai over rumours of second lockdown." *The Telegraph*. April 2, 2021. https://www.telegraph.co.uk/global-health/science-and-disease/migrant-workers-rush-leave-mumbai-rumours-second-lockdown/.

Wanyonyi, Sophia. "Homelessness in Germany on the Rise." The Borgen Project. https://borgenproject.org/homelessness-in-germany-on-the-rise/.

Water Drop Los Angeles. "Welcome to Water Drop LA: Combatting water insecurity in communities across Southern California." https://www.waterdropla.org.

Wehner, David. "Facebook Commits $1 Billion and Partners with the State of California to Address Housing Affordability." *About Facebook* (blog). October 22, 2019. https://about.fb.com/news/2019/10/facebook-commits-1-billion-to-address-housing-affordability/.

——. "Facebook Invests $150 Million in Affordable Housing for the Bay Area." *About Facebook* (blog). December 9, 2020. https://about.fb.com/news/2020/12/facebook-invests-150-million-in-affordable-housing-for-the-bay-area/.

Whyte, William Hollingsworth. *The Social Life of Small Urban Spaces*. Washington, DC: Conservation Foundation, 1980.

Wikipedia. S.v. "Costanera Center." Last modified April 23, 2021. https://es.wikipedia.org/wiki/Costanera_Center.

——. S.v. "Horst Paulmann." Last modified April 23, 2021. https://en.wikipedia.org/wiki/Horst_Paulmann.

Williams, A. Park, John T. Abatzoglou, Alexander Gershunov, Janin Guzman-Morales, Daniel A. Bishop, Jennifer K. Balch, and Dennis P. Lettenmaier. "Observed Impacts of Anthropogenic Climate Change on Wildfire in California." *Earth's Future* 7, no. 8 (2019), p. 892.

Willse, Craig. *The Value of Homelessness: Managing Surplus Life in the United States*. Minneapolis: University of Minnesota Press, 2015.

99% Invisible. "Unpleasant Design & Hostile Urban Architecture." July 5, 2016. www.99percentinvisible.org/episode/unpleasant-design-hostile-urban-architecture/.

LECTURES

Kousoulas, Stavros. "The Problem with Problem-Solving." New Urban Questions or Minor Infractions lecture series, TU Delft. November 21, 2019.

Maltzan, Michael. "Addressing Homelessness: What Can (and Can't) Architecture Do?" John T. Dunlop Lecture, Harvard University, October 13, 2020.

Radman, Andrej. "Groundless Grounds." New Urban Questions or Minor Infractions lecture series, TU Delft. December 12, 2019.

Tammaru, Tiit. "How to Better Understand Sociospatial Segregation? The Concept of Vicious Circles of Segregation." Social Inequality in the City, Diversity and Design lecture series, TU Delft. February 21, 2019.

Weel, Taufan ter. "Abstract Machines in the Production of Space (or Architectures of Control)." New Urban Questions or Minor Infractions lecture series, TU Delft. December 19, 2019.

Zammataro, Andrea. "Urban Informality: A Metropolitan Question Redefining the Agency of the Architect." New Urban Questions or Minor Infractions lecture series, TU Delft. November 28, 2019.

FILMS

Grant, Lee, dir. *Down and Out in America*. 1986.

Groteclaes, Julia, dir. *Mittendrin*. 2019.

Ho, Matthew, dir. *Urban Nomadism: The City as a Space of Exclusion*. 2019

Schwartz, Daniel, dir. *What It Takes to Make a Home*. 2019.

Wiseman, Frederick, dir. *Public Housing*. 1997.

Statistical Sources

The numbers in the statistics have been gathered by the respective city researchers from the following sources:

New York City

– United States Census Bureau, QuickFacts New York City, New York, https://www.census.gov/quickfacts/newyorkcitynewyork.
– New York City OpenData, DHS Homeless Shelter Census, https://data.cityofnewyork.us/Social-Services/DHS-Homeless-Shelter-Census/3pjg-ncn9/data.
– Coalition for the Homeless, "Basic Facts About Homelessness: New York City," https://www.coalitionforthehomeless.org/basic-facts-about-homelessness-new-york-city/.
– New York State Labor Department, https://dol.ny.gov/labor-data.
– NYU Furman Center Blog, https://furmancenter.org/thestoop/entry/snapshot-of-homeownership-in-new-york-city.
– Castle Avenue Real Estate, https://www.castle-avenue.com/new-york-flat-trends.html.

San Francisco

– City and County of San Francisco SF.Gov: San Francisco Performance Scorecards, https://sfgov.org/scorecards/benchmarking/homelessness.
– United States Bureau of Labor Statistics, Western Information Office: San Francisco, https://www.bls.gov/regions/west/ca_sanfrancisco_msa.htm.
– Bay Area Census: San Francisco City and Census, https://www.census.gov/quickfacts/sanfranciscocountycalifornia.
– San Francisco Homeless Count & Survey 2019, https://hsh.sfgov.org/wp-content/uploads/2020/01/2019HIRDReport_SanFrancisco_FinalDraft-1.pdf.
– Statista.com, https://www.statista.com/statistics/1234783/average-sales-price-of-condos-and-single-family-homes-san-francisco-districts-per-square-foot/.
– Department of Numbers: San Francisco–Oakland-Fremont California Household Income, https://www.deptofnumbers.com/income/california/san-francisco/.

Los Angeles

– U.S. Census Bureau, Population Estimates Program (PEP), updated annually, https://www.census.gov/programs-surveys/popest.html. See also: https://www.census.gov/quickfacts/fact/table/losangelescountycalifornia,losangelescitycalifornia/PST045219; https://www.census.gov/prod/www/decennial.html; http://censusviewer.com/city/CA/Los%20Angeles; https://www2.census.gov/library/publications/decennial/1990/cp-1/cp-1-6-1.pdf.
– Los Angeles Homeless Services Authority (LAHSA), http://documents.lahsa.org/planning/homelesscount/2005/HC05-full_report.pdf. See also: http://documents.lahsa.org/planning/homelesscount/2011/HC11-detailed-geography-report.PDF; https://www.lahsa.org/documents?id=3437-2019-greater-los-angeles-homeless-count-presentation.pdf; https://www.lahsa.org/data?id=45-2020-homeless-count-by-community-city.
– Welfare Info Organization, https://www.welfareinfo.org/poverty-rate/california/los-angeles.
– State of California Employment Development Department, https://edd.ca.gov.
– U.S. Department of Commerce, Bureau of the Census, https://www.commerce.gov/bureaus-and-offices/census.
– Constantine Valhouli, "Opinion: L.A. housing is expensive, sure. But are you paying too much for your rental?," Los Angeles Times, January 14, 2016, https://www.latimes.com/opinion/livable-city/la-ol-housing-los-angeles-20160112-htmlstory.html.

São Paulo

– Instituto Brasileiro de Geografia e Estatística, https://cidades.ibge.gov.br.
– Prefeitura de São Paulo, Assistência e Desenvolvimento Social, "Pesquisa Censitária da População em Situação de Rua em São Paulo 2019," March 21, 2020, https://app.powerbi.com/view?r=eyJrIjoiYzM4MDJmNTAtNzhlMi00NzliLTk4MzYtY2MzN2U5ZDE1YzI3IiwidCI6ImE0ZTA2MDVjLWUzOTUtNDZIYS1iMmE4LThlNjE1NGM5MGUwNyJ9.
– Centro de Pesquisa e Memória Técnica, https://www.prefeitura.sp.gov.br/cidade/secretarias/assistencia_social/observatorio_social/pesquisas/index.php?p=18626.
– Prefeitura de São Paulo, "Taxa de Desembrego, Município de São Paulo," https://www.prefeitura.sp.gov.br/cidade/secretarias/upload/urbanismo/infocidade/graficos/18_taxa_de_desemprego_1991_10267.pdf.
– Suzana Pasternak and Lúcia Maria Machado Bógus, "Habitação de aluguel no Brasil e em São Paulo," Caderno CRH – UFBA, Salvador 27, no. 71 (2014), https://www.scielo.br/scielo.php?script=sci_arttext&pid=S0103-49792014000200002.
– Proprietário Direto, "Média de preços REAL do m2 em São Paulo," https://www.proprietariodireto.com.br/preco-m2-sao-paulo.
– Fundação Sistema Estadual de Análise de Dados, "São Paulo diversa: uma análise a partir de regiões da cidade," January 2020, https://www.seade.gov.br.
– Nicola Abé, "Consequences of Corona: The Skyrocketing Homeless Population of São Paulo," Spiegel International, January 28, 2021, https://www.spiegel.de/international/tomorrow/consequences-of-corona-the-skyrocketing-homeless-population-of-sao-paulo-a-bc469f46-1ac1-4a2c-a4a6-e39418bb9ece.

Moscow

– The Federal State Statistics Service, Moscow, https://fedstat.ru and https://rosstat.gov.ru.
– Andrei Pentiukhov, "The mortality of homeless people from the cold has decreased 10 times in eight years in Moscow," RIA Novosti, February 21, 2011, https://ria.ru/20110221/336987369.html.
– Nina Kaishauri, "The ideal homeless person is a sober Muscovite aged 55–60," miloserdie.ru, October 22, 2018, https://www.miloserdie.ru/article/idealnyj-bezdomnyj-trezvyj-moskvich-55-60-let/.
– Information Center of the Moscow Government, "Almost 30 thousand homeless people in the capital received help from the mobile service 'Social Patrol' in 2018," January 16, 2019, https://icmos.ru/news/pochti-30-tys-bezdomnykh-v-stolitse-poluchili-pomoshch-ot-mobilnoy-sluzhby-sotsialnyy-patrul-v-2018-godu.
– Sergei Gurianov, "Invisible deaths: How the pandemic increased the number of homeless people," Izvestia, November 19, 2020, https://iz.ru/1088425/sergei-gurianov/nevidimye-smerti-kak-pandemiia-uvelichila-chislo-bezdomnykh.

Mumbai

– Office of the Registrar General and Census Commissioner, India, https://censusindia.gov.in.
– Linah Baliga, "1 in 5 Mumbaikars below poverty line," The Times of India, September 23, 2011, https://timesofindia.indiatimes.com/city/mumbai/1-in-5-Mumbaikars-below-poverty-line/articleshow/10086050.cms.
– Statista.com, https://www.statista.com/statistics/271330/unemployment-rate-in-india/.
– Knight Frank and Khaitan & Co, "Institutionalising the Rental Housing Market in India – 2019," https://content.knightfrank.com/research/1004/documents/en/india-topical-reports-institutionalising-the-rental-housing-market-in-india-2019-6718.pdf
– Tanya Thomas, "Home prices unlikely to drop in Mumbai," Mint, January 14, 2021, https://www.livemint.com/companies/news/home-prices-unlikely-to-drop-in-mumbai-11610589763822.html.
– Surbhi Gupta, "What is the cost of living in Mumbai?," Housing.com, September 3, 2021, https://housing.com/news/cost-of-living-in-mumbai/.

Shanghai

– Shanghai Census Data, http://service.shanghai.gov.cn/SHVideo/newvideoshow.aspx?id=493AE1AA672849E9.
– China's National Bureau of Statistics, "Shanghai 2010 Sixth National Population Census," February 28, 2012, http://www.stats.gov.cn/tjsj/tjgb/rkpcgb/dfrkpcgb/201202/t20120228_30403.html.
– Hexun, "Registered Urban Unemployment and Unemployment Rate," http://calendar.hexun.com/area/dqzb_310000_D0230000.shtml.
– Baidu, "More than 180,000 people are covered by low-income insurance in Shanghai, and more than 20,000 people were terminated this year," September 9, 2019, https://baijiahao.baidu.com/s?id=1644177855753467288&wfr=spider&for=pc.
– Sohu, "Shanghai house price ranking by district," July 21, 2020, https://www.sohu.com/a/288434841_100146875.
– QQ.Com, https://new.qq.com/rain/a/20200620A09HGB00.

Tokyo

– Tokyo Metropolitan Government, Statistics Division, Bureau of General Affairs, https://www.toukei.metro.tokyo.lg.jp/jugoki/2013/ju13qf0001.pdf.
– Tokyo Metropolitan Government, https://www.metro.tokyo.lg.jp/tosei/hodohappyo/press/2020/12/25/06.html.
– Ministry of Health, Labour and Welfare of Japan, https://www.mhlw.go.jp/toukei/list/63-15b.html.

Image Credits

Agência Brasil / Photo: Rovena Rosa 133

Fanny Allié 170–171

Pascal Angehrn 204, 205

Simon Jappel / gaupenraub+/- 206

Arolsen Archives 59

Association Vendredi 13 69

Laurie Avocado 124

Yuri Avvakumov 140

Iwan Baan 192, 193, 194–195, 230, 231, 232–233, cover

Jakob Bahret 24–25

John Bare 244, 245

Robert Benson Photography 216, 217, 251

Aicha Boutayeb 77, 78, 79

Andrea Branzi 90

Brooks + Scarpa Architects 213, 214–215

Tara Wujcik / Brooks + Scarpa Architects 212

CCA 186, 187, 188, 189

Levi Clancy 123

Everton Clarindo / Secretaria municipal de Direitos Humanos e Cidadania (SMDHC-SP) – Prefeitura de São Paulo 132

Clifford Beers Housing 238

Courtesy of georgecohenphoto.com 174

Steve Devol 120

Cory Doctorow 125

John d'Oh 8–9

Tatiana Efrussi 143

Nikolay Erofeev 144

João Bittar Fiammenghi 134

Jocelyn Froimovich 71

Glenna Gordon 180, 181

Mark Gorton/RSHP 202–203

GoSleep 70

Grendelkhan 84–85

Tim Griffith 210, 211

Bobak Ha'Eri 253

Don Hamerman 175

José Hassi 255

Thomas Hawk 110, 115

He You 156, 158, 159, 160

Here And Now Agency 239, 240–241

Hertha Hurnaus 218, 219

Hiroaki Imai 164, 168

Amir Jina 69

Valéria Jurado 93

Prathmesh Kharatmal 150, 151

Kurt Kuball / gaupenraub+/- 228, 229, 208–209

Fred Laurès 247, 248–249

Peter E. Lee 112

Jeanchristophe Lett/Manifesta 13 Marseille 80

Armando Lobos 73

Norman McGrath, courtesy of Lo-Yi Chan 105

Jonathan McIntosh 102, 104

Memoria Chilena, Biblioteca Nacional de Chile 88

Christopher Michel 16–17

Michael Moran Photography / OTTO 224, 225

Myr Muratet 247

Amy Murphy 253

Myrzik and Jarisch 13, 26–27

Marcus Pietrek 242, 243

Maria Pokrovskaya 143

Projetemos – Rede Nacional de Projecionistas Livres / Photo: @vjmozart 130

Stephen Przybylinski 43, 44, 45, 46

Tiago Queiroz/Estadão 94, 97

Marcus Repa: image from Fraya Frehse, "A Rua de Máscara (São Paulo, 5 de novembro de 2020)," video documentary 95

Wilfredo Rodríguez 50–51

David L Roush 106

Sumita Roy Dutta 148

Valentina Rozas-Krause 113

Luisa T. Schneider 53, 54, 55, 56

Florian Schreiber 196, 197

Markus Schreiber / picture alliance / ASSOCIATED PRESS 66–67

Sebastian Schubert / gaupenraub+/- 207

Morley von Sternberg 200, 201, 234, 235, 236–237

Emile Straub 255

StreetWise, Inc. 37, 38, 39, 40

Studio MC 220, 221, 222–223

Nicolás Stutzin 89

Stav Tsur, as part of the course "TS18 – Tokyo Studio and Seminar – Initiates for Negative Spatial Growth," by Bezalel Academy of Arts and Design, Jerusalem 166, 167

Mike Vogl – vogl-perspektive.at 226, 227

Rajesh Vora/The Kinetic City & Other Essays 152

Nicholas Worley 198, 199

All dollar ($) amounts stated in the book are US dollars (unless otherwise specified).

Who's Next?

HOMELESSNESS, ARCHITECTURE, AND CITIES

Editors: Daniel Talesnik and Andres Lepik

Assistant editor: Ella Neumaier

Project management: Sonja Bröderdörp, Ella Neumaier, Cristina Steingräber

Design: Julia Wagner, grafikanstalt

Copyediting: Dawn Michelle d'Atri, Camila Schaulsohn

Translation into English (texts by Juliane Bischoff and Andres Lepik): Amy Klement

Architectural drawings: Ilyas Kerem Yilmaz

Reproductions: Eberl & Kœsel Studio, Altusried-Krugzell, Germany

Printing and binding: Eberl & Kœsel GmbH & Co. KG, Altusried-Krugzell, Germany

© 2022 Architekturmuseum der Technischen Universität München (TUM), ArchiTangle GmbH, and the contributors

Architekturmuseum der TUM
in der Pinakothek der Moderne
Barer Str. 40
80333 Munich
Germany
www.architekturmuseum.de

ArchiTangle GmbH
Meierottostraße 1
10719 Berlin
Germany
www.architangle.com

ISBN 978-3-96680-017-4

Cover image: Star Apartments, Los Angeles, California © 2014 Iwan Baan
Graphic spread on pp. 4–5: Kathryn Gillmore